PRAISE FOR THE FIRST EDITION OF
DAYS IN THE LIVES OF SOCIAL WORKERS:

When I read the first story, "Social Work in the ER," I found myself saying, "What an exciting day!"

Delores Shirley, MSW
Faculty Liaison/Advisor and Director of Recruitment
University of North Carolina-Chapel Hill School of Social Work

DAYS IN THE LIVES OF SOCIAL WORKERS was extremely informative for me. Before reading this book, I had no idea social workers were involved in so many different settings. Working to get my BSW and not knowing exactly what area I would like to work in, *DAYS IN THE LIVES OF SOCIAL WORKERS* has planted many ideas and options in my head. I recommend this book not only to social work majors, but also to those who don't exactly know what social workers do.

Emily C. Christopher
BSW Student
Shippensburg University

The students loved it!

Naurine Lennox, ACSW, LICSW
Associate Professor and Chair
St. Olaf College
Department of Social Work

Days in the Lives of Social Workers

50 Professionals Tell "Real-Life" Stories from Social Work Practice

Second Edition

Days in the Lives of Social Workers

50 Professionals Tell "Real-Life" Stories from Social Work Practice

Second Edition

Linda May Grobman, Editor

White Hat Communications

Harrisburg, Pennsylvania

Days in the Lives of Social Workers
50 Professionals Tell "Real-Life" Stories from Social Work Practice
Second Edition

Edited by Linda May Grobman

Published by:

White Hat Communications

Post Office Box 5390
Harrisburg, PA 17110-0390 U.S.A.
717-238-3787 (voice)
717-238-2090 (fax)
http://www.socialworker.com

First printing: 1996
Second printing: 1998
Third printing (2nd edition): 1999
Fourth printing (2nd edition): 2001
Fifth printing (2nd edition): 2002
Sixth printing (2nd edition): 2003

The editor can be contacted by e-mail at: *linda.grobman@paonline.com*

ISBN 0-9653653-0-1
Library of Congress Catalog Card Number: 99-66001

Note: The names and identities of social work clients mentioned in this book have been carefully disguised in accordance with professional standards of confidentiality.

Chapter 17: "The opinions or assertions contained herein are the private views of the author and are not to be construed as official or as reflecting the views of the Department of Army or the Department of Defense."

Portions of Chapter 34 are reprinted with permission of the New York City Chapter of the National Association of Social Workers. They were published in the May 1996 issue of *CURRENTS* of the New York City Chapter NASW.

Table of Contents

About the Editor

Linda May Grobman, ACSW, LSW, is the founder, publisher, and editor of *THE NEW SOCIAL WORKER®*, the magazine for social work students and recent graduates, and the co-author of *THE SOCIAL WORKER'S INTERNET HANDBOOK*. She has practiced social work in mental health and medical settings, and is a former interim executive director of the Pennsylvania and Georgia state chapters of the National Association of Social Workers. She received her MSW and BM (Music Therapy) degrees from the University of Georgia. She and her husband Gary, an author and consultant to nonprofit organizations, play flute duets and brag about their son Adam in their "spare" time.

About the Contributors

Joan M. Abbey, MSW, is an adjunct lecturer at the University of Michigan School of Social Work and Eastern Michigan University Social Work Department. She serves as a consultant in fiscal, policy, and program evaluation to state and local governments and private agencies. Her recent publications include *Making Change: The Cost to Michigan's Children* and "We Know Better Than We Do" in the *Michigan Journal of Law Reform*.

Ronald M. Arundell, Ed.D., ACSW, LISW, is Associate Professor of Social Work and Program Director for the BSW program at the College of Mount St. Joseph in Cincinnati, Ohio. He also maintains a small private practice specializing in the treatment of adolescent sexual offenders. Dr. Arundell has worked as a clinical social worker with children in residential and psychiatric inpatient settings.

Dr. Marjorie A. Baney, LCSW, is retired from her position as Chapter Relations Associate at the National Association of Social Workers in Washington, D.C. She was also executive director of two state chapters of NASW. She holds a doctorate in adult education from NOVA Southeastern University. Currently, she teaches computer courses for senior citizens as a SeniorNet volunteer. She is secretary of the Coordinating Council for the Williamsport (PA) Learning Center at the James V. Brown Library.

Staci A. Beers, MSW, LSW, is employed at the state level in the victim services field. She received a BS in Criminal Justice/Women's Studies from West Chester University and an MSW from Marywood College School of Social Work.

Amy Blake, MSW, CSW, ACSW, has a private practice in Ferndale, Michigan, where she is also vice-president of A Woman's Prerogative

Bookstore. She earned her MSW from the University of Michigan in Ann Arbor. She has received several awards, including the Detroit Chapter, National Organization for Women's Loretta Moore Award for contributions in raising consciousness on issues of concern to women.

Beth Boyett, MFA, CMSW, is an outpatient therapist at Spectra Behavioral Healthcare Systems in Memphis, Tennessee. Prior to earning her MSSW degree from the University of Tennessee-Knoxville (May 1995), she was an assistant professor of English at Rhodes College (Memphis), Franklin Pierce College (Rindge, New Hampshire) and Visiting Writer-in-Residence at St. Albans School (Washington, DC). Beth is a native of Mobile, Alabama and has published fiction and essays in small literary magazines.

Angela Marie Brinton, BSW, received her degree from Missouri Western State College in 1992. She was previously employed by the State of Missouri in Kansas City.

Taylor Burns, LCSW, was the Clinical and Administrative Director of Northern Lights Recovery Center in Nome, Alaska from 1994 to 1998. He has worked in a variety of substance abuse, mental health, and domestic violence intervention settings as a social worker and recreation therapist.

Asherah Cinnamon, MSW, LCSW, is a national associate and director of the National Coalition Building Institute, Southeast USA Region. She also maintains a private practice in clinical social work. She has received many awards, including the New England United Methodist Award for Excellence in Social Justice Actions. She is a member of a local FBI Hate Crimes Task Force, and previously served as a member and Co-Chair of the Portland (Maine) Police Department Bias Crime Task Force. She founded the Second Generation of Maine/Children of Holocaust Survivors.

Kenneth Cohen, BS, Social Welfare, is Ombudsman for the Franklin County Children Services in Grove City, Ohio. He has been employed by Franklin County since 1974, previously as an Investigative Social Worker and an Ongoing Social Worker. In his role as Ombudsman, he has worked with a client base approaching 10,000.

Madeline B. Cohen, MSW, CISW, graduated cum laude in 1976 from Emory University with a BA in psychology. She went on to the University of Georgia and received her MSW in 1978. She currently works for the Tucson Jewish Community Center as the Senior Adult Coordinator. Her previous clinical experience encompasses mental health and medical social work. Among her professional awards are Outstanding Young Woman of America and Who's Who Among Human Services Professionals. In addition, she is a freelance puzzle designer with publications in several national magazines.

Cami L. Cooper, MSW, received both her BSW and MSW from Arizona State University, having earned her graduate degree in May 1996. She has been employed as a school social worker since 1993, having previously worked as a case manager for at-risk high school and middle school students and an in-home counselor for pregnant teens. She speaks fluent Spanish and sings in a gospel choir in her spare time.

Michael Crawford, MSW, RSW, has taught welfare theory and family practice in the School of Social Work at the University College of the Cariboo in Kamloops, British Columbia since 1991. He previously taught at Grant MacEwan Community College in Edmonton, Alberta. His clinical and research interests are in the area of family violence, and he has worked with physically and sexually abusive men for more than 15 years. He received his BSW from the University of Manitoba and his MSW from the University of Calgary.

Catherine Lau Crisp, MSW, is a clinical social worker at the Medical College of Virginia Hospital in Richmond, Virginia. She is a member of the National Association of Social Workers and the National Association of Lesbian and Gay Alcoholism Professionals (NALGAP) and is a co-leader of Bridge Builders: Acting for Justice and Liberation in Richmond.

Judith C. Czarnecki, MSW, LISW, is President/CEO of Family Service of Northwest Ohio, where she has served in various administrative capacities since 1985. Her professional experience also includes direct practice in family service and child protective service settings. She is actively involved in many professional and community organizations, including the Ohio Chapter of NASW, where she was awarded the local Social Worker of the Year Award in 1990 and the State of Ohio Outstanding Service Award in 1989.

Amber Daniels, MSW, is Youth Center Supervisor at Latino Family Services in Detroit, Michigan. She has held various youth development positions and serves on several youth-related task forces and advisory boards in the Detroit community.

Merle T. Edwards-Orr, Ph.D., LICSW, is the Neonatal Intensive Care Unit social worker at Fletcher Allen Health Care in Burlington, Vermont. He also is an Adjunct Assistant Professor of social work at the University of VT. He received his MSSW from the University of Tennessee and his Ph.D. from the University of Wisconsin-Madison. He previously served as Chair of the Department of Basic and Applied Social Sciences at Trinity College of Vermont.

Janice Fristad, ACSW, LSW, CAE, is Director of State Services at the American Association of State Social Work Boards. Her former positions included Chapter Development Associate at the National Association of Social Workers in Washington, DC and Executive Director of the Pennsylvania Chapter, National Association of Social Workers.

Susan Dodd Gaylor, MSW, ACSW, is Area Training Manager for the Virginia Institute for Social Services Training Activities (VISSTA), Piedmont Area Training Center. She also maintains a small private practice in Salem, Virginia. Her previous experience includes working as a child protective services social worker in Washington, DC; Atlanta, Georgia; and Roanoke, Virginia.

Alfreda Paschall Gee, MSW, is a public health social worker for a high risk maternity clinic in North Carolina. She received her MSW from the University of North Carolina-Chapel Hill and is a member of the National Association of Social Workers, North Carolina Public Health Association, and the North Carolina Association of Public Health Social Workers.

Patricia Gleason-Wynn, Ph.D., LMSW-ACP, is currently the BSW Director and Assistant Professor in the Department of Social Work at Southwest Texas State University, San Marcos, Texas. She has worked with older adults, particularly in nursing homes, since 1980.

Gretchen Gross, LICSW, ACSW, NCADC, is a Social Worker II and Staff Counselor at the Division of Reproductive Endocrinology and Infertility at Women's Health Services, Fletcher Allen Health Care in Burlington, Vermont. She is a clinical instructor at the Department of Obstetrics and Gynecology, College of Medicine, University of Vermont, and is a clinical social worker and certified alcohol counselor in private practice in South Burlington.

Joann Hansen Haggerty, MSPH, ACSW, CCSW, is currently doing freelance public health work in the areas of qualitative research, needs assessment, and program evaluation. She completed a Master's in Public Health with an emphasis in research methods in Maternal and Child Health. In her thirty years of social work, she has worked in a wide range of service areas, with the last ten in the AIDS field in various capacities from clinical to research. Her recent interest in research came as an increasing wish to help document the needs and strengths of those with whom she has interfaced.

Carol A. Heintzelman, DSW, is a professor in the Social Work Department, Millersville University, in Millersville, PA. She has been a social work educator since 1971, having worked in child welfare and services to senior citizens prior to that time.

Carol Hendler, MSW, LCSW-C, LICSW, LCSW, now maintains a full-time private practice in Bethesda, MD. While maintaining a part-time private practice, she worked full time in the U.S. Army's Family Advocacy Program, treating child and spouse abuse at both Walter Reed Army Medical Center and at Ft. Meade. She is licensed as a clinical social worker in three states and the District of Columbia, and was president of the Metro DC Chapter of the International Society for Traumatic Stress Studies for three years.

Laura Crawford Hofer, MSSW, LCSW, ACSW, BCD, is a counselor at the Counseling Center of Western Connecticut State University in Danbury, CT. After graduating from Harvard University with a bachelor's degree in history, she served as a VISTA volunteer before returning to school at Columbia University for her MSW. She has been a clinical social worker since 1976.

Christian Itin, BSW, MSW, Ph.D., is an Assistant Professor with the Greater Rochester Collaborative MSW Program in Rochester, NY. He is a past program director with both the Colorado and Hurricane Island Outward Bound Schools. He continues to contribute to the linkage between social work and adventure-based practice.

Jerry L. Johnson, Ph.D., is assistant professor at the Grand Valley State University School of Social Work. Before teaching, he spent 13 years as a therapist, administrator, community organizer, and consultant in Detroit, Grand Rapids, and across Michigan.

Judith J. Lacerte, MSW, LISW, G.S., is a home health services team leader at the Department of Health and Environmental Control in Anderson, South Carolina. She is certified by the SC Department of Mental Health as a geriatric specialist and received special training in geriatrics at the University of North Carolina, Center for Aging Research and Education Services. She was the South Carolina Public Health Social Worker of the Year in 1995.

Daniel Liechty, Ph.D., D.Min., LSW, formerly psychosocial coordinator with a hospital-based hospice program, has joined the social work faculty of Illinois State University at Normal, Illinois. He is a member of the National Association of Social Workers, the Academy of Certified Social Workers, the Association for Death Education and Counseling, and the Ernest Becker Foundation. He is a graduate of the Bryn Mawr College Graduate School of Social Work and Social Research.

Carol M. Line, BS, ACSW, is currently in private practice as a social worker and physical therapist. She practiced as a school social worker with the Eastern Upper Peninsula Intermediate School District in Northern Michigan for nine years.

Kim R. Lorber, MSW, CSW, is a social worker at a nursing home in Bronx, New York City. She is enrolled in the DSW program at Wurzweiler School of Social Work, Yeshiva University, and is conducting research on AIDS/HIV issues for women, lesbians, couples of mixed-HIV status, and HIV-positive paid professionals working with HIV-positive individuals.

Susan Mankita, MSW, LCSW, was director of social work at Vencor Hospital in Coral Gables, Florida until recently. She left that position to pursue completion of her Ph.D. at Barry University. She is an adjunct faculty member at Barry University, and serves as Social Work Forum Leader on America Online.

Toni Murphy, MSSW, CCSW, is currently in part-time private practice in Raleigh, North Carolina. She specializes in counseling services for families of children with special needs, adolescents with special needs, and adults with disability-related issues. Before opening her private practice, she was employed as the Director of Social Services for a nonprofit agency in the Southwest that provided services for children and adults with developmental disabilities. She was nominated for an adjunct faculty position at the University of Texas School of Social Work as a result of her educational supervision of graduate students.

Lisa Orloff, ACSW, is a forensic social worker at the Legal Aid Society, Capital Defense Unit, in Brooklyn, New York, where she previously worked in the Criminal Defense Division. Before her employment at Legal Aid, she worked in several settings with crime victims, including a domestic violence shelter and a rape crisis center. She received her MSW from Florida State University in 1992.

Andrew J. Peters, CSW, MSW, is Project Director at Pride for Youth Project, Long Island Crisis Center.

David C. Prichard, Ph.D, is Associate Professor of Social Work and Associate Dean of Assessment in the College of Health Professions at the University of New England in Portland, Maine. His practice experience includes 15 years of clinical treatment and supervision, specializing in work with survivors of primary and secondary trauma. He received his Ph.D. in 1996 from Virginia Commonwealth University in Richmond, where he resided for 10 years. He now lives, writes, bikes, and kayaks on the coast of Maine.

Ogden W. Rogers, Ph.D., CICSW, ACSW, was formerly a clinical social worker in emergency medicine at the Johns Hopkins Hospital, Baltimore, Maryland. He currently is Assistant Professor and Program Director of Social Work at The University of Wisconsin-River Falls. He is engaged in consultation and research on issues of disaster mental health, refugee assistance, and international humanitarian law.

Glenda Dewberry Rooney, MSW, Ph.D., is Associate Professor in the Department of Social Work, Augsburg College, in Minneapolis, Minnesota. She has over 20 years' practice and administrative experience in academic and human service organizations, including an employee assistance program. In 1994, she completed a study that examined the concerns of employed women and the service provisions of employee assistance programs. The focus of her current research is practice ethics and the use of focus groups as a qualitative research method in social work.

Seth Rosenberg, MSW, is a clinician with the Homeless Program at the Veteran's Administration in Tucson, Arizona. He began working in the field of social work in 1982 as a "Neighborhood Youth Worker" for the Tasmanian Council for Youth in Hobart, Tasmania. He worked for a number of mental health agencies in Australia and in Tucson, primarily as a counselor, before taking a job as a Supervised Release Specialist with the Superior Court Pretrial Services. He received his MSW in 1995 from Arizona State University, graduating Phi Kappa Phi and *magna cum laude.*

Diane Rullo-Cooney, MSW, LCSW, CADC, is a social worker in private practice with Rullo Psych Associates in Hazlet, New Jersey. She is also an adjunct professor at Rutgers University in New Brunswick, New Jersey, and has completed coursework toward a doctorate in social welfare at Fordham University.

Fred Sacklow, CSW, R, is a social worker with the New York City Board of Education. He also maintains a private psychotherapy practice in Queens, New York.

Gerhard J. Schwab, Ph.D., teaches social work at the University of Guam. He received a Ph.D. in social work and psychology at the University of Michigan. He has practiced social work in Austria (his home country), Papua New Guinea, Michigan, and Guam.

Scott P. Sells, Ph.D., LCSW, LMFT, teaches MSW students at Savannah State University and is clinical director of the Savannah Family Institute. He serves as a consultant to the Department of Juvenile Justice, and has written a book entitled *Treating the Tough Adolescent: A Family-Based, Step-by-Step Guide.*

Michael Shernoff, MSW, CSW, ACSW, is in full-time private practice primarily with gay men, and teaches "Social Work with Today's Lesbians and Gay Men" as an adjunct faculty member at Hunter College Graduate School of Social Work. He has edited four books, co-edited two books, and written over 50 articles, all on psychosocial issues of HIV/AIDS and mental health for gay men. Many of his writings can be found on his Web site, and he is also the online mental health expert for The Body, the world's largest HIV/AIDS Web site. In addition, he has served on the boards of the National Social Work AIDS Network (NSWAN) and the National Lesbian/Gay Health Foundation.

Kenneth G. Smith, MSW, LCSW, received his BA in Social Welfare from Old Dominion University and MSW from the University of Tennessee-Knoxville. He is Partial Hospitalization Coordinator at St. Anthony's Hospital in St. Petersburg, Florida and has 19 years' post-graduate experience as an inpatient therapist, program chief, and chief social worker in a psychiatric hospital; private practitioner; and community mental health clinician. He earned a Diplomate in clinical social work in 1994.

Roberta (Rusty) VanSickle, MSW, continues her "snail paced" recovery. She now works with the Florida State Vocational Rehabilitation Council, coordinating other state disability advocacy groups. She has become credentialed as a Certified Disability Consultant, and is scheduled for training in Civil Court Mediation. She feels that her personal experiences as she walked herself through the various disability service systems have qualified her as a professional with much to offer others. Roberta also coordinates an online stroke support group and online consumer advocacy efforts. She was formerly editor of *Job Training and Placement Report*, a newsletter about supported employment services.

John D. Weaver, ACSW, LSW, is a Casework Supervisor and Mental Health Disaster Response Coordinator for Northampton County Mental Health and a part-time therapist for Concern Professional Services, both in Bethlehem, Pennsylvania. He also has a private consulting practice. He is currently ranked as an American Red Cross (ARC) Disaster Mental Health Coordinator and is a volunteer DMH instructor for ARC, having received its Clara Barton Honor Award for Meritorious Volunteer Leadership. He is the author of *Disasters: Mental Health Interventions*, published by Professional Resource Press.

Timothy S. Wight, MSW, is a Social Science Program Specialist with the U.S. Department of Justice, Office of Justice Programs, Office of Juvenile Justice and Delinquency Prevention. He formerly was employed as a Correctional Treatment Specialist/Drug Treatment by the U.S. Department of Justice, Federal Bureau of Prisons.

Pamela J. Wilshere, LSW, is mental health services director at the Dauphin County MH/MR Case Management Unit in Harrisburg, Pennsylvania. She worked with a migrant child development program in Central Pennsylvania in the mid-1980s.

Jack Yatsko, MSW, LSW, is Program Director at Friendship House, a clubhouse model psychosocial rehabilitation program operated through the Kauai Community Mental Health Center, Adult Mental Health Division, State of Hawaii. He received his MSW in 1994 from the University of Hawaii.

Introduction

If variety is the "spice" of life, then social work is one of the "hottest" careers around. Variety is one of the things that make social work practice exciting for so many members of the profession. It's also one of the reasons so many people don't fully understand exactly what it is that social workers do.

A story was told at a social work conference I attended. The speaker related the difficulties he had in explaining to his mother what he did professionally. Finally, after years (maybe even decades) in the social work profession, he took a professorship at a university. His mother was relieved—when her friends asked what her son did for a living, she simply said, "He teaches."

Indeed, it is sometimes difficult to articulate exactly what one does as a social worker, and social work is a profession that is sometimes misunderstood. So, when I set out to publish a book about social work, I wanted to convey a sense of not only what it is that professional social workers do, but what their lives are like on a day-to-day basis.

This book is about real life social workers. It goes beyond saying, "I'm a social worker," and says, "I'm a social worker. Spend a day with me and see what it's like." It takes a first-hand, close-up look at the roles social workers play every day in places from hospitals to prisons to universities. It celebrates the joys and rewards of social work, and it presents a realistic view of the challenges of being a social worker. In it, real life social workers describe their days—not necessarily "typical" days, since most say there is no such thing, but days that are representative of the essence of their work.

Whether you are about to receive your social work degree (or are thinking about it), are already a social worker, know a social worker, or just want to know more about the profession, reading *DAYS IN THE LIVES OF SOCIAL WORKERS* is sure to clear up any misconceptions you may have and will certainly broaden your view of what a social worker can do. Maybe it will help you decide what area of social work to specialize in, to articulate why social work is important to you, or to explain to your mother what it is that you do now that you're grown up.

As you read **DAYS IN THE LIVES OF SOCIAL WORKERS**, you will discover that the career possibilities in social work are virtually endless. You will read about social workers who are employed by state and federal governments, social workers in private practice, social workers in other countries, social workers working for communities, and on and on. In each chapter, you will find something different, while you will also notice that many of the same core social work skills are used across settings.

This book is divided into fourteen parts, each focusing on a specific population or type of setting. Not every social work specialty is covered specifically, but there is much rich material from which social workers in any setting can learn. Within some specialties, such as mental health, you will read about several subspecialties, because there are many very different settings and roles in which social workers work with these populations. I have grouped the chapters of this book into what seem like neat categories, but in reality, many of these stories could easily fit into more than one.

My hope is that you will use this book as a starting point—an introduction to the variety of roles social workers play every day. Use it as you would the opportunity to literally follow and observe 50 different social workers for a day. Soak up as much as you can from each experience, decide what you would like to explore further, and then take it from there! Use the appendices in the back of the book to find additional resources and information on the areas of social work that interest you the most.

Then you can create your own unique days in social work—days that I trust will be filled with much success and many rewards.

Linda May Grobman, ACSW, LSW, Editor

Acknowledgments

DAYS IN THE LIVES OF SOCIAL WORKERS evolved from an idea to a reality as manuscripts poured into my mailbox from social workers around the country (and beyond). My excitement grew as each story revealed the vital roles social workers play in people's lives, as well as the role the profession plays in social workers' lives.

I was especially struck by the many social workers who said, "I really love my job," and the sense of excitement conveyed in their stories. This book was possible only with the participation of the social workers who took time out of their busy days to write about what happens during those days. I would like to thank each of these professionals for the work they do, and especially for their contributions to this book.

Thanks also go to those chapters of the National Association of Social Workers that published the call for manuscripts in their newsletters and to the SOCWORK, BPD, SW-FIELD-WORK, AASWG, FEMSW-L, and other e-mail mailing lists that provided a forum for getting the word out about this project.

I want to thank the many, many social work educators and students who have read and used the first edition, and who have taken the time to give me their input by mail, telephone, e-mail, and at conferences throughout the country. Their comments helped shape the new content in this expanded edition.

I am appreciative of Judy Margo's assistance in updating the information in Appendix A, *Organizations of Interest to Social Workers*, for the second edition.

I am especially grateful to my husband Gary for his meticulous proofreading, editorial input, and support of this endeavor.

LMG

PART I:
HEALTH CARE

Chapter 1
Social Work in the ER

by Ogden W. Rogers, Ph.D., CICSW, ACSW

In early December, the air is gray and cold. What starts as a modest breeze off the harbor gets funneled by the faces of multi-story buildings on Monument Street, whipped into a biting blast that always seems to be in one's face. As I walk the blocks from the parking garage, I pass underneath the canyons of the Johns Hopkins Hospital. Towering above me stand many floors of surgery, therapy, and patients. Thousands of people bustle about in a brisk pace that insiders call "a Hopkins Walk." I am headed to the end of the block, the corner of Monument and Wolfe Streets. Of this huge medical complex, this is the basement. This is the Hopkins Emergency, and I'm the social worker on the 10 a.m. to 7 p.m. shift.

There are five ambulance doors, and by this time in the morning, four of them are already filled with the orange and white "cracker boxes" of the BCFD (Baltimore City Fire Department). I walk toward the big electric street doors of the department, emblazoned with the logo of the lofty Hopkins "Dome," and the very clear words, "DO NOT PUSH." I smile inwardly as I think about how later tonight, I'll be giving 4th year meds a lecture on ethics and the emergency room. I will ask them to stand outside with me, read those words, and consider all the possible messages they imply.

The waiting room is packed, as usual. Despite all the efforts of bright paint on modern architecture, it still has the ambiance of a bus station. There are about 80 sullen, tired, and mostly black people, hunkered in coats and plastic chairs.

Around them whiz physicians, residents, nurses, med students, and me, mostly white, and mostly looking like they are always in a hurry. I know that some of these people will be sitting here, still waiting, when my shift ends.

I throw my coat in a corner of the closet that is my office and see the notes that have piled waiting for me this morning.

A nurse has donated some clothes for a "clothes closet" I have set up for our homeless patients (who are not an uncommon population, but tend to be treated at times with less than a full measure of respect). I stack them according to blouses, shirts, pants. I secretly hope she will see these clothes walk out a few days from now on the frame of some now-nameless person. I hope it will decrease the distance between them.

Sleeping in the holding area is a young man with no apparent medical problem who says he is seventeen; a runaway from San Diego. I tell him I'm here to help. He has had breakfast, and I am arranging an early lunch while I try to offer him opportunities to tell his story. It is a detailed and confused tale, and the few bits of fact that emerge don't add up. I make some phone calls and find out that none of the addresses in San Diego exist. I go back and forth a few times while getting a new piece of information with each visit. Seeking some resources for possible referral, it seems this young man has already spent some time telling slightly different stories at both the city Department of Social Services and Traveler's Aid. Confronted with this information, and a continued offer of assistance, he indicates he's not really from San Diego, but is an undocumented alien from Jamaica. He asks for bus fare to the Consulate in Washington, D.C., forty miles away. I am incredulous, as the accent he has sounds pretty American to me. We have a nurse in the unit from Kingston, and I ask her to help me interview the young man. It becomes quickly apparent that he's lying again and he gets angry. I tell him I figure he's probably in a pretty tight spot, and I'd like to help him.... I don't need the whole truth, but he's gotta come close enough so that I can find his best way out of this emergency room. He stares at me angrily. Silent.

The klaxon goes off and a garbled radio voice says we have five minutes to two incoming medical emergencies via ambulance. I tell the angry fellow to enjoy lunch, and I'll be back in an hour. Before I even get back to my office, one of the cases is coming through the ER doors on its way to Critical Care Bay One. Shortly after, Bay Two is also filled with activity. I have flagged down the paramedics from both units to get what little I can on addresses, names, and any family who may have been present. I have donned gloves and go through the critical care rooms, picking up the cut-off clothes and searching for identifying materials. I find a purse in Bay 1, a wallet in Bay 2. The wallet in Bay 2 tells me a lot about a Mr. Tolliver. He's a barber, a mason, a husband, and he's been to this ER many times in the past three years with heart problems. There is a well worn photograph of him and a woman when they were both much younger and happier.

Through the elbows and tubes and paddles, I can look into both bays. I can see that both patients are elderly and unconscious. I set up the family rooms for relatives—quiet places where anxious, waiting people can be located. A small elderly woman and her adult daughter come looking for the patient in Bay 2. I inquire if she is Mrs. Tolliver. I offer the orientation and support that this crisis usually calls for. I prepare them for a "medical episode." The little woman's coat smells of mothballs and the faintest hint of stale cigar. They are quiet, trembling, and tragic.

The patient in Bay 1 recovers from the brink of death in 30 minutes, and is stable enough to be sent upstairs to a cardiac care unit. Bay 2 appears to be DOA and the resuscitation effort seems to go on forever. It is "early in the month"—a euphemism that means the ER is staffed with new residents and interns, and they need the practice trying to keep people alive. I guess it's better they practice on somebody who's pretty much dead than somebody who's pretty much alive. I am never easy with this decision.

After well over an hour, Weaver, the medical resident "calls it." I will help him break the news. I help a nurse with the quiet task of tidying up the body. Weaver is on the phone and smiling. His patient has died, but the blood gases and electrolytes induced during the resuscitation effort are the mimics of viability. "Harvard Lytes, man, we got Harvard Lytes!" Weaver says to me. I reach and touch his arm in the enthusiasm. "That's great, Martin," I say. "You are very good at what you do. Now, you need to take a moment, switch gears, and go with me to the family room to tell this patient's wife that her husband is dead." Weaver stiffens and I continue my hold on his elbow. My grasp has shifted from one of celebration to one of support. "Uh... yeah, yeah. Let's go do it. Uh, what was this guy's name?"

In the family room, Mr. Tolliver's survivors sit quietly. I have been in and out in the past hour and have kept them informed. They are prepared to hear that he has died, but until it is said, there is always a prayer upon hope. I have done this with Weaver before, many times. His style is to hem and haw, and when he's really uncomfortable, he starts to go into intricate detail and use medical jargon. He's getting better. Today, he skips the jargon and offers only a moderate amount of highlight about the rescue effort. I offer a brief clarification to the family that both prods him and allows for a moment to catch his mental breath. He enters back into the conversation simply: "I'm sorry, Mrs. Tolliver, we did everything we could, but your husband's heart just gave out. He's gone."

"Johnnie's dead?" she asks quietly.

"Yes ma'am," Weaver replies.

I ask the wife and daughter if they'd like to go back with me to the treatment room to see him and they numbly agree. I look over my shoulder and find that Weaver has gone. He has done his job with Bay 2. He goes back to work with the living. I will go with Mrs. Tolliver and her daughter to face their loss.

Back in Holding, the sullen young man looks a little less sullen, perhaps now a bit resigned. I figure he figures he's run out of time and stories. He's not been hassled by anybody in the last hour, and he got a meal, so maybe, just maybe, this worker will play it square with him. The story that emerges this time is vague enough in the details that it has more of the ring of truth to it. He's from Philadelphia, and has gotten into some trouble with "associates," to whom he sold some crack. He left Philly in a hurry. The car he stole broke down, and he was lucky to get it off I-95 and not attract attention from the Toll Authority police. He has a grandmother in D.C. and he's trying to get to her house. I tell him this one "sounds like it could just be a phone call away," if he gives me the grandmother's telephone number. He hedges for a bit, and then says that he burned her before, and he's not sure she will help. I tell him why don't we give it a try, it's just phone calls.

The klaxon goes off again and some disembodied dispatcher's voice reports that we have 12 minutes to prepare for a pediatric chopper incoming from the Eastern Shore. The peds nurses start preparing a bay. A resident calls up to peds-neuro to get a team on the way down to the ER. Over the radio, a medic starts firing a report. On board is a little girl, apparently run over as somebody backed out of a driveway. One can hear the medic coming in over the static with numbers and facts about her condition that reveal she is strong, but hovering. There is attention in his voice. Somewhere over the Chesapeake Bay, he is focused on this bleeding child, and yet he knows it is just a matter of time and space before what was a situation on a driveway becomes a medical episode in the trauma center. All the people and scenery shift around except for the little girl in front of him.

Back in Holding, I am talking to the seventeen-year-old's grandmother. At first she is angry that I am bothering her about this grandson who has-no-respect-and-he-lies-and-he-cheats-and-he-steals. Then she catches her breath and she wants to know why he's in-the-hospital, and is-he-hurt and is-he-gonna-be-okay? I take a moment to reassure her about his present medical condition without elaborating on his potential social or legal status. I want to put them together on the phone. I ask if she can talk with him for a little bit, and she agrees. I cover the mouth piece as I hand him the phone. "Be nice to this old lady," I warn. "She cares more about you than anybody in Baltimore does."

The child from the Eastern Shore is now an unconscious case in Bay 3. Except for the thin red trickle from her right ear, and faint bruise above her right eye, she seems an otherwise unmarred 4-year-old. She is the center of an ever-expanding audience that is the hallmark of a pediatric critical care case. The room fills up with interns and residents and nurses from trauma teams that all own some piece of her recovery: Neuro, Internal Medicine, PICU, Surgery. The Peds trauma team is involved in all the work of initial assessment, and consults take place, being fired over shoulders. She is a well of attention, absorbing eyes and hands and thoughts about her vital signs.

Many of these people are "players," but many more are just "watchers." They have an "interest in the case," as a strategy develops to put this broken little girl back together. Those in the outermost rings crane their necks to see. They momentarily join into brief conversations with another spectator who is not central to the action. This is a teaching university hospital, and this is one of its pick-up classrooms. I watch a young surgical resident, who is backed into a far corner, and make a mental note about him. He is standing on a chair so that he can see. His hands are gloved and hold each other.

The beautiful child who looked "like a keeper," begins to "go sour," and what seemed mostly a head trauma goes into a full court surgical press. Before this is over, the floor will fill with blood and fluids, trash and terse words will fly freely, and a young woman will cut open and reach into the child's chest and squeeze her unmoving heart, hoping to make it move. When the collective hope is exhausted, someone in Attending's clothes says softly, firmly: "Thank you everyone. We're done here." There is a quiet embarrassment, and the once densely packed room becomes almost instantly empty. I turn to prepare a family room.

On my way back through the waiting room, I am flagged down by the sullen teenager, who is now not sullen, but smiling and waving and looks as if he has become my best friend. "Hey man! I'm outta here," he says. "My moms n' pops is on the way."

"You got a ride," I say.

"I got a ride." he smiles back.

"You be straight with that old lady," I wave my finger at him. "She loves you."

"Thanks, man," he says. "I owe you."

I ask him to tell me where he left the car he took from Philadelphia, and without a beat he gives me a corner about six blocks away. I shake his hand and walk back to the critical care bays.

Bay 3 has been cleaned, and is empty except for two figures. I look in from an adjoining room. Beneath the white-green hospital light, the dead child lies under stark white sheets; all the tubes and machines are gone. The young surgical resident I had noted earlier is the only person in attendance. He has bathed the little girl's face, and is trying to pack her leaking right ear with some nasal gauze. He is silent, and there are tears on his face. The packing will not stay put and keeps spilling out of the dead child's ear. He keeps trying to push it back in and keeps failing. He repeats this process over and over and seems stuck at the task. His hands have the slightest tremble. I move noiselessly up to the young resident and add a hand to his packing. In a moment it is secure. I offer my hand, "It's Doctor Menedez, isn't it?" "Yes," he grips me back tightly, still fixed upon the little girl's face, "Reuben."

"Let's get some coffee, Reuben," I say, "I need a cup."

"Yeah. Thanks," he nods.

I am called a while later to the triage desk. A large, soft black man who is well known to me is standing across from the nurse. She has a slightly exasperated smile and she makes a motion of introduction with her hand. He has apple butter cheeks and a blank stare. He wears a racing cap.

"I don't feel so good. I don't feel so good—uh hum, uh hum," he quietly drones.

"I don't feel so good. I don't feel so good—uh hum."

"Turn off the machines. Turn off the machines—uh hum, uh hum."

"Turn off the machines. Turn off the machines—uh hum."

I know this man as Willy. I smile and offer my hand that he takes limply. "Okay Willy, let's look around," I say, and we start to walk around the intermediate care unit. We peek in at the Asthma Room. We look into Holding. I make some reassuring observations about the environment around us, and nod at the people who pass by. People who know me and Willy make smiles and nod back. It becomes clear after five minutes that any machines of any concern are all turned off. Willy's shoulders relax and I walk him out onto the street. He will come back in two weeks after his Prolixin clinic appointment and we will do this inspection again.

Morrison, the sector "cage officer" has swung by, looking for this nurse he wants to date. He gives me a wink and says I must be Willy's best friend. I wink back at Morrison and tell him I'm everybody's best friend. We hang out together at the triage desk and shoot the breeze for a while. All the time, Morrison has an ear cocked to his radio.

The cage car officer patrols the entire Eastern District. He responds to sectors where officers have made an arrest, and transports the arrested person to the district lockup for booking. Morrison moonlights as a police officer in the ER, and over time I have come to know him as a go-between for myself and some of the other sector officers. When issues of domestic abuse arise, the police and I have needs from each other, and Morrison has helped me make small breaks into the blue line. About every other month or so, I go on a "ride-along" for a shift with somebody in the district. I use the time to get tested by the officer at the wheel, and make some points about how we can help each other in those sticky situations. Afterwards, we will go to the Police Union Club and have too many beers. There have been some times now when I have been called from my office to go to some address in the neighborhood and help the officer on the scene. I feel good that these relationships are working.

"Hey Morrison," I punch lightly at his shoulder, "If you promise not to ask where I got it, I'll give you a present." Morrison thinks for a moment and then bites, "Okay, what?"

"There's a green Jeep Cherokee with Pennsylvania plates near the corner of Broadway and Eastern Avenue. It's outta gas and it might be hot from Philadelphia. I'm psychic."

"Cool," says Morrison, and he bends down to his radio.

After hours, the little girl's mother has arrived. While escorting her to the family room, she asks me if the child is all right. When I hesitate, and tell her that I am going to get Dr. Silvertson to come and talk to her, she knows her daughter is dead and she begins to wail and fling about, beating me on the chest. I wrap her with one arm, while waving off security guys with the other. We shuffle into the quiet of the family room to face some facts.

Sometime later, when she has composed herself and had a conversation with the physician in charge, we go into the quiet of Bay 3 and spend some time with the dead girl's body. The mother strokes the little girl's forehead. "She looks like an angel now," she says quietly, "in heaven." I nod and hold her other hand. She wants to know if I want to see some pictures of the little girl from her wallet. At this moment nothing is more important to me, and we share the photographs.

When we are done, I send the child's body off to the morgue, and I place the mother in the care of her people, who traveled hours away from this ER, back to the rural place where they came from, knowing their lives are changed forever. I am starting to get tired, and I hope there are no more child deaths tonight. I then quash the thought with my own magical prohibition about such desires, as they tend to backfire upon me. It's a struggle with magic, I always face, here in the ER. I sit behind the only electric doors in this neighborhood that look constantly onto poverty, death, and tragedy. I am buoyed at times by the human strength that emerges. The humor, courage, and compassion that creeps into those spaces in-between. I am always tugged by my wishes and hopes, against the hard facts of life in East Baltimore. I find a constant struggle between wishes and reality. I go get another cup of coffee, and as I sit looking out onto the ambulance dock, I see this little homeless guy shuffle out of the hospital, wearing a shirt I stacked in the "clothes closet" this morning.

I laugh to myself as I see this bit of serendipity walking down the street. No matter the costs of tragedy, there are little moments of quiet heroics as well. The ER is a place of disorder, and the worker who works best is the one who can go with the flow. Sometimes hours of boredom are punctuated by minutes of terrific activity. One has to think fast on one's feet. Up in the rest of "the house," life has more order. Workers get to schedule appointments. Even in the intensive care units, where death is a common visitor, there is a greater sense of control. One is deeper in the hospital; one is on the hospital's turf. The ER is more like a beach, where the sea and the land meet, changing each other over and over. To do social work in the ER takes the heart and mind of a surfer; each new person off the street is another wave to meet well.

It is six o'clock, and the fourth year meds are in a pile at the triage desk, waiting for me. Soon, they will be starting their rotation in the ER, and I get three hours in this week to talk ethics, the state of welfare, and social services in the emergency room. They are dressed in street clothes and these little white jackets that some call "clerk coats." Some of them have developed an officious defensiveness, while others just look lost and bewildered. I meet each one of them well, handing them a donut. I start off by making a joke that this is one of "two places that's open 24 hours a day and has cops: Dunkin' Donuts and the ER." We laugh for a moment, and then get ready for a little conversation.

"To understand emergency medicine, you have to understand the street," I say, motioning for them to follow me onto the sidewalk outside, where we can look up and face the leviathan of the hospital. "Now... look at these doors and consider what they say: DO NOT PUSH...."

Chapter 2
Managing a Hospital Social Work Department

by Susan Mankita, MSW, LCSW

Hospital social work department management is wonderful work, if you can get it. While social work in health care is still a flourishing area of practice, many of my colleagues from around the country have fallen victim to massive restructuring efforts that eliminated social work management positions. The good news is that many departments, like mine, remain intact, and quite a few health care social work leaders have moved higher up the health care ladder.

For six years, I have managed the social work department at a small long-term acute care facility. There are two kinds of days here—the atypical and the insane. As I walk into the large building, I wonder which kind this will be. Sometimes, the challenge of doing more with less and the severity of human need combine in just the right way with my social work thinking, creating nothing short of an internal explosion. There is fiery passion borne of this kind of work, and it fuels me daily. I love my job, because I can effect powerful and lasting changes in the lives of catastrophically ill people, in the way other professions see their roles and, given the right issue, in the way services are delivered in the community.

As a "working" department manager, I wear two hats. I am responsible for ensuring that the department's objectives are carried out *and* for carrying a caseload. The social workers are responsible for assessing and addressing the many psychosocial needs of patients and their loved ones. We "follow" them during the course of their hospitalization, which in social work-ese means we develop and maintain supportive relationships. We work with them to identify strengths, cope with crises, and adjust to loss. We help them make the transition from the hospital to a continuing care plan that maximizes their independence and quality of life. This is called discharge planning. I am ultimately responsible for ensuring that patients in our facility move through the health care continuum appropriately.

There are messages waiting for me today. I know that as soon as I listen to them, I will be off and running in response. My calendar reminds me that we have a management meeting this morning, and I have scheduled supervision for our MSW intern in the afternoon. I enter my code and the mechanized voice that greets me each morning informs me, with no apology, "You have nine new messages."

The first message is from my administrator, advising that we will need an Ethics Committee meeting today, now scheduled for 4:15. She's also wondering when the abuse policy will be ready. Next, our CFO wants a prediction of discharges for this month. The Quality Review Manager reminds me that statistics are due on Monday. Three messages are lengthy expositions from marketers hoping for an appointment this week. A physician requests help with a challenging family member, and the very family member who challenges him calls to request help with the physician. This one, from the nursing supervisor, draws my attention immediately.

"Please send someone up to see Mr. Diaz. He's a nervous wreck today."

Of course he is. His insurance company has been trying to transfer him to a nursing home all week. Each morning, he has prepared himself psychologically to go, and each afternoon, one of the social workers has told him his transfer arrangements haven't been completed.

"Perhaps tomorrow," he says each day.

I make a mental note to send someone up to see him as soon as possible.

Mr. Diaz has been through hell and survived. Far too sick to go anywhere else at first, he has been ventilator dependent and badly infected. His nightmare began after surgical removal of cancer in his gastrointestinal tract. Seems they got most of the cancer, but they weren't able to wean him from the machine that inflates his lungs with the air that keeps him alive.

Sick as he is, he is totally aware of his environment. His tracheostomy, which acts as his airway, pushing in and sucking out his breath, before it can vibrate past his vocal chords to make sounds, has forced him to become adept at mouthing words and using a letter board to make his needs known. Not unlike the game of Charades, he uses his hands wildly to make people understand him. Luckily, it is summer time, and his two teenage granddaughters hold vigil daily, playing cards and talking about boys. They serve as his voice, turn him if he gets too uncomfortable, and entertain him when boredom comes. My colleague walks in and I ask if she will run up and visit with Mr. Diaz and place a follow-up call to his insurance company to see if they have completed the steps necessary for his transfer. I relax knowing he will be attended to. I tally some of the outcome data. The 10 a.m. management meeting arrives quickly.

A Voice at the Table

Team meetings are a mixed blessing for a department manager. Hospitals hold them frequently, and there is an expectation you will be present even if you are a vital practitioner in a three-person department, as I am. Despite this tension between addressing management issues and providing direct patient care, the opportunity for input into how the facility operates is unparalleled. My social work values have played an important role, earning me a reputation as a "voice of reason." Having a social worker on the management team is one way to make sure that no patient is labeled "difficult" without acknowledging the contribution of the hospital environment or the impact of the disease, that no family's concerns are minimized, and that the patient's needs are always primary.

Today's meeting lasts most of the morning. We are preparing for a big survey and dividing the many remaining preparations among us. We are updating our policy manuals with the latest adjustments and brainstorming about how we can best present our strengths.

Managing Risk

In this litigious day and age, criticism of health care delivery runs high. Social workers can be critical players in managing risk, by observing for indicators that might lead to a lawsuit and starting the facility to work to correct problems and undo damage, if possible, before they intensify.

As I make rounds on the medical floor, before heading down to lunch, I see Katie, Mrs. Johnson's daughter. I know Mrs. Johnson will probably be medically stable for discharge soon and stop in to make sure the family has no new questions about her impending transfer. I soon realize that Katie's responses to me are not her usual friendly ones.

"Are you OK?" I ask.

"Just fine," she responds with a controlled voice that at once confirms my suspicions that she is extremely angry about something.

Because I know Katie from the family support meetings, I take a chance and reach in.

"I can see whatever it is, you're trying hard to keep it inside. I care about you and your mother and I'm here to listen and help if I can."

"Maybe a lawyer can help," she blurts out, her anger finding expression before a willing audience.

Floodgates open, and as her anger finds a voice, she starts to cry. She is angry with everyone right now, especially Dr. Salerno. No phone calls for over a week and she found out about her mother's new infection by accident. Everyone has "written her mother off" with discharge pending. She'd hoped her mother would be better when it was time to leave the hospital. She feels helpless and no one seems to care.

We agree that one way of improving the situation will involve the communication among her, the doctor, and the staff. A meeting with our Interdisciplinary Team is set for tomorrow. I advise my administrator of Katie's distress, and she calls the physician herself. Several staff members rally, making empathetic, information-filled visits to the room. Tomorrow, I will engage team members, family members and physician in a problem-solving session that will satisfy Katie's concerns. Another crisis soon averted...for now.

Preparing the Next Generation of Leaders

The bulk of the caseload is divided among social work staff, consisting of a full-time MSW and a social work intern. When I am sitting at meetings, they are rushing between patient rooms, juggling phone calls. I count my blessings daily for my coworker, Maria, whose skills are sharp and whose competence makes my job that much easier. She is a fairly new social worker, and I provide her with clinical supervision she can apply toward her license. In my view, it is a manager's responsibility to prepare social workers for professional advancement. I momentarily fantasize about leaving work to finish my oft-neglected Ph.D. How well-prepared is she to run the department in my absence? Quite prepared, I decide. She has participated in the management team during my occasional absences and in the supervision of our intern. When she began working here, I encouraged her to participate in one of the many quality improvement teams, and she joined the Information Management Team. She quickly rose to a leadership position on the team and has earned respect. She is organized, compassionate, has great communication skills, and has shown flexibility in situations requiring it. It's delightful to watch her blossom.

Our intern from the university, Ana, has some natural gifts and insights that make supervising her a delight. At 3:00, we meet for her individual supervision, and she shares her anxiety about one client on her caseload. The spouse of a patient in ICU seems unwilling to bare his soul to her; in fact, she believes he actually finds her annoying. She recounts multiple efforts to engage him in a discussion of his feelings, all to no avail. It becomes apparent to her that her desire to please him has superseded his needs, and that leads to a productive discussion yielding additional insights and a plan to make another try. She saw her first dead person this week. She had ample opportunity to leave the room, but chose to stay and support the grieving new widow, a woman in her 80s whose relatives live in Argentina. Ana will be an excellent social worker.

At lunch, my mind returns to Mr. Diaz. If he *is* going to leave, we should get him a cake. He is one of our success stories.

The team worked with him throughout the summer. The speech therapist helped him practice his swallow so he could once again eat the Cuban rice and beans that made him salivate, instead of relying on the tube feeding that the dietitian monitored for adequate intake. The skin and wound care nurse taught his teenage granddaughters how to care for his skin so it wouldn't become red and raw or break down into ulcers. Nurses hung IV bags, checked the sites through which medication goes in, gave him his medication, and continually reassessed his condition. The respiratory therapists managed his airway, making sure that he got enough support, while at the same time, advancing the balancing act called weaning— learning to breathe on his own to avoid being attached to the ventilator for the remainder of his life. Physical therapy worked with him twice a day and strengthened his muscles, so now, he can walk around the nurse's station with assistance, tubes and all. It has been a long road, but even *he* has begun to experience brief moments of optimism...perhaps, *perhaps*... he WILL live through this.

End of Life Decisions

Ana and I sit with members of a family who have requested that their loved one be removed from life support. Our ethics committee considers all cases that involve "end of life" decisions, offering ethical guidance to patients, families, and physicians. This family has come to believe there is no chance of a meaningful recovery.

We explore with the family what "meaningful" would be from the patient's perspective, if he could tell us. We help the family identify benefits and burdens of continued treatment. They say the patient was a proud and independent man who disliked doctors, hospitals, and pain. His wife is convinced that he would not want to live like this. His daughters sob softly in the background and agree. I am crying a little, too, but inside so no one else sees.

Challenges to Balance and Perspective

When I finally get the call from Mr. Diaz's insurance company, I am sitting in the office rewriting the hospital's abuse policies. This is a priority because the Joint Commission on Accreditation of Healthcare Organizations (JCAHO) will make its visit soon, and failing the survey is too horrible to imagine. I know Mr. Diaz's insurance company is anxious for him to leave the hospital. Hospital care is extremely costly. He has, in fact, been ready to go since last week, from his physician's perspective. Though I have had several pleasant chats with Monique, the nurse case manager who's been monitoring his progress, the woman who calls me today is Monique's boss. We have a manager to manager chat about Mr. Diaz's benefits. She wants to be completely sure that I know that as soon as she resolves a paperwork glut, she will be sending an ambulance to transport him to a nursing home.

He has been waiting for them to finalize his transfer arrangements all week, and now it's Friday. She advises me that her final approval may not come until evening. I request that if the approval comes down from her higher ups after 7:00 or 8:00 p.m., they send the ambulance the next day. She informs me that she will send him at 8:00, if the paperwork comes through at 8:00, 11:00 p.m. if it comes through at 11:00 p.m., or 2:00 in the morning if she decides she wants to. Unless, of course, I want to keep him in the hospital for free.

My blood is boiling... I am ready to say something extremely un-manager like when she says...

"...and I don't have the time now to debate this with you," and hangs up.

Have you ever looked straight at a phone, cradled in the receiver and yelled "YOU'RE SICK" at the top of your lungs? You now know that I have.

Fuming, I run half-crazed into administration, ready to pounce on my bosses for all the woes of the health care system. Relating this story, skin and face burning, I ask them to back me up on this. We cannot possibly release this man under these circumstances, regardless of cost to the facility. I prepare for the worst.

"Of course, we won't [release him]," she says. "We are responsible for this man's well-being. He is not going anywhere until you tell me it is safe."

I feel the adrenaline rush slipping away, and my heart rate goes back to near normal. Somewhere in the back of my mind, I remember saying something similar about safe transfers at a Monday morning management meeting.

"What are you going to do about this?" asks the Assistant Administrator, who has overheard. He knows me well enough to know that I won't let this slide.

Making Health Care Humane, One Policy at a Time

At day's end, I drive home, deliberately avoiding the radio so thoughts of the day can settle in, some finding resolutions, and some inscribing a mental note amidst the rubble that is my brain for tomorrow's attention. I remember my boss's question. That case manager needs education, for sure. I wonder if she is the only person so jaded by the bottom line focus of today's health care environment, that she sees people as assets to be moved between accounts. First thing Monday morning, I will write a letter to the company's president questioning their transfer policy. Certainly no publicity-conscious managed care company would dare admit to transferring patients during late evening hours, I realize. I smile victoriously as I think about how I will have an impact on safe transfers throughout the community by writing to all the managed care companies, showcasing the offender's statement that they would never put one of their enrollees at risk in that way. Tonight, revenge is rich for the hospital social work department manager, but only because it can improve access to safe, appropriate care for people who cannot advocate for themselves.

Chapter 3
Social Work in the Neonatal Intensive Care Unit

by Merle T. Edwards-Orr, Ph.D., LICSW

It was January in Vermont. It was cold. It was Monday. That meant I had two pagers to carry on this day at the University Hospital where I work. I had attached to my right side pocket my usual pager so the Neonatal Intensive Care Unit (NICU) could track me down. On my left side, I carried the pager for the Emergency Room, as I do every other Monday. I felt rather like a gunslinger in a '50s western.

All by itself, the NICU had been keeping me busy. Two sets of twins and one single, not a one of them over 2 pounds, had been admitted to the unit over the last week. This along with the usual run of babies with pneumonia, birth defects, and less serious prematurity. In case I had forgotten those five new little ones over the weekend, there were the five Supplemental Security Income (SSI) applications lying on my desk to greet me as I opened my office door.

Since all children born under 1200 grams, or about 2.5 pounds, are automatically eligible for SSI, I fill out a fair number of these forms. Since they are relatively simple forms, as Federal forms go, I can knock out one, including the supporting paperwork, in about 10 or 15 minutes. I have found it takes me about twice that to teach a parent to fill one out, so I figure I might as well just do it. But that logic presupposes that I won't find myself staring at five of them first thing one gray January morning. It did not look like it was going to be a great day.

In truth, I quite like my job. I love working around babies. I also like that critically ill babies equally befall the rich and the poor, the wicked and the virtuous, and the smart and the stupid. So I get to see a range of people.

I find being the only social worker in my unit a touch lonely. I look forward to my morning coffee time with my social work colleagues as a chance to talk about our own children, complain about the trials of working in healthcare in the '90s, and share information about the hospital and what's new in the professional world. So, armed with my computer-generated list of all babies in the NICU, I gathered up my coffee cup and crossed over the parking lot to the main building and the employee cafeteria.

I was about halfway there when my pager sounded. "Which one?" was my first thought. I am not frightened of the ER like some of my colleagues, but it still represents the unknown more than the NICU pager does. In this case, it was the NICU. The relative known. I responded and a pediatric intern told me she wanted to send young Heather Suitor back to her local hospital, Westlake, in far Upstate New York. This was a good idea, because it meant the child no longer needed NICU care, she would be closer to home, and our very high census would decrease by one.

Reverse or "back" transports, as returns of babies to local hospitals are known, are a microcosm of the administrative and protocol end of the health care system. No one doubts that it is best for babies to be near their parents. Equally, no one wants babies to receive inadequate care. Putting those two principles into practice can be a complicated task.

When I heard the resident say that the team was planning to transport young Miss Suitor to Westlake Hospital, I sighed and began to check whether the process was being followed and whether it even could be followed, since it was Martin Luther King Day and I was not sure the administrative staff at Westlake was even working. "I'll call Dr. D. at Westlake and make sure I ask him about the administrative staff when I do," said the intern, annoyed by my reminders that red tape is there (and babies end up hanging around ERs and parents get huge bills as a result of transfers that don't respect that red tape).

"Give me a holler when you hear, but I'm on my way up and I'll see where we are on this," I said by way of a sign-off.

When I arrived at the NICU, the father of one of our new micro-preemies greeted me. Roger Innis was somebody's fantasy of backwoods Vermont: laconic and honest with just a touch of deference which you could tell made him angry. Now he found himself and his 1.5 pound baby in the land of high-tech in what was, to him, the big city. He was not unintelligent (nor unadaptable, as the weeks would reveal when by discharge, he could talk supplemental oxygen needs and feeding schedules with the best of them) but was way out of his element and was needing to talk to me about two items.

First, it was Monday and he was broke and did I remember the $25 check and hospital meal card I usually brought on Monday. I hadn't, which I regretted, since I knew how much it hurt his pride to ask and how much he needed it. Second, he needed to tell me that the baby's maternal grandmother had been admitted to their local hospital with cancer and was not expected to live much longer. That meant he would be on his own up at the hospital for a while during the time his wife tended to her mother's needs. At the same time, the baby had taken a turn for the worse and the doctors were making no promises about the outcome. He just, in his at once laconic and roundabout way, needed to talk. So, we talked. About the baby, about his mother-in-law. About his relationships with his family (not good) and his with Sarah's family (on-and-off). About his not drinking and how hard that was. About what a big town this felt like to him. About how he wanted a job so he could support his new family. I didn't say much. There wasn't much to say. He just needed to know someone was noticing him and his worries. After a while, I told him I would bring by that check and he nodded sort of mournfully but strode off to find a way to kill the time, since looking in an isolet at your tiny baby is not a full-time job.

Back to Suitor. In the minutes between phone calls and talks with medical staff, I filled out some SSI applications. Name (got to make sure I don't get the twins mixed up). Condition (I almost could write "prematurity at 27 weeks gestation with a birth weight of 750 grams" for all of them). Demographics about the doctors and hospital. A little bit on tests. A couple of releases and that was about it. Not very hard, but five times was decidedly tedious. By the time I had gotten through one set of twins, the transfer looked ready.

The final step was to call Heather's mother to confirm this is what she wanted to happen and give her the arrival times. Yes, she was indeed pleased that we were sending her daughter back to Westlake. That way she would have a chance to visit.

"So travel is a problem?" I asked.

"Oh, yes, my husband uses the car for work and I need to be with my two older kids anyway. I haven't gotten to see Heather in two weeks, since just after she was born," Ms. Suitor replied.

"Have you talked to Medicaid to see if they will help with the transportation costs and maybe even give you a ride?"

"Can they do that? How does that work?"

"I will write a letter of medical necessity and fax it to Medicaid in your county and then you can get transportation help."

"But what about caring for my older kids?" she asked.

"Have the folks from Public Health checked in with you? They should have, and they often help with that kind of thing."

"No," said the mother.

"Let me give Jean a call at Public Health in your county, and she'll check back with you about child care. Also, have you checked with any of your kids' aunts or grandparents to see if they'd help?" I asked.

"Oh, I couldn't impose," was the predictable response.

"Whatever you feel is right in your family, but this is a real crisis and Heather needs you. Families are often happy to pitch in at these times," I suggested.

This was a routine conversation, helping people locate and sort out resources. Only it was happening about 10 days too late. It had been Christmas and I had been off a fair amount, plus the unit had been very full. As a result, if you weren't in my face, like Roger Innis, you didn't get attention. We sometimes forget the importance of the routine. Here was a family that really needed "Resources 101" but hadn't gotten it yet, and time with their baby had been lost. The baby was out the door by a little after noon. Not perfect, but all told, not bad work.

I grabbed a bite of lunch where I read my several days' mail and generally tried to make sense of my life. Lunch tends to be my quiet time. A chance to read an article and generally chill out. If possible, I give my wife a call (she is also a social worker, in private practice) and remind myself of my life outside the hospital walls.

Just as I wrapped up my lunch remains, my pager went off, this time from surgical ICU. *Why SICU?* I wondered. Not my outfit any longer. But, as a dutiful soldier, I called. They had a 19-year-old woman who was very sick with pre-eclampsia (a very dangerous disease of late pregnancy) who was almost certain to lose her baby at 22 weeks into her pregnancy. My colleague who handled Labor and Delivery was only half-time and had left at noon, so that meant this conversation fell to me.

My job was to discuss with the mother and whatever family she had with her what to expect from the delivery. Did they want to hold the baby after she (in this case) was stillborn? Did they want to name her? Did they want a funeral or the hospital-provided cremation? These were issues they had to begin to think about and be as ready as one can be at the time. This is a particularly grueling and yet satisfying part of my job. Grueling because people who are losing their babies are always profoundly sad. Satisfying because it is one of those times when a social worker knows that he (in my case) is really doing some good. Losing your baby is overwhelming, but a chance to talk and be sad and get information is an important gift another person can provide.

Another beep on the pager. Did I know about the Lonergans? asked Sue from the NICU. Well, I knew something. What did she mean exactly? It seems Sue had just gotten off the phone with Jane Lonergan, baby John's mother, and she was making veiled suicidal comments. No, I didn't know about that specifically. I knew that Jane had a history of depression but that she had been doing well over the last several years. I had hoped she wouldn't fall into a new depression sparked by the post-partum period. Maybe I'd better give her a call.

She wasn't there (or wasn't answering). I called Nancy Jones, the public health nurse for her area. As it turned out, Nancy had just seen Jane this morning, and she was worried.

Yes, Jane had made veiled suicidal statements, but had denied real suicidal intent. Nancy knew Jane far better than I did. What did she think? Well, Nancy noted she was not a mental health professional, but she felt that Jane, while not immediately suicidal, clearly had it on her mind. We discussed psychiatric resources available in her area, and they were fairly sparse. I noted that we had psychologists available to provide mental health supports to families and children and maybe I should try to get them to see Jane. Nancy liked that idea, so I tried Jane again.

She answered this time. I made small talk and made sure she was updated on her baby's condition, but quickly got to the point of my concerns. Jane was embarrassed but agreed that she had wondered from time to time whether she wasn't just causing trouble being around. We discussed this for a while with my agreeing that, while she had suicidal thoughts, she was probably not an immediate risk. She agreed that she did not plan to kill herself, and she knew who to call if she felt a strong urge to do so. She also agreed to see our psychologist when she came over to see John tomorrow. I paged Louise, the psychologist, who agreed she could see Jane. I then just hoped my assessment was right and Jane was telling the truth.

Off to Surgical ICU. Janelle Houseman was there in her bed, with her boyfriend, Mitch, at her bedside. Janelle looked very sick and spoke with difficulty. Mitch was exhausted and scared but trying hard to be strong. They talked about their lives, their hopes for the baby, how they had learned things were going wrong, their expectation that the baby would be born dead or die upon birth, but their hope for the best. I am often struck by how powerfully people struggle to understand and overcome a situation they had never dreamed would happen. Here was a young couple that would survive. They would hurt, but they would find a way to come out the other end whole.

The day was winding down. This all had happened between miscellaneous phone calls, SSI applications, pages from the pharmacy for permission to approve Social Work Department payment for prescriptions, and the rest of the little stuff that no one remembers but takes up minutes and hours in a day. No meetings today. That was unusual.

And charting. I needed to make sure each of these major contacts had a note in the chart, so other team members were aware of my observations. This takes time, but it is a commonplace thought in medical settings that "if it isn't documented, it didn't happen."

It was well past dark when I returned to my office to finish the day's paperwork, pass the ER pager (it had been quiet today) on to the next day's worker, and head home. Not a bad day. Some sense of accomplishment. Certainly some frustrations. Plenty to look forward to for tomorrow.

Chapter 4
Social Work in an Infertility Clinic

by Gretchen Gross, LICSW, ACSW, NCADC

L ife in a medical clinic setting is vastly different from my initial experiences as a hospital-based social worker. In those days, working in the Emergency Room, with the Burn/Shock/Trauma team, in a chemical dependency treatment center, or with the inpatient gynecological oncology service meant that I was married to my beeper, and needed to be a jack of all trades, able to go from a family meeting set up to decide on possible organ donation to a discharge planning session. Compared to those days, my current position as a counselor in a University-affiliated outpatient medical clinic provides me with much more autonomy and control over my professional life, my case load, and diversity of population and services offered.

Each day, I see a variety of couples and individuals who are referred to me by the physicians, midwives, and the other practitioners who provide reproductive services to our patients. My office is in the Department of OB/GYN, and I provide services in the same manner that I do at my private practice. I schedule my own clients, attend weekly in-vitro fertilization (IVF) team meetings, present at Resident Didactics (meaning I train OB/GYN residents and fellows in the psychosocial aspects of reproductive medicine and women's health care), and present at department Grand Rounds. I consult with physicians on troublesome cases, and treat or refer clients as needed.

Since working in this medical subspecialty, my clinical repertoire has grown significantly, providing me with a diverse experience of reproductive medicine, which I find to be stimulating. Although I meet with infertility patients, I also provide counseling services for depressed women, women who are having postpartum depression, pregnant women with a history of bulimia or sexual abuse, women and couples who experience sexual dysfunction, multiple miscarriages or fetal losses, and those who are considering treatment alternatives, such as adoption or stopping treatment and leading a "childfree" life.

I perform clinical/psychosocial assessments on couples who, for any number of medical reasons, have been diagnosed with some form of infertility, and are proceeding with reproductive technologies in hopes of becoming pregnant. I meet with every couple considering in-vitro fertilization (IVF), therapeutic donor insemination (TDI—with an anonymous or known donor), and donor egg procedures (both known and anonymous donors) through our clinic. A couple must have this assessment as a part of their pre-treatment work-up to assess their marital and individual stability, their coping skills and support networks, their understanding of the psychological, financial and time demands placed on them during treatment, and their comprehension of their chances of becoming pregnant. Depending on the treatment needed, there can be up to a 75% failure rate, which each person must understand prior to starting treatment.

These procedures, though offering hope for genetic offspring and the experience of pregnancy, often challenge a couple's ethical beliefs about levels of medical intervention. Each couple should consider this aspect of treatment before starting treatment. If a Catholic couple is considering IVF, and they have found significant strength in their religion, how do they expect that proceeding with IVF (not sanctioned by the Catholic Church) might affect their religious belief, practice, and participation? In some sense, I slow couples down a bit, in order to engage them in decision-making processes that are ethically and spiritually compatible. It is far more advantageous to encourage these patients to make a slow and thoughtful decision, rather than to allow them to rush into decisions on procedures that might directly contradict their religious or ethical beliefs.

Infertility treatment has a significant potential to highlight and exacerbate any previous relational difficulties and individual pathologies, rather than to initiate problems. Because of the duration and type of emotional and physical stress, treatment fans the slow burning embers more often than starts a new fire for couples. For example, if the male partner has a history of an anxiety disorder and is finding that as treatment progresses, he is experiencing more frequent and severe panic attacks, he needs to be identified and treated. His anxiety will affect various levels of treatment, from semen collection and quality of the ejaculate to marital communication and functioning during and after treatment. Now, consider that the wife might begin to blame him for bringing this up if it slows down the process or prevents them from starting treatment immediately. He might blame himself for their infertility, or she might punish him for asking for help. Couples in infertility treatment will experience more marital and intrapsychic stress than they had anticipated. Their ability to communicate this to friends, family, and staff, as well as to each other, is paramount to diminishing their sense of isolation.

The assessment sessions provide patients with a forum to begin to discuss some of these concerns, myths, fears, and expectations while learning that they are not alone in the infertility experience. Current statistics estimate that 15-30% of American couples will experience some level of infertility. However, because of the intimate nature of infertility, few people share their diagnosis, and fewer receive social support for infertility. Many couples will come to sessions fearful that they are abnormal, because they are shying away from malls and grocery stores where there are likely to be more children and families. Simply normalizing the couple's experience of this process, validating their experiences, and providing them with a safe place to talk about their anger, frustrations, and sense of being out of control can help significantly.

Another facet of this position involves helping couples come to terms with ending treatment, to living without children in the case of their not going on to adoption. Because there are so many treatment options, with more developing rapidly, it is difficult for a couple to say "we are through with treatment." However, that can be as therapeutically appropriate as continuing with treatment, which might exhaust them and their resources. The counselor may be one of the first people to raise this option as an acceptable and healthy choice. Helping couples explore their definitions of "family," their expectations of their relationship without children, and to make some sense out of their experience is central to good infertility practice.

I have found work in this subspecialty very exciting, stimulating, and demanding. It requires a significant level of medical knowledge of each procedure (couples do not need the added stress of "teaching" their counselor about their treatment process, expected outcomes, surgeries involved, and so on), an awareness of the possible impacts of fertility drugs on mood states, an ability to work as a member of a multi-disciplinary team where you may be the only mental health professional, and a significant working knowledge of differential diagnosis. Work in infertility is similar to, but not the same as, working with a chronically ill population, in which there is an experience of waxing and waning treatment, changes in mood and affect depending on the phase of treatment, and an understanding of the effects of the process on a marriage, and other significant relationships.

Further, in such a cutting edge medical setting, the ethical dilemmas that arise continue to challenge all members of an infertility treatment team. Clinical social workers must constantly check in on themselves to assess their own potential for projection and overlap on the issues and treatment of each couple. Infertility counseling brings the future into the present. Dilemmas and opportunities that most of your social work colleagues consider "science fiction" will repeatedly present in your office!

For example, a young man diagnosed with cancer banks sperm prior to surgical, chemical, and radiation treatments. His prognosis is good, and the couple feels that they can consider fertility issues at a later date, when he is well. That patient dies of complications, and his wife presents six months after his death wishing to be inseminated with his sperm, in hopes of getting pregnant. You are asked to meet with her, to assess whether she is making a rational decision at this time. The clinic team is unsure about their participation in this process, as it challenges several of them ethically. When you meet with this woman, she is clearly in acute grief, still emotionally numb, and expresses some levels of guilt about the relationship. She tells you that just prior to his death, she and her husband had separated because he had learned of an affair she had started while he was in treatment for cancer.

Difficult ethical questions are now raised, such as: Would this man, if he were alive, choose to have a child with this woman? What are the legal considerations? Did this man include his frozen sperm in his will? Do his parents and family know about her interest? Would she tell them? What is the woman's level of emotional stability? Although a composite of many cases of which I am aware, this is not an unusual situation. Medically, physicians are now able to extract sperm from a man in a coma. Is this ethical? Is this legal if the man is unable to give consent? Is this rape? What rights does the wife have to having offspring by her comatose husband? Though again futuristic, these cases have been raised a number of times in hospitals and infertility clinics.

On a more familiar level, couples undergoing IVF can easily freeze embryos not returned to the woman's uterus for later use. Are both partners equally interested in this possibility? Do they consider that these embryos may become a bone of contention should the marriage dissolve? It is difficult but necessary to raise these subjects with this couple prior to their IVF attempt. Knowing when and where to refer to collaterals— whether to a lawyer familiar with reproductive law or to a psychiatrist who can help a patient come off a medication (or start on one) in the best interest of a healthy treatment process and possible pregnancy—is so important when working with infertility.

Though I have always worked in and around the medical setting, this is the most challenging and stimulating arena yet. I must always learn more, to keep up with developments and changes in many areas. I must always challenge my own ethical standards. Can I work with a couple who have recently conceived quadruplets through IVF and are now interested in terminating two fetuses? How do my own feelings affect my work with this population? I rely on my team members, specifically the IVF Nurse Coordinator and Research Nurse, who always have an open door for conversation. These developments happen much more quickly than we generally anticipate. Being able to talk over our own issues, concerns, and ethics is imperative to maintaining a level of self-awareness and effectiveness in this field.

One drawback to this field is that I miss working with other clinical social workers (most clinics have one staff counselor), and therefore I relish membership in supervision and professional groups. Specific professional memberships of great importance are somewhat limited to the American Society of Reproductive Medicine (ASRM), and the ASRM Mental Health

Professional Group, which is made up of clinical social workers, psychologists, psychiatrists, and ethicists who specifically meet to address the changing demands of these positions.

Finally, awareness of one's own reproductive expectations, abilities, and interests is tantamount to working in this field. If you are experiencing infertility and are in treatment or have been recently, and have not been in counseling yourself, I strongly suggest that this would be a challenging and difficult arena in which to work. Similarly, being a counselor who has children or is pregnant and is sitting daily with patients who are expressing anger at "the fertile world" provides its own set of challenges.

We must ask ourselves, "What is the value of parenthood in this society? Do I understand my own biases one way or the other? Can I be effective in helping to minimize the splitting between the 'haves' and the 'have nots' in a society where 'family' is defined by the number of children in a relationship?" Questions such as these cycle and recycle and can help one become a more effective and compassionate care provider.

One final word. If you are interested in this area of subspecialty, please be sure you are aware of the myths of infertility, which continue to circulate. Be sure to get an extensive background in the medical side of treatment, so your patients do not have to spend session time describing IVF, and become expert in grief and mourning. Without these as a minimum requirement, you are more likely to be unhelpful than helpful to your clients.

Chapter 5
Working with Pregnant Women in Public Health

by Alfreda Paschall Gee, MSW

I work with pregnant women. That is an easy, safe, and accurate assessment of my job that works well in most settings. It immediately distances me from the "I take children from their parents at my own whim" stereotype that I used to live with a few years ago. My work is public health oriented, pro-active and yes, even appreciated by various, though not all, schools of thought.

I work in a small city that grows with tourism, the movie industry, and other light industries. It grows in poverty for far too many, with seasonal laborers, and the very young giving birth too soon. Sound familiar?

I am paid by the county from funds I generate by billing Medicaid for the contacts I make with patients in the maternity clinics. I follow each patient from the time I meet her until roughly two months after her pregnancy ends, regardless of the pregnancy outcome. I work in two settings: the local hospital's OB/GYN clinic, and a newly-formed private OB/GYN office, just exploring all the ins and outs of Medicaid reimbursement and patients.

The job has specific requirements set out by state guidelines, but affords a good deal of autonomy and professional judgment. There are four social workers involved in the maternity team, and we work with nurses and are supervised by a nurse. This has provided challenges in the true sense of the word. It has worked very well, and we have been able to carve out our own areas of expertise. It is also helpful, as our team becomes a part of the larger medical community, which includes other disciplines, such as doctors and administrators.

My friend, Barbara, and I coined the phrase that we are "born again social workers." It is a term we use with care and affection. And yet, we use it more some days than others.

Below, I have included some excerpts from a few of my days as a "born again" public health social worker.

Tuesday: Dr. McIntyre, a second year OB resident, calls from the ER about a patient who was just taken to the Birth-place to be monitored. Facts: Nova is 36 years old, has four kids, weighs 350+ pounds (can't be weighed on scales), had two previous C-sections, was gestational diabetic last two preg-nancies, and her last delivery was 15 months ago. She has no car, no phone, lives 15 miles south of the hospital. Husband is "away working." Closest relative is her critically ill father, for whom she is the primary caretaker. Nova's main support is a cousin who lives 18 miles west of the hospital. Nova learned three days ago that she is seven weeks pregnant, and has two appointments Thursday: one at the OB clinic and one at the abortion clinic, and a decision to make about which one she keeps. She is tearful, but calm and ready to talk. Dr. McIntyre introduces me to her, saying, "Ms. Gee is a social worker. She can help." (NOTE: Gasp!)

I let Nova know what I have been told, let her fill in some details, and check to see if I was accurately informed. I do my best listening, offer referrals, if not solutions, and encourage her to take some time to think. The decision about the preg-nancy needs to be made soon, and we agree it is her first priority. We discuss some ways that she has used in the past to make hard decisions, and I teach her one of my own tech-niques that has worked at times. She agrees to call me or see me Thursday, or sooner as needed. (NOTE: Procured a box of tissues for Nova, as tangible evidence for myself that I was helpful. It is Nova who has the tough job.)

Tuesday afternoon: Sharon, 29, stops by the clinic to show me her 6-month-old baby boy. She's still breastfeeding, still in her apartment, and still clean. She still sees John, who "hasn't hurt me since the baby came," and still has little con-tact with her family. "I quit going to the [drug treatment] pro-gram, but I'm doing fine." (NOTE: Build on the obvious posi-tives. Bite your tongue against sharing what your instincts tell you. She came for a reason. Water that seed you planted with her 10 months ago.)

Tuesday later: Julia is 14 years old, second pregnancy, with one miscarriage earlier in the year. She is tired of living at home, does not like her mother's boyfriend, and wants to live with the father of her baby. "He's 19 or 20 and he makes good money" with no obvious employer. Julia is suspended from school, again. Her mother works swing shift at the sewing mill, and "sits for some old lady sometimes." Julia always comes to clinic alone, goes to *Baby Talk* class for teens, loves the health educator, and considers herself a group leader.

Today, in clinic, Julia is upset that her boyfriend has been turned in to the D.A. for having sex with her (a minor). She suspects the hospital staff made the report. She is not as concerned that her test of cure for syphilis is still reactive, which she has never told her mother about.

We review all the literature on Sexually Transmitted Diseases and prevention. I discuss the idea of abstinence, which makes her smile. I'm not sure if this is because she considers it stupid, or if it's an option she does not think she can choose. I encourage her to talk to her mother.

I tell Julia that I made the report to the D.A.'s office, which nearly ends the meeting then and there. I give the position of my legal obligation, but I doubt if she hears much of it. She leaves the pamphlets on STDs on my desk. (NOTE: Hope she will continue her prenatal care. Get help from the health educator, whom she trusts.)

Wednesday: Charted all the stuff from yesterday. Wrote "creative" job plans and goals for next year. Followed up on that call to the D.A.'s office. Asked Cyndi for help about Julia. Prepared referrals for the Child Service Coordinators and presented cases. Spent time with Cathie about her patient who is HIV positive.

Thursday: Nova chose the OB Clinic, and says she feels "It's the right thing for me." Her husband came "back to town from working off somewhere." Her cousin will move in to provide help with her father and kids and will bring a car. Nova is less tearful. "I'm not used to having others do for me." (NOTE: We'll work on that.)

Sharon's boyfriend was in the newspaper in the Police Blotter for assault and battery. They didn't print the victim's name. Maybe she'll call. Maybe she's upstairs in the hospital. I won't have time to go by her house today. Maybe she'll call.

Signed Toni up again today. Keyetta is only eight months old; this is a different father of baby and "this one is really special." Toni is off her meds, if she ever used them. She is vague. She only fed Keyetta juice today ("She likes juice!"); and left her in the stroller for the entire three hours except to change her diaper (which I provided) and when I held Keyetta to model for Toni "one neat way to help Keyetta go to sleep." (NOTE: Keyetta is beautiful and very alert. She liked *Simple Gifts* and I think Toni had heard it before.)

Saw six other folks, including a frustrated mother about her daughter who is in need of homebound school. I made phone calls about this year's Fall meeting with the school staff. Instigated to trash a friend's office for her 40th birthday.

Friday: Barbara and I kiss our desks today. (A ritual of "born again social workers.") Her patient, whose two children have been in foster care, has been granted custody, and Barbara did not have to testify. I am reminded that I have not set foot in a court room in five years, and we both rejoice that a good decision was reached. Her patient has worked hard and is ready.

Home visit to Julia's house. The first good sign is that she lets me in the house. She says, "I talked to my mom." The investigation prompted her and her mother to talk. She chooses not to share the content of that conversation with me, but doesn't say anything about moving out, either. Julia says little, but asks, "Will Cyndi be having *Baby Talk* on Tuesday?" I tell her I am sure she will and give her a bus ticket to get there.

Phone mail message from Sharon: It was not her this time. John is in jail, but she expects he'll be out soon. "Can we talk Monday?" (NOTE: I know this could mean anything. Hope it means she's ready to leave, and don't even think she wants a way to get him out of it. But she called, and it was not her, and that seed is still growing.)

Chapter 6
Managing in Managed Care

by David C. Prichard, Ph.D.

I park my car in the black asphalt parking lot and stroll at a brisk pace into the newly constructed managed health care office building just off the highway. It is one of many mirrored glass and red brick buildings prevalent in the corporate business park of the posh West End of the city. I take the steps, two at a time, to the second floor, and punch in the security code to gain entrance to the very large office space that, with padded blue partitions, has been divided into four pods of eight cubicles. As clinical supervisor of one pod, I am responsible for the clinical supervision of eight clinical case managers.

It is 8 a.m. sharp, and already there is the gentle trill of the digital phones, the buzz of voices taking calls. I check in briefly with the crisis worker in a corner pod. She's on the phone. A tap on her shoulder and an inquisitive look provides me with the smile and a thumbs down that tells me I have no emergencies from the previous night. Strolling past the receptionist, I'm informed that there is a call on hold for me, and am handed a stack of 15 phone messages taken by crisis workers the previous night, apparently routine calls, or so I hope. I rifle through these as I walk briskly to my cubicle in the far corner of the rectangular room. The ivys in the window provide a splash of green; the ficus floor plant has shed its few remaining leaves, its brown branches stark and accusatory.

The shorthand of the receptionist makes sense to me, though it would appear to be a foreign language to one not familiar with the cryptic lingo of the managed care industry; I translate quickly in my head. Smith needs five sessions to terminate; Waklowski needs two sessions for initial intake; Barrow needs authorization for two clients in need of psychological testing; Meldrum needs inpatient evaluation for a suicidal client; Milton is appealing a denial for authorization for inpatient detoxification...the messages go on. Seeing nothing out of the ordinary, I put the messages at the bottom of a stack of 18 messages left over from late yesterday. I will need to get these taken care of immediately. On a typical day, I will receive 40 phone messages, on top of the calls that I pick up while at my desk.

I settle in, tip back in my padded chair, prop my feet on the desk, and begin to sift through the 50+ client charts stacked in several piles on my cubicle table top. The medical records coordinator will stroll by at 10 a.m. and 2 p.m. to drop off records that need review. Providers have mailed in treatment plans, updates, and discharge summaries that will need to be reviewed to determine the medical necessity of mental health treatment. In the case of initial treatment plans, I ascertain whether or not the client has been provided a diagnosis that is covered by his or her particular insurance policy. The diagnosis must be supported by specific symptoms, and the therapist needs to be very specific in presenting a plan for reducing the symptomatology reported by the client. Finally, I need to be certain that the provider has included outcomes measures that will indicate the success of treatment and suggest when treatment may be appropriately terminated.

I turn on the computer, gazing out the window as it warms up. I will spend much of the day here, fielding calls from mental health providers seeking authorization to provide treatment for clients. My job is controversial. There are those who believe that managed care is simply another example of corporate America discovering a means to increase profits for shareholders of insurance companies, at the expense of individuals seeking mental health treatment. To a large extent, I agree. The corporate administrators who run the company appear to be much more concerned about the financial health of the company than the mental health of the clients, or policy holders. I do believe, however, that there are excesses in the system that need to be managed. I recall disturbing cases of fraud and unethical treatment—the recent case, for example, of a psychiatrist billing Medicaid for weekly sessions for a client who had died two years previously. And the case of the psychoanalyst who, after two years of treatment with a client diagnosed with an adjustment disorder, requested 1700 additional sessions. I feel conflicted, torn between opposing the profit-driven corporate greed that drives the managed health care industry, and supporting the need to screen out unethical, inefficient, ineffective treatment, that at its best does no harm to clients, and at its worst creates considerably more distress and fosters unhealthy dependence.

I reflect back to my work in community mental health and the indignation I experienced by decisions made by managed care. As did many social workers, I rebelled at the thought of an outside person "dictating" to me how to provide the most effective treatment for my client. And, indeed, with some companies, it did feel as though the managed care case managers were more intent on cutting sessions and reducing costs, than providing ethical, effective treatment. I recall a woman who I evaluated for inpatient hospitalization. She was floridly psychotic and experiencing command hallucinations—voices telling her to run her car into the side of a bridge. The managed care company refused to authorize the voluntary inpatient treatment, and encouraged her to drive to the community mental health center to be evaluated for treatment. Their refusal to authorize treatment for a voluntary client disempowered her, and could easily have resulted in the injury or death of herself and others. The latent function of their negligence resulted in the necessity of an involuntary hospitalization, with the state of Virginia paying the bill rather than the managed care company—another example, I felt, of corporate greed taking advantage of a governmental loophole to line the pockets of company stockholders at the expense of taxpayers.

Sighing, I turn back to the computer, lean into the screen, and dive into my stack of client charts, many containing requests by providers for authorization for initial assessments. The first request is typical. The provider is requesting two initial sessions for an assessment and to develop a treatment plan. The client is a 25-year-old single mother whose husband abandoned the family a month ago. Since that time she has experienced significant weight loss, is unable to concentrate at work, and reports that she has spells of uncontrollable crying throughout the day. She is not reported to be suicidal, but appears hopeless, overwhelmed, and states that her life is worthless. The precipitant is clear, symptoms well-defined, and the provider suggests a course of action that includes crisis-oriented treatment. The situational symptoms suggest an adjustment disorder, which is covered by the client's insurance policy, and I suspect the client will benefit from the solution-focused treatment proposed by the provider. It has taken me two minutes to review the chart, enter authorization for treatment and a short note into the computer, and send the chart back to medical records to be processed and the authorization mailed.

With 10 phone calls interspersed among the reviews, in two hours I have processed 20 charts, all of them requests for initial authorizations for treatment. I have pulled aside three charts that I will present at the team staffing at 10 a.m. The team I supervise meets with the agency medical and clinical directors once a week for two hours to staff more difficult cases. Today, we will also be addressing concerns regarding two providers. One provider appears to have a proclivity toward diagnosing clients with dissociative identity disorder (DID), and is requesting $20,000/month inpatient treatment for a highly functional client; the other relies on hypnosis and past life regression to treat incest survivors. The issue in the former case is whether the provider is properly diagnosing clients and is providing cost-effective and efficient treatment; in the latter case, with what research-informed treatment modalities are considered appropriate.

While most providers appear to be very competent and ethical, there are those few that take up much of our time and energy as we seek to provide the most effective and efficient treatment to clients. The meeting is interesting. The clinical director has done her homework and we spend much of the two hours reviewing DID and the current research on effective treatment for incest survivors. We strategize how best to educate and communicate with these providers. While we do not want to be accused of dictating treatment, we also have an ethical responsibility as professionals to insure that clients are receiving competent, effective, and efficient treatment by qualified, competent mental health professionals. There are no easy answers.

Lunch arrives quickly, and I eat at my desk while reviewing the weekly training manual on brief and solution-focused treatment. Tomorrow, I will be meeting with a group of 38 providers in the region to whom I provide clinical case management. I know that it will be a difficult two hours. Providers are struggling to adapt to the managed care system, and there is a great deal of resentment, born largely from resistance to change, fear of the unknown, perceived loss of clinical control, and loss of income. There is a sense among providers that managed care equates to forced unethical, restricted treatment. Later in the week, I will be meeting with the entire clinical staff of a community mental health center to discuss their concerns around managed care, and to provide training on how to provide ethical treatment in a managed health care environment. The presentation will focus on the ethics of managed care and the fundamentals of solution-focused treatment, which is the language of most managed care companies. I will draw largely on my experience in community mental health, private, and managed care practice.

On Fridays, I spend the day in the clinic on the first floor. My specialty is in crisis intervention and trauma, and therefore, I select cases in which clients have clear precipitating events that have led to the presenting symptoms. My treatment is crisis-oriented and focused on reducing the immediate symptoms of the trauma. The deeper work may come later. For now, my work is to help clients regain their equilibrium after a particularly traumatizing life event. The focus will be on normalizing the reactions being experienced by exposure to a difficult, "abnormal" life event and in working with clients to find effective coping mechanisms to adjust to changing life circumstances. It is not unusual for me to see clients in intensive treatment several times per week over a few weeks. Once major symptoms have subsided, and the client appears to be back at previous levels of functioning, we will decide mutually on termination.

I spend much of my afternoon on the phone with providers, discussing cases. Although many providers appear to view me as someone whose job it is to restrict treatment, I see my role as one of collaborator, providing free, collegial, peer supervision. I receive a call from Heather, one of my favorite providers. While many providers are hostile and demanding when they call, questioning the ethics of anyone who could work for managed care, Heather appears friendly, communicative, and direct. We have developed a mutually respectful, professional relationship, and when she calls, I trust Heather to be forthright and honest. For that reason, our call is short. Heather is requesting eight additional sessions for her client who is experiencing trauma reactions from a rape that occurred three weeks ago. The request is clearly reasonable, the treatment appropriate, and most importantly, I have come to trust her professional judgment and integrity. She specializes in and works well with trauma survivors. Continued treatment is authorized. We spend a few minutes talking about plant care—she has no trouble with ficus, and offers several suggestions for determining proper light and water.

I am relieved when 5 o'clock arrives. I feel as though I've been on the phone and computer all day, yet there remain many charts and unanswered phone messages scattered on my desk. These will need to wait until tomorrow. I gather the charts to return to medical records, where they will be double-locked to insure confidentiality. Turning off my computer screen, I water and mist the ivy plants on my window sill. The plants are healthy, of the sort that flourish well with little care and regular doses of water. The ficus on the floor has given up; although I have bought several, I never seem able to coax them to survive, much less flourish—too much water, I suspect, and death by over-attention!

As I head home, driving down the azalea-lined boulevard, I reflect on my last call with Heather. Interesting discussion on plants, I muse. Indoor plant enthusiasts need to acknowledge their limitations with plant care; so too do mental health practitioners need to know their clinical limitations, areas of expertise, and they should practice within these bounds. In a nutshell, that is at the core of my work as a managed care clinical supervisor—assuring that the most qualified, experienced, competent, efficient, and effective practitioners are providing treatment to clients that are, indeed, in need of medically necessary care.

PART 2:
HIV/AIDS

Chapter 7
Private Practice with Urban Gay Men:
With a Subspecialty in HIV/AIDS

by Michael Shernoff, MSW, CSW, ACSW

I work out of the second bedroom in my Manhattan apartment. After spending 45 minutes on the Nordic Track early in the morning, I see my first client, B, who is a fifty-year-old fireman whose partner of 27 years died almost a year ago of cancer. Neither he nor his partner were infected with HIV. He is stumbling through life adjusting to being a widower and trying to learn how to do for himself all of those things that he once counted on his partner to do for him. I spend the session empathizing with and validating his feelings while simultaneously trying to keep my feelings in check, even though it has been more than four years since I buried my own beloved partner after his death from a series of AIDS-related lymphomas. I jot a note to remind myself to bring the intensity of the feelings stirred up by this session into my own supervision and therapy later in the week.

My second client is L, a youthful HIV-positive man who is also grieving the loss of his partner, C, from AIDS less than a year ago. Additionally, L is dealing with a flare up of Chronic Active Hepatitis B, for which he is preparing to undergo a liver biopsy. During the session, he is in tears, lamenting that while he has his family and friends to provide support, he does not have the special attentions of a partner "to do for me all that I did for C during his various hospitalizations." My heart goes out to him, as I have thought those same things at various times since Lee died.

The third man I see is M, who is also HIV-positive and though never having experienced any physical symptoms of HIV disease, the level of virus in his blood stream is detectable and increasing. So far, he has chosen not to take any medication, but he feels that the time is approaching when he will need to begin some form of therapy. Our sessions are filled with his discussing all of his feelings about how his condition is progressing and the uncertainties associated with taking the powerful new medications. After M, I go to the gym for an hour and a half to help do something purely physical that takes my mind off of the work I have already done and that lies ahead.

The landscape of my life, personal history, memories, and dreams is littered with the corpses and ghosts of loved ones, clients, colleagues, and just fellow members of my tribe and community who have died in this plague. Being a middle-aged HIV-positive gay man living and working in Manhattan's Chelsea neighborhood, which is literally one of the ground zeros of the AIDS epidemic in North America, there is no way it could be any different. Since the early 1980s, when the AIDS plague began to spread within the gay community, I have been surrounded by illness, death, and grief. My best friend and colleague in my private practice, Luis, died of AIDS in 1989. Six men in my apartment building have died of AIDS over the years, as have more than 100 of my clients. In the face of so much loss, those accounts of a tunnel of white light or the soul's triumphant escort by a chorus of angels seem like a child's story devised to soothe and comfort. I've had to become matter-of-fact about how the body inevitably fails us, and most of the time I don't worry about what happens when we die. I try to stay focused on how to live life well and how to help my clients live well.

This is nothing like what I expected I would be doing when I was training to be a therapist. Back then, I had certain young and hopeful ideas about the potential of human beings, within a normal life span, to grow in self-awareness. My job as I saw it was to help them make changes that would allow them to lead happier lives. But by the mid-1980s, I suddenly found myself with a clientele made up largely of gay men who were either symptomatic with AIDS or anticipating the onset of symptoms, many of them under the age of 40.

Beginning in 1983, as a volunteer at the Gay Men's Health Crisis (GMHC), which is the world's oldest and largest community-based AIDS service organization, I have worked with dozens of gay men with AIDS, and supervised a team of volunteers caring for the then desperately ill and dying. At that time, GMHC was sounding the alarm that this illness was going to become an epidemic in the gay community. Even those of us working with AIDS clients every day could not wrap our minds around how this illness was devastating our community. As an action-oriented person, the hardest thing for me was knowing that despite my most creative and skillful clinical maneuvers, I was not going to change the essential fact that these men were dying. I had not been trained as an oncological social worker. Since the onset of the AIDS plague, I have been learning how to do this work while simultaneously being immersed in providing both patient care and training to other professionals who knew even less than I did about the essentials of HIV, working with gay men, injection drug users, young people who were dying, and their families.

Today is a special day, as it will be the final session of a support group I have been leading for over six years for the social workers on the AIDS team at St. Luke's Roosevelt Hospital Center in Manhattan. When I was first hired to run this group, these professionals were in a constant state of crisis because of the staggering number of client deaths they regularly experienced.

Despite the excellent supervision they received, the hospital and department were in an enormous period of change and transition that left none of the social workers feeling well enough supported professionally or secure about being able to maintain their jobs. With the advent of the new triple combination anti-retroviral therapies available, client deaths became increasingly rare, even among the inner city injection drug-using population that made up the majority of the individuals on their caseloads. Today, while the various fiscal cutbacks still create a climate of job uncertainty for these skilled and dedicated social workers, they have become a cohesive team and have learned how to weather the varieties of personal and professionally demanding situations that are a routine part of HIV social work. While we have discussed that there will always be some need for an ongoing support group, most of the members and I have come to the general consensus that the group has really run its course. Riding the subway back to my office, I review the work this group has done and my role in helping them provide services to some of Manhattan's most disadvantaged and difficult-to-serve individuals. I allow myself to feel proud of the part I have played in facilitating the process and the crucial work these wonderful people have engaged in for the previous years.

The first session after returning from the hospital is a lunch time appointment with a male couple. R and T, who have been together seven years, are a mixed HIV antibody status couple with R being the person with AIDS and T being his HIV-negative partner. When I first began working with them, R was critically ill and most of our sessions focused on helping them adjust to R's deterioration, share their feelings about what they were going through, begin their mourning individually and as a couple, and plan for greater levels of caring for each of them. At one point, I referred them to a group at GMHC for couples in which one or both partners have HIV. Their regular attendance in this group provided them with an enormous amount of support, both from the two social workers leading the group and from the other couples who were also struggling to learn to survive and thrive as best they could with one or both partners suffering from this life threatening illness.

Now the picture is entirely different. R has regained his health entirely as a result of the triple combination therapy referred to as HAART (highly active anti-retroviral therapy). He has returned to work full time and is as robust, strong, and energetic as he has felt in many years. This resurgence of his health has had some unexpected side effects, primarily the destabilization of his partnership with T. As he began to grow stronger and accept the fact that he was not going to die soon, he recognized that though he felt strongly for T, he did not want to spend the rest of his life coupled with him. T is understandably hurt, but also recognizes that had R not gotten ill so early in their relationship, they might not have developed into anything more than a passing affair. The work at this point consists of encouraging them each to honestly express to one another their feelings about the relationship and its likely ending. Amidst the tears, pain, and fears, there is a lot of genuine love and acceptance that this upcoming transition will inevitably and likely be in both of their best interests.

Next, my session with S is especially trying. S is a 29-year-old superstar hair stylist who is making enormous amounts of money. At the time of his last HIV test, he was still uninfected despite repeatedly having unprotected anal intercourse while high on amphetamines. He has not been able to cease or reduce his drug binges and only attends AA or NA for three or four meetings. During sessions, he confesses his most recent lapse and vows that it will be the last time. Therapy has helped him see that though he is not physiologically dependent on the drugs, he behaves like an addict and is frequently behaving in highly impulsive and self destructive ways. Even the recent deaths of two of his close friends from overdoses of a "recreational" drug they all were doing has not motivated him to enter a drug treatment program.

S enters the session looking pale, wasted, and obviously recovering from the effects of "partying" on drugs. Before I even say anything to him, he reports that he has partied again. "I'm not surprised. You really look like sh--. Do you know that you look like you have AIDS?" I say to him.

"Do I really look that bad?" he responds.

"I'm not exaggerating at all, and I'm surprised that your clients aren't reacting to how badly you look."

"Actually, my bookings are down."

With that, I proceed to remind him that I do not feel I am helping him any longer. In fact, I believe that our sessions are enabling him by allowing him to think he is doing something to help himself when, in fact, he is not. He just nods in agreement. When I tell him this will be our last session unless he either goes into a rehab, or commits to staying drug free and going to at least one 12-step meeting a day, he just looks at me.

"S, I can't just sit here and watch you kill yourself with the drugs and unsafe sex. You need an intensive drug treatment program before we can do the work in therapy that you need. If I continue to work with you, I will be an accomplice to your death."

"You really think that if I don't stop I'll be dead?"

"Remember F and V," I remind him.

The session ends with my telling him that the only way I will be willing to see him again is if he wants my help in getting into a rehab or he has been clean and dry and working a program for at least six months.

I have four other sessions with people whose issues do not directly relate to HIV or AIDS. Colleagues and friends often ask me how it is that I've been able to work in AIDS for so long, dealing with all the pain and suffering endemic to this patient population. Others ask whether it's overwhelming to have intimately known and worked with so many people who have died or who are dying. I have had to struggle to learn that I am indeed doing something by simply sitting with clients, caring about them, and encouraging them to share any and all of their feelings about what is happening to them. Of course, I am unable to change the outcome of their illness. Accepting this reality, more than anything else, has taught me how to tolerate discomfort.

The discomfort I experience is about many things. Often it arises from a genuine empathetic connection with clients who are honestly experiencing feelings about their loss of health, career, lover, and their own imminent death. Once I have grown to care about a person, I feel all the accompanying discomfort about losing that person. Sometimes there is simply the uneasiness of being close to a person who is very ill or who is dying, simply because this reminds me of the fragility of my own good health. Before the onset of AIDS, active alcoholism, drug addiction, and Hepatitis B were the only life-threatening illnesses likely to kill my patients.

My first professional experience with AIDS was in 1981, when a psychotherapy client began exhibiting symptoms of what we now know is HIV illness. At that time, AIDS was unknown, but shortly thereafter, the syndrome was labeled Gay Related Immune Deficiency (GRID). It soon became clear to me that the men who were sick with this new disease had lived no differently than I had for many years. I assumed that if these people were getting sick, there was an excellent chance that the same thing could or would probably happen to me.

Beginning in the earliest days of the epidemic, there was the problem of burnout: everyone I knew, it seemed, was on death's doorstep. The first few deaths of my clients were terribly traumatic. Even as I grieved and went to the funerals and memorial services, I grew angry and frustrated that my clients' lives had been cut short. Some of them were tremendously gifted and creative, and the loss seemed unspeakably tragic. Then, after so many deaths, I went through a period of numbness and couldn't grieve for anyone. People would tell me about someone who had died—someone who may have been my client for a time—and I wouldn't be capable of calling his lover to express my sympathies. I was overwhelmed and shut down, not just to loss but to every kind of connection. I didn't know how to deal with it and felt like a passenger on the Titanic as it began to take on water, running from end to end offering my meager ministrations as the ship kept sinking. As treatments began to improve, the crisis and siege mentality of the work began to abate.

Therapy work with people with HIV and AIDS can seem banal as we discuss everything from wills to bowel movements. It may not seem as if much is going on as I sit with clients in their hospital rooms talking about their medical treatments, or just murmur soothing words as they endure intense physical pain. My simple questions to clients with dementia may not penetrate their mental fog. But I truly believe that just being there and caring about them is extremely healing.

There are different stages of therapy with clients who have AIDS, and each stage may be radically different. Clients who have just found out, or are just dealing with their positive HIV status, I encourage to talk about their fears, their regrets, their anger. I tell them about long-term survivors and nonprogressors—people like me who have HIV but don't become symptomatic. When it seems clinically appropriate to do so, there have been clients with whom I identify myself as a long-term survivor to give them some living embodiment of hope.

This work has changed me profoundly. It has caused me to lose the illusion of my own mortality that so many of us hold on to irrationally. The work has helped me tolerate enormous amounts of uncertainty and discomfort, both in clinical and personal situations. Most of all, it has humbled me. I feel proud to have been among the first social workers in the world who were there working with individuals and families affected by AIDS. I feel extremely privileged and blessed to still be here and doing this work when so many of my colleagues are now gone...way too soon.

Chapter 8
A Very Special Nursing Home in the South Bronx

by Kim Lorber, MSW, CSW

Each morning, I travel to a nursing home in the South Bronx. This is a unique setting for people with AIDS who are in recovery from substance abuse addiction. Treatment is offered by an interdisciplinary team comprised of a permanent staff of social workers, doctors, nurses, a dietitian, substance abuse counselors, case managers, recreational therapists, an education department, and a bevy of consultants. Interdepartmental relationships are strong, reinforcing effective team treatment for residents while also modeling cooperativeness and mutual affection. Many employees have been employed here for most if not all of the program's eight years. Improvements in medical treatment have changed the direction of practice from sobriety for limited survival of residents to a skills-building program for the vast majority, who will graduate to live in society. The annual death rate has been reduced from 30 deaths to less than six.

I am buzzed into the facility and receive the smiles and greetings of those residents whose responsibility it is to monitor the "front point" and document the goings and comings of their peers. Some I know better than others from our work together in groups or individual therapy; most I know fairly well from our initial psychosocial assessment interview. I marvel at the growth they have accomplished in only a few months.

Residents range in age from their early 20s to late 60s. Many grew up in the foster care system and are survivors of physical, emotional, and sexual abuse. The majority are African American or Hispanic. Most have not finished high school. Some have never worked. All have little self-esteem and belief in their own abilities to change. Most are mandated to the home by a legal agency as an alternative to incarceration.

Often, the date of arrival is their first time substance free. Over time, the symptoms from withdrawal will wane, but it is not a fast or easy process.

Our program requires abstinence from illicit drugs and alcohol use. It promotes recovery and a change of behaviors, attitudes, and perceptions. It has a 3-phase structure. Orientation lasts for approximately three months, during which residents participate in in-house activities and develop cohesiveness as a supportive group. Primary Care is a 4- to 6-month phase during which residents begin to attend appointments and recreational outings unescorted. Re-Entry is the third and final phase, requiring completion of an 8-week discharge planning group, which I co-facilitate. Upon completion, mandating agencies will be notified that residents have completed the program and are ready to return to the community.

They will now begin to look for housing, a process that can take two or more months through the Division of AIDS Services (DAS). Their support systems, including family, support groups, Narcotics Anonymous or Alcoholics Anonymous meetings, medical care, individual therapy, and a food pantry, must be in place. Registration with a local agency offering case management and many of these services is essential. These networks will replace the support inherent in our structured program and are coordinated through the social work department.

I check the marker board in the clinic to see who is on bed rest. A review of the "House Changes" clipboard notes Debbie's hospital admission. I call the hospital to find out Debbie's room and telephone numbers. I fax a request to hook up her television and then call her. She sounds exhausted and tells me about the tests she is expecting and her frustrations at being hospitalized again. This is her fifth stay in as many months. She is in pain, lonely, and feeling isolated. Debbie tells me about toiletries and clothing she needs and asks me to contact her brother in New Jersey. She earlier signed a consent form permitting me to speak with her family as needed. Her brother is not at work, and the home number Debbie gave me is incorrect. With her permission, I contact her mother, who knows very little about AIDS. She is concerned about her daughter's treatment and cannot understand why Debbie continues to be plagued by various serious illnesses. I remind her that Debbie's vulnerability is due to her compromised immune system, and that Debbie has returned "home" to our facility feeling better following each hospitalization. Debbie's mother tells me she will kill herself if Debbie dies. I listen, appreciating her worry. There is little more I can say. I offer Debbie's telephone number, but she hesitates. "I live on a fixed Social Security income. I can't afford to call," she says. I suggest taking it for Debbie's brother or daughter. She accepts and thanks me for calling. I call Debbie to let her know I reached her mother, but I do not tell her it is unlikely she will hear from her. I am relieved to learn later that she has called, after all. Debbie hopes for a reunion with her family but, after 25 years of heroin addiction and abandoning her six children, their support has been minimal. They came to visit for the first and only time during a previous hospitalization when they thought she would die. I contact our substance abuse department and relate Debbie's supply request.

Rachel arrives eager to know if I have heard anything from her lawyer, who has left me angry voice mail messages. I listen as she describes last night's dismissive and unhelpful phone call. Rachel is also a mother of six, all boys, who have been raised by others for most of their lives. She is eager to appeal the termination of her parental rights (TPR) and to gain custody of her 2-year-old son. I have written to the judge and her lawyer and left several messages on the latter's voice mail asking about the status of the appeal process. We are waiting to receive papers for Rachel's signature to be submitted to court. A new attorney will be assigned for this phase. Rachel is eager to "have my baby back." She has seen Richard once in almost two years; he has lived since birth with a foster care family eager to adopt him, as they have his three older brothers. I feel conflicted between my professional responsibilities to help Rachel in her self-determination efforts and my personal preference to leave the child with his brothers and the only family he has ever known. I remind Rachel she should be patient and that she is doing everything she can, having begun a Parenting Skills Class run by the Administration for Children's Services (ACS) and my in-house Parenting Support Group. She has been drug-free for nine months. I forewarn her that ACS is concerned with Richard's well-being. Rachel leaves and I jot a note, which I will transcribe later into her chart in the clinic, regarding the progress of her case and our latest efforts on her behalf.

Mitchell needs a letter to help his 18-year-old daughter and her baby find housing. They live in a shelter and lived with him prior to his readmission to our facility. I document his current status, date of admission, and the dates of his admission and discharge during his previous stay.

Lawrence wants to vote in today's primary elections. He has been in the program for a week. I advise him to speak with his counselor to arrange for an escort. Residents are not permitted to leave the facility within the first 30 days of admission, with the exception of legal and medical appointments. Later, Lawrence tells me he has decided not to vote. Meanwhile, I have called the Voter Registration hotline to order forms for other residents.

At 10 a.m., I co-facilitate the Re-Entry discharge group with my office mate. We begin with a review of the importance of keeping a schedule. We solicit updates about the clients' developing outside support networks and distribute calendars for the coming week. I remind them that half of our discharged graduates have relapsed when they lacked outside support. We review the changes they will find from living within an institutional environment to independent apartment life. I remind them of their complicated medication regimens, which most still have dispensed to them throughout the day. Some residents take 40 or more pills daily. They are encouraged to seek self-medication status in order to become familiar with this responsibility before they are also required to shop for groceries, cook, and have meals ready.

Residents typically are excited to be phase-advanced to Re-Entry and see that as the time to find an apartment and "get out." They are eager to be independent, feel good about having been clean for approximately seven or more months, and are tired of living in a structured environment offering little privacy. While their frustrations are understandable, it is the purpose of this group to help them prepare for independent living. Some will have their own apartments. Others will wait for a city-furnished scattered site apartment. They are encouraged to begin going independently on recreational outings. Sometimes we are forceful in our comparison of what they are doing versus what they say they will do once they have moved. Those who think they will join groups and go to movies later when they haven't during their time with us, probably won't. We conclude with a discussion of reestablishing family ties, and residents candidly discuss their family histories, shame of having lied and stolen from their relatives, repeated attempts to be forgiven, and what often feels like final rejection. They are encouraged to be patient with others with whom they need to renegotiate relationships. They are reminded of the importance of focusing on their own recovery and goals, to avoid bad feelings that might trigger a relapse.

I next meet with Michael, a poetic, sensitive man who enjoys writing, reading, and classical music. He is a member of my Creative Writing Group. We periodically meet to discuss literature or something Michael has written. Today he is tired from an unrelenting bout of pneumonia, and he offers me a poem he has written. I accept it gladly and assure him I will read it soon. I do not make any effort to edit or critique his work; I will share with him the parts I understood and enjoyed best and compare it to other things he has written or we have both read. This is a lovely break before lunch.

During lunch in our cafeteria Elsa approaches me. I make an afternoon appointment around therapy and group commitments. After lunch, I check my voice mail messages. Elsa arrives eager to know if I have communicated with the foster care agency about her scheduled child visits and next court date. Elsa's son Johnnie is five years old; she left him with his father three years ago. Johnnie entered the foster care system one year later, after his father abandoned him, and has been living with the woman he knows as "Mommy." Elsa is mandated to our program and arrived newly "clean." She located Johnnie with the help of our family social worker. I began to work with her and arranged a visitation schedule with the monitoring agency, one hour every two weeks. The agency had been ordered by the judge to begin the process of terminating Elsa's parental rights, which they postponed with her reappearance. At her request, I arranged for her to attend an ACS Parenting Skills Class and my in-house Parenting Support Group. She completed and received certificates for both. Elsa is currently in the frustrating situation of waiting for the next court hearing, in two weeks. The last one, two weeks earlier, brought some surprising results. The supervising agency and the foster mother are eager for the eventual re-unification of Elsa and Johnnie. The caseworker, eager to present to the judge this rehabilitating mother and documentation supporting her success, was instead held in contempt of court for not having begun the previously requested TPR process. She is to return with her own attorney. The judge has also ordered that Johnnie be moved to a preadoptive home, in order to become eligible for adoption sooner. Elsa is understandably distressed. I assure her we will find her an attorney to arrange adequate representation. I give her a referral slip to the Bronx Family Court, where she can request to see the court record and find out her attorney's name. Elsa is most concerned about Johnnie being uprooted while she pursues custody. She is waiting for news from the supervising agency but knows little will happen before the next court date.

Jennifer arrives for individual therapy. Her boyfriend has been discharged and did not leave any contact information. She is very sad, certain he will live with his son's mother and that their relationship is over. While relationships are discouraged within our environment in order to prevent distractions and other "addictions" during the recovery process, they happen regularly. She is the House Coordinator, the highest level within the residential structure, overseeing all resident responsibilities. Jennifer wants to be alone now and discusses how to negotiate some privacy while she deals with her feelings. We discuss how she will be able to do this now and later when she is working and having her daughter, temporarily in kinship foster care, living with her again. She is overwhelmed by the thought of these responsibilities. We focus on developing her outside support system and discuss her frustrations in securing an apartment. She is articulate and insightful and we reflect on her ongoing growth. I encourage her to continue attending her codependency and stress management groups, and we hug at the end of her session.

I return to my office and check my voice mail. There is a message about a lease for a resident to sign and take to her DAS worker. I call the front desk and, learning she is out of the facility, leave a note for her with the pertinent information and a referral slip so she can get a pass for tomorrow. I have checked the DAS worker's availability and the resident's schedule for any conflicting legal or medical appointments.

It is 3:00 p.m. and time to prepare for my Parenting Support Group. This 8-week certificate group allows residents the unique opportunity of being validated as parents by discussing their experiences. Most have not raised their own children or have done so while using substances. The process of recovery includes reconciliation with family whenever possible. Painful memories and current confrontations can make this especially difficult with children. We focus on familial patterns and how the clients as parents are watching their grandchildren being raised as they were raised themselves, and as they raised their children prior to separation. They have genuine concerns about understanding the cycle and how they can create change in their own lives and those of their loved ones. Rachel does not come. Gloria cries as she shares her amazement at the evolution in her relationship with her two daughters. She came to the facility angry that her 14-year-old daughter had told her school social worker 10 years earlier about Gloria's drug use, which resulted in her children's removal from her home into the foster care system. Gloria was unable to look at her own responsibility until a recent relapse, during treatment, which helped her to focus on her need to grow and become a role model for her daughters. Their relationships have improved significantly.

Group is over at 4:15 p.m. I go to the clinic to complete my chart notes. I am ready for my last meeting, an interdepartmental daily review at 4:30 p.m. with the substance abuse team. There are no significant resident problems to discuss today, and I head back to Manhattan at 5:00 p.m.

Chapter 9
Pediatric HIV Research

by Joann Hansen Haggerty, MSPH, ACSW, CCSW

I am a Research Instructor working for an NIMH-funded longitudinal exploratory research study of the patterns of caregiving for infants seropositive for HIV. My day starts early.

6:00 a.m. Ryan, who still thinks he is a kitten, gives me a whiskery kiss. It's time to get up. Oh no, it's Monday. How am I going to get it all done today? First there's a home visit, then data collection at the Pediatric Infectious Disease (PID) Clinic, then preparation for an update from our computer data for tomorrow's staff meeting. Better start.

8:00 Meet my coworker to drive to the home visit. On the way, we talk about Twana, the mother who we will see today. She is one of the 75 biological moms with HIV in our study. They are generally African-American, asymptomatic, but struggling with poverty, being a mom, and facing their dying every day, often in secret. In addition, we have 25 kinship or foster mothers enrolled. (I prefer the term "mom" to "study subject," although terms of "client" or "patient" are equally problematic.) Twana is a 28-year-old mother of a two-year-old child, Tyronne, and his two siblings, ages five and eight. Like 92% of the children in our study, Tyronne has seroreverted and is no longer HIV antibody positive. His mother is not so lucky.

9:00 We arrive in this small town, trying to decipher the directions to this mom's new house. "Go down Main Street to Hardee's. Take a right at the tire place" lands us at the mall. We stop at the Quick Stop convenience store for a few carefully worded directions, trying not to draw attention to why these white women might be going to that street.

9:15 We find the home. A young man is sitting outside. Hopefully, Twana told him we are coming, so we won't have to explain too much. Twana comes out, smiling much more broadly than when we were in clinic. Little Tyronne, now two years old, comes bounding out to the porch. We try to look friendly and organized, but not too officious. Twana tells the fellow on the porch to go to the store and get her something. He disappears and we head in. Twana and Tyronne seem comfortable with us now, since we have visited them twice before.

This exploratory research study focuses on parental caregiving with children seropositive for HIV. We collect data at five time periods from the child's birth to age two years in clinic and on home visits. We administer questionnaires, do a nonparticipant observation of the interaction between the caregiver and child, conduct a semistructured taped interview, do language screening and heights and weights on the child. Home visits can take between two and four hours.

Today, we start with the naturalistic non-participant observation of mother-child interaction. We tell Twana to do whatever she would do if two strangers weren't there. We synchronize our timers, then put the earplug in one ear. Hearing the beep every 10 seconds, we record every action and sound of the child and the mother or whoever interacts with the child. Tyronne delights in the circus train toy we brought. We busily write codes as the mom teaches this curious little guy how to use it. Tyronne becomes very active, climbing on the couch, then runs around. Then he pulls up his little chair, and sits, watching us. We unsuccessfully stifle our giggles. Then squealing, Tyronne runs outside, his mom chasing him down the street. We hustle as we try to keep scribbling our codes. Several neighbors watch and laugh from their front porches. Back inside, Twana feeds Tyronne a bowl of canned noodles which he pokes at, and he continues to cruise around the room.

10:30 We finish the observation and put away our timers. It was an exciting hour of observation, not as wild as some. Now

I administer a variety of questionnaires, some standardized, on issues of the mother's feelings about her child, her own health, and her use of support and resources.

Finally we come to my favorite part as a social work researcher, the collection of qualitative data. For this audiotaped semistructured interview, our interview guide moves from general to more personal questions—"How has the baby been since we last saw you?" to "How do you manage to live with HIV?" Here our caregivers digress into their current stresses and past remorses; they reveal their souls. Twana talks about her family, which doesn't help with the children and gets down on her, a boyfriend who has a substance abuse problem, and some guys on the street yelling out to her as "the Bitch with AIDS." I feel her sadness and fight my tears, then I join in her anger.

I balance between listening and documenting, and not probing too far to alienate this mom, between wanting to hear of her pains and not wanting to open them up beyond what she can handle. Frequently, I need to refrain from moving into the social work interventionist role. At the end, I direct her back to the clinic social worker, the health department, and her doctors, and hope she'll go. She has said she won't go to the AIDS agency until she is really sick.

In working on this research project, I have switched roles from clinician to researcher. I use a different type of interaction than when I was in clinical work. I have had to learn to respond to the poverty, the stories of abuse, to the increasing symptoms with a carefully paced listening, to tease out the whys of their lives, without prying or trying to change things. I try to elicit their own self management efforts. If they have not found a way to solve the problem, I direct them to their workers. We will break confidentiality and notify workers only if the situation seems dangerous. Sometimes we see switches; sometimes children are belittled. More often, we see moms struggling with barely a home with furniture. We see them sad as they talk about dying and not being able to raise this child, but then turn and smile when the kids come in again, and we know they won't let themselves think about it until they come to clinic again. Somehow, they manage to make their lives work.

12:30 p.m. We say goodbye to Twana and Tyronne. I find myself getting a catch in my throat. This is one strong woman. I don't know if I will see her again, since this completes our study contacts. She thanks us for coming, saying that we really helped her, but she did all the talking. She promises she will go back to the clinic for herself. She is so hungry to talk about HIV, but doesn't very often because she doesn't want to upset the few people that do know, and there is no support group in her city. She even called us her support group.

12:35 We stop at the first fast food place, since we feel a need to take care of ourselves. We only wish we could have brought this mom and child with us.

1:00 On the ride back, we talk over the visit, and decide that today we are more worried about her poverty than the HIV. Her food stamps were stolen, and her mother is refusing to drive her anywhere, because she "mouthed off" to her mother's boyfriend. What will become of her? My experience in writing clinical assessments has helped me write field notes of research contacts. I will document this mom's depression and her coping to avoid returning to drinking. I am also glad to document her strengths in functioning despite her problems. My coworker and I inevitably begin discussing the unemployment, neighborhood drugs, and lack of support that trap this mother. I appreciate the close knit study team, where we can process our varied reactions, since we are from different professions—nursing, health education, social work, and psychology.

2:00 On the way back, I stop at the PID clinic. One of the babies, Whitney, is scheduled. Hopefully, I will be able to administer a set of clinic questionnaires and an interview to her mom, Genine. The crowded waiting room indicates another hectic day for all the clinic staff, especially the social workers. Problems abound, especially limited space and time to see patients. Some children are very sick, wasting and neurologically impaired, and difficult to see. In addition, some of the mothers avoid clinic, because they are in denial about being HIV positive.

Genine is glad to see me. She's twenty and is HIV positive. She and her partner are trying to make a life with their one child. In a talkative and upbeat manner, she reports that Whitney is negative on her HIV testing today. Genine gets more serious in explaining that she thinks her mother will reject her if she finds out about her HIV diagnosis. Genine is glad she went back to work, even though she hates to leave her baby. We complete the questionnaires and most of the interview before Whitney is seen by the doctor.

3:30 Back at the office, I decide my priority is getting a soda and catching up with the team. My overflowing mailbox beckons—memos, letters, stuff. First are the newsletters from NASW and the Society for Clinical Social Work. I like to stay in touch with social work, especially because my work is so different now. I file the newsletters on the "Later" pile. When in doubt, make a list: write field notes, edit today's observation, score the language and developmental screening, track letters from subjects, administrative details from the University, and the data the Project manager requested. That's first; the rest can wait.

3:45 I sit down at the computer to work on the Paradox database. I need to do an update on our progress: a table of total subjects by race and caregiver and how many contacts completed. I add new data and then fight with the Paradox program a little.

4:10 A coworker comes in to discuss a research question that would make a good paper. I share my views on today's moms. Sure Twana is depressed, but she is managing. How can we document her strengths, her self-management techniques, and what she needs? While I am predominantly a data collector, and not an investigator on this study, I am able to offer psychosocial background which has helped add to the understanding of these caregivers, and formulate research questions.

4:45 Graduate student comes in describing her progress on a paper. I direct her to the verified SAS data set.

5:00 I push print out and log off, giving the table of data to the secretary to make copies for the morning.

5:05 I pack up my disks to take home—to write my field notes. I like to capture the essence of my contacts on the same day. Sometimes I take work home and do it, and sometimes not, but it feels better if I have the option. Fortunately, I do have another day in the office before I go out on another home visit.

5:35 As I unlock my front door, Ryan uncurls from his day on the couch, and bounds over circling me, demanding food. I think about the little cheery Tyronne running circles around his mom. I have a twinge of sadness for her plight, but remember that she seemed earnest in thanking me for talking with her. In fact I know she felt supported from my listening. We do have debates on whether research can be an intervention.

I am glad that I can go to choir tonight. I push out the feelings of guilt that Twana can't go out—she doesn't have a babysitter. I hope she will talk with her social worker about getting more help. I am glad that I am listening and analyzing, but not serving as her clinical worker. I have been the direct service worker, case manager, therapist, and advocate. Now my job in research is to document the hows and whys of her life, so we can all learn how to help her and others like her.

PART 3:
SCHOOL SOCIAL WORK

Chapter 10
Elementary School Social Work

by Cami L. Cooper, MSW

My first experience as a school social worker was my undergraduate internship in an alternative high school. I often refer to that experience as "social work boot camp." As a result, I aspired to become a school social worker. I am now employed full-time at Washington Elementary School in Phoenix, AZ. Some of my colleagues are envious of the three-month summer vacation, but I am quick to inform them that it is well-earned.

School social work has other advantages, besides the generous vacation time. The working hours (I work 7:30 a.m. to 2:30 p.m. Monday through Friday) are also excellent and allow for time to engage in activities outside of work. The typical working day is also an advantage, if you enjoy being continually challenged and never repeating the same day twice. But, in my opinion, the kids are the greatest advantage. There is nothing in the world more precious than a small child delivering an "I love you" note to your desk at the end of a tiring day.

School social work also has its disadvantages. They may include having to work at more than one school and having a tremendous caseload. The job description is limiting and does not permit for in-depth therapeutic interaction with students or families. Also, you are often the only social worker present on a school campus. It can be somewhat isolating not to have someone close at hand who shares the same background and knowledge. However, I meet once a month with the other social workers in the school district, which helps eliminate feeling completely isolated.

With such a big caseload (I average around 120 students), the most important characteristic a school social worker can possess is organization. It is virtually impossible to be effective and get the job done in a chaotic and disorganized work environment. Good time management skills are also important, if one is to manage several different activities at one time. Creativity is also a valuable personal characteristic, particularly for elementary school social workers. Persons with artistic abilities can put them to use to create group and classroom activities for the students. But I believe the most important characteristic a school social worker should have is genuine love for children. They are the foundation of the job.

The salary is competitive with those for other social work positions, ranging somewhere between $25,000 and $40,000 annually, depending on level of education and experience. The National Association of Social Workers features a specialty section of school social workers and often provides excellent workshops and networking opportunities which are designed specifically for school social workers.

No two days are ever exactly the same in school social work. The following is a step-by-step account of a typical day in my life as an elementary school social worker. This is actually a composite of several days, but will give you the general idea of what I do.

7:15 a.m.   I arrive on campus just in time to assist a teacher in pulling apart two students on the playground who are engaged in a minor physical altercation over a basketball. Since I am already heading in the direction, I offer to escort the two students to the office. After writing up two quick disciplinary referrals for the Assistant Principal, I check the mail that has accumulated in my mailbox: several student referrals from teachers, a request from another teacher to conduct a home visit on a chronically absent student, a note from the principal reminding me of an important meeting with a parent later in the day, and a videotape I ordered from a catalog on conflict resolution, which I intend to use for group.

7:45 a.m. I am stopped by three teachers on my way to the office. One wants a phone number to a local homeless shelter for a family and the other two want to discuss difficult students in their classrooms. I encourage each teacher to complete a Social Work Referral form and place it in my box, and I promise to review them as soon as possible.

8:00 a.m. I open the door to my office/group room just in time to catch the phone. A parent on the other end asks if I would be willing to write a brief statement regarding his child for a local psychiatrist. I agree and press the "Play" button on the answering machine as I hang up. The first message is a confirmation of a guest speaker who has agreed to share with the sixth grade classrooms about his career in professional sports. As the second message plays, reminding me of a meeting later in the day with a parent, a student enters my office, crying. I ask her what is wrong. She tells me that her parents got into a fight over the weekend, and her dad went to jail. We discuss her feelings regarding the incident, and I sit with her as she continues to weep. When she feels ready to return to class, I send her off with a written pass to the teacher.

8:30 a.m. I quickly locate the parent permission slips for the students signed up to go to School Bell. I leave my office, locking the door behind me, and walk to several classrooms, retrieving students. We all pile into my compact car, seatbelts fastened, and drive ten minutes to the Phoenix Urban League office. The students skip up the stairs and down the hallway to the special room filled with new clothes. The students take their seats at the tiny tables, digging into the bins of crayons and paper. The volunteers assist the students one by one, trying on brand new clothing. Each child leaves with a giant bag filled with new shirts, pants, shoes, and underclothes. I wave thank-you to the kind volunteers and we pile back into the car. Back at school, I escort the proud students back to their classrooms and return to my office.

9:30 a.m. I listen to the new message on the answering machine. After the message ends, I pick up the phone and dial the principal's office to verify that the time she suggested to conduct home visits works with my schedule. I open the filing cabinet and pull out a folder of group activities, quickly sorting through the papers until I find the one I want. I return to the office to make copies of today's group activity. On the way back, another teacher stops me to say that the behavior modification point system I arranged for one of her students appears to be working. I arrive back in my office in time to unlock the door and let the students coming to group file in and take their seats on the couches arranged in a circle.

9:45 a.m.   We begin group by rating our week (five is high, one is low) and each student shares one good event and one bad event that occurred over the past week. I introduce the day's topic, peer pressure, and distribute the worksheets. After completing the worksheets, several students volunteer to role play situations dealing with peer pressure. A brief discussion is generated from this activity. I initiate the close of group by asking each member to summarize what he or she learned from today's session. On the way out the door, they each choose a prize from the prize bag.

10:45 a.m.   I sit down at my desk to document the events that took place in the group session. The phone rings, and someone in the office informs me that a parent has arrived requesting my assistance. I walk up to the office and escort the parent back to my office. After some informal conversation, the young woman begins to cry and shares some of the struggles she is facing as a single parent. When she is ready to leave, I assemble a small food package from the supply of canned goods I keep in a cupboard. I encourage her to attend the free parenting classes I arranged to have offered on campus and give her one of my business cards.

11:30 a.m.   I quickly gulp down a sandwich and some fruit juice just before heading out to the playground. When I arrive, the person completing her duty shift hands me the two-way radio and jokingly wishes me luck. I stand under a shade tree. A girl on my caseload joins me under the tree and informs me that her family was evicted over the weekend and that she may be moving back to California with her grandparents. I tell her how sorry I am to hear the news and we discuss the impact of the changes on her life and her feelings toward the situation. I blow the whistle shortly after she turns to leave, and signal for the students to return to their classrooms. On the way, two students get into a fight. I pull them apart and escort them to the front office. After completing the disciplinary referral forms, I lead the two boys into the back conference room and conduct a brief mediation. They discover the altercation was actually the result of miscommunication and resolve the conflict by shaking hands. I make a brief note of this on the referral forms and return to my office.

12:30 p.m.   I enter my office and find the necessary paperwork for home visits and return to the principal's office. No one answers the door at the first home. At the second home, the mother answers the door but does not invite us in. We discuss her child's poor attendance through a tattered screen door. She explains that her child has had a severe case of head lice but will be back in school tomorrow. We thank her and return to the car. I make a brief note in the Home Visit Log as we head back to the school.

1:00 p.m.   I return to my office and sit down at my desk to prepare for the upcoming lesson on Substance Abuse I will be teaching to a second grade class. A few minutes later, the three sixth grade students recruited to be the puppeteers for the program arrive, and we briefly go over the lesson.

1:30 p.m.   The three student puppeteers and I walk to the second grade classroom. We are greeted at the door with hugs and applause. As the sixth graders are setting up for the puppet show, I review last week's lesson with the class. I read today's lesson, as the puppeteers bring the story to life. We distribute the worksheets to the children and discuss the important parts of the story. When the lesson is finished, the puppeteers pack up their supplies and we return to my office.

They return to their classrooms just as the final bell of the day is ringing.

2:30 p.m.   I make a quick call to the front office for someone to make an announcement reminding the teachers on the Social Work Advisory Committee that there will be a brief meeting in the group room.

2:45 p.m.   Eight teachers arrive. I distribute a brief agenda and commence the meeting. We discuss some of the challenges I have been facing. The teachers offer some helpful feedback and suggestions. For example, the sponsor of the Student Council offers to recruit some of her students to assist me in organizing a canned food drive to replenish the campus food pantry. Another teacher suggests I make a brief presentation during each staff meeting to describe the various services I provide, for those on the faculty who are still somewhat unfamiliar with the role of a school social worker. I thank them for their support and helpful suggestions. After a brief discussion, the meeting is adjourned.

3:30 p.m.   I pack my things and prepare to leave for the day. I stop by the office to run some copies of worksheets to be used in a classroom lesson I will be teaching first thing in the morning. As I pull out of the parking lot, I honk my horn and wave at several students playing on the basketball courts. Today was a good day. I wonder what tomorrow will bring.

Chapter 11
An Inner-City High School

by Fred Sacklow, CSW, R

A student calls first thing in the morning. It's Raphael. I'm surprised, and I sense that this can't be good news. He says that he won't be coming to school today. I was expecting to see him today as one of the usual 15 students or so that I see in a combination of individual or group counseling on a daily basis. Raphael says that his grandparents hit him. His grandmother even used a broomstick. Now he is at his girlfriend's house waiting for the City child welfare caseworker to call, because his girlfriend's father reported the incident. I gather the necessary information from Raphael and let him know that I will call his grandmother and the caseworker and try to help him sort this out. We make an appointment to see each other tomorrow at school. I can't help but have strong feelings about this situation. Poor Raphael has already been "kicked out" by his mother and now this. He is hurt and depressed and has a poor hold on his anger. Such impulsiveness and rebellion against "adult" authority is typical at this time for many teens, but it can be too much for some family systems to bear. The school social worker often has to intervene in the student-family system. Such conflict often makes it hard for students to learn and, in Raphael's case, increases his depression which often gives rise to hopelessness and suicidal thoughts.

Since I work in a vocational high school that teaches aircraft mechanics, most of the students I see are boys. They come from all over the city and represent all nationalities and cultures. My present case load is about 70 students, although it can go up to 100 students a week. My first discussion today is with Gina. She is a refreshingly sweet girl who is very lively. But she tells me that she has not eaten since about a day and a half ago. Yet she insists she is not hungry. She has her chewing gum and plans to live on that until she gets home in about six hours. My instant reaction is to want to feed her. But, of course, she would resist this vehemently. I would also like to give her a parental type lecture about getting a good breakfast and the importance of a well-balanced meal, but she already knows this. Gina also likes to wear only black, with dog collars around her neck. If people don't like it, she says it's too bad. Since Gina is only a freshman and our relationship is new, all I can do right now is to try to get her to trust me and feel comfortable with me.

I wonder if Gina has some kind of serious eating disorder. She also has strange likes and dislikes when it comes to foods. She seems of average weight for her size and has no medical problems. I wonder how food may get translated into adolescent identity issues for a young girl trying to find her place in the world.

Not only do many of the kids I see have personal or family issues they struggle with, but many like Raphael and Gina also have learning problems. Both are in "special education" programs. Raphael is in a Resource Room. He goes there once a day for small group tutoring and remediation. Gina is in a more restrictive setting because of her learning disabilities. She is functionally grouped with similar students who share the same special education teachers. Both students recently received their report cards, and each failed two subjects.

Gina says she can't pay attention, because the boys bother her. I have had to intervene with certain boys who never seem to run out of questions for Gina as to why she is so different. They all wear the same baggy jeans and name brand tops and so look like each other, so why can't she dress like the other girls? They also wonder how she can like heavy metal music when everyone knows that rap music is "in."

Raphael says he failed because it was the teacher's fault. He doesn't know how to teach and plus the teacher doesn't like him. Many students seem to share the same explanations for why they fail. Dealing with students' frustrations and dissapointments when it comes to their education is a big role for the school social worker. The students have a history of failure and some have become so hopeless and discouraged that they drop out of school. These students need to be motivated and supported and sometimes even led to a goal.

It so happens that today, Gina's mother is coming in to speak to one of the teachers. I make arrangements to see her as well. She comes in with her son, Gina's older brother. The mother is pleasant and verbal. I bring up Gina's eating habits. Her mother is very concerned about this and pleads with Gina often to eat better. She says that Gina is in psychotherapy where this is also being addressed. Her mother says that Gina misses her father a lot. Her parents are divorced and he does not keep in contact with her. I also learn that Gina's brother has just split with his wife, someone with whom Gina was very close. After they leave, I reflect on the difference between school social work and psychotherapy. My goals here are much more practical, it seems. Help the student get his or her high school diploma and then move on. Help them plan for the future, be it the military or college or a job. Many may need referrals to other agencies and institutions for continued training and assistance.

Danny knocks on my door and comes in with two students I do not know. They hover in the doorway as Danny sits down and then asks when he is supposed to see me. I am surprised, because I make it clear to all students at the beginning of the term when our appointment is. I refresh his memory and then give him a pass so he can let his teacher know why he is leaving class. Danny, like all my students, is mandated for counseling. When evaluated by the School Based Support Team, it was determined that counseling could aid his adjustment to school and better his chances for success. Counseling was indicated on his Individualized Education Plan (IEP). This is a plan that is developed for all students in special education. This does not mean that students are volunteers for counseling or that they know why they are given the service in the first place. Some students take to it with apparent ease and have issues they want to discuss. Others come because they feel that at least it is better than being in class, and still others are more ambivalent and may say "go away." Danny is being resistant these days. He feels he doesn't need counseling any more. He can handle his own problems. This wasn't the case just a few short weeks ago, when he was having trouble with his sister and needed to talk about it. Sometimes confronting this teen resistance and ambivalence can be very frustrating. Don't they see that I just want to help? Am I the enemy or what? If you try too hard, you push the teen away, and if you don't try at all, it seems as if goals are not being met. You have to walk a fine line.

I get a call from the Special Education dean. Robert has been talking constantly in class and throwing balls of paper. They want me to talk to him. I meet with Robert. He is initially quiet and does not look at me. We have known each other a while now. He is a junior this year. It is surprising to watch these young people grow up. It is sometimes remarkable the changes that can be seen when you first see a student when he is 14 or 15 years old and then when he is saying goodbye to you at around 18, 19, and sometimes even 20 years old. Robert is growing up and changing, too. He is becoming more aggressive and less likely to take any disrespect (as the kids are fond of saying) from others. He tells me that he is unhappy being in special education. He feels that he is not progressing, and now he is worried about his future. We discuss the possibility of his taking classes in the mainstream. Many students are in special education but still take so-called "regular" classes. Robert is not confident that he could compete with those kids. I tell him that we will see how he does this term and we will look at mainstreaming options for him next year. Robert is labeled Emotionally Disturbed. This usually means that the student is intelligent and has at least an average IQ but that his behavior is sometimes beyond his control.

I decide to go to my mailbox to see if the form that Raphael's caseworker said she was going to fax me is there. I only have a few minutes, because the bell will ring soon. Then I expect to have a group of four students. Sometimes it seems that I never left high school myself. I am so geared to the bell. My only break is the forty minutes I get for lunch each day, and sometimes even that is taken up by a student or parent meeting. There is nothing in my mailbox, but I pass many kids wearing hats in the hallway. They are not supposed to wear hats. It is not part of the dress code. Do I confront them or mind my own business? Should I enforce the rules or just try to work with the kids I am responsible for?

Which social work hat to wear is the question. Working in a school puts you in multiple roles. Many students cut a class, sometimes consistently. They question whether they really need to know earth science. Why should they go to art when they say they can't draw? Some even refuse to go to gym. They are not coordinated or good at basketball or maybe just plain scared. These students need a dose of reality, so they know what to expect and can understand the consequences for breaking the rules. The school social worker has to help a student take greater self responsibility, even as he or she assists them in improving their coping skills and maturity levels.

The bell rings and in walk four students for a group session. It is a new group, although some of the students know each other from class or other groups that I have run with them. It is hard to keep a steady group going. Kids' schedules change and then they have to be seen at a different time. The fifth member of this group had to be taken out, because his teacher objected to my seeing him during his class. This happens sometimes. A competition occurs between a class and counseling. I try to explain the service to the teacher in question and we talk of compromises. I usually end up being accommodating since, after all, this is a school. It does have a price in group continuity and cohesiveness.

Mario tells the group that he does not feel good today. His girlfriend broke up with him two days ago. He only knew her for about three months but was sure he wanted to marry her. He can't sleep and has trouble concentrating on his class work. One boy tells him that he should just forget about her and that there are plenty of other girls, but Mario is not so sure. He went out last night and got drunk. He does not remember how or when he got home. Mario has a history of excessive drinking. Andrew tells him that he is crazy. *Doesn't he know what alcohol will do to him?* he asks. The discussion continues and the bell rings. If only the problem ended there. I give Mario some literature on alcohol and teen relationships. We agree to continue to talk this next period privately.

The school social worker is often confronted by students with very self-destructive behaviors. Mario needs immediate and intense intervention. He has already been hospitalized for depression and is on medication. Teen relationship issues can often push vulnerable teens to the edge. Mario is in need of friends. Hopefully the group can help. Here, the students can talk to and hear each other in a safe environment, and although they sometimes ignore each other, they very often support each other as well.

The last period is finally over. I have about forty-five minutes to finish the paper work for the day. The attendance for each student has to be recorded. I have two counseling reports to finish, because tomorrow there are two Educational Planning Conferences I will attend. These conferences occur after the School Based Support Team finishes their testing and is ready to sit down with a student's parents to review the results, as well as to determine the most appropriate placement. We also discuss counseling issues at that time and whether or not the service is being utilized by the student and if it should be continued or not.

Many school social workers perform social intakes and evaluations on students as part of their team duties. This helps the team formulate a broader idea about the student's psychosocial functioning and lends itself to determining the student's proper placement and service needs. This is especially critical when the student is first referred for testing. My job is to provide the mandated counseling, not a full social assessment. The team members, the psychologist, and the educational evaluator are often the people the social worker interacts with most in his professional capacities. These relationships can be rewarding and also conflictual. For the last two years I have found myself in the middle of two professionals who are at war with each other. It is difficult to remain neutral, but I try to be supportive to both in my own way. A typical day may find me giving advice to one about the other.

It's finally three o'clock. Now I just have to brave the traffic home. I think of the ways I can relieve some stress. At least the sun is shining. Before I leave, I think I will call the teacher's union hotline. We have no new contract, and with the City finances getting worse every day, I wonder what kind of contract and salary increase we will get and when.

School social work is certainly about kids and not money. Many colleagues I know have to work part-time to make ends meet. We often have to work in less than adequate settings with less than adequate supplies. Helping kids grow, develop, and learn is the name of the game. Sacrifice seems to come with the territory.

Chapter 12
Social Work in a Rural School District

by Carol M. Line, BS, ACSW

I had always been a city dweller. For forty years, I thought that no one could or should live anywhere but in an urban area, and Detroit was my choice. After receiving my MSW, I immediately went to work as the director of a day program for mentally challenged adults. Within two years I had a new job supervising the development of community placements for institutionalized clients. Both of these jobs demanded many working hours and generated a great deal of stress. My husband, also a social worker, worked for the then governor of Michigan, William Milliken, staffing his urban affairs office. His job was also pressure-filled and time-consuming.

We both decided that, although we both loved social work, we would very much like to "smell the flowers" as we practiced our profession. We longed to be able to live in a pristine environment, without the stresses of pollution, traffic, crime, and competition for space and services. So, we made a decision to do the unthinkable, leave our very prestigious jobs and try a new lifestyle in a rural area of Michigan.

One of the first jobs that became available was in the Upper Peninsula, about as rural an area as one can get. Some would even call it a wilderness area. The job was with an intermediate school district (ISD), a regional body that served a three-county geographic area, covered 4,000 square miles, including several inhabited islands, and had more deer than people. There were 13 local school districts within the ISD. The smallest of these districts had less than 10 children; the largest had 3,500. At the time I began working for the ISD, there were only three social workers covering the entire school district, and they were all relatively new. Most of the residents of this area had never seen a school social worker and the schools had little or no idea about what school social workers were supposed to do.

My first challenge came when I realized that the people who lived in this area were very independent and proud. They had been used to working their land, bartering for their needs with their neighbors, and surviving as a result of their own efforts. They all lived like one big, extended family and helped each other without being asked. It was very difficult for them to request or to accept help from "outsiders." They did not feel comfortable with governmental systems or people who had not been born and raised in the area. Winning their trust and confidence was my first major goal.

Even though the school was the focal point for community life, families in trouble tended to distrust school staff and school authorities. As a result, I found it more fruitful to meet with families in their own homes, rather than at the schools themselves. This necessitated a lot of driving, in all weather conditions and on all kinds of roads. Some of the home visits were *memorable*, to say the least.

Directions to homes were given by landmarks, not by miles or road names. One went to a home based on: "It is the first white house on the right, after the dairy farm. If you go up the hill, you have gone too far. There is a blue pickup in the driveway." I became very good at following these kinds of directions, and when someone gave me a direction with an actual road name in it, I continued to ask for landmarks, because there was no guarantee that the road sign would still be standing after the latest storm.

I used to think that urban slums were the worst housing I had ever seen. I still think that, because even though the homes I visited in the U.P. were often very poorly constructed and had minimal amenities, their occupants never had to worry about whether the gas or electricity would be turned off or the toilet would be clogged. They could always use kerosene lamps, wood burning stoves, and outhouses. In the city, when the landlord fails to fix these basic systems, one often goes cold and hungry. Here, there are always options.

My first home visit one day brought me to a small structure with no windows. I knocked on the door and was met with a cheerful: "Come in!" I noted, when I looked for the door-knob, that THERE WAS NONE, just a big hole where the knob should have been. So, I gave the door a push, figuring that it would open smoothly. To my surprise, the unhinged door fell inward, hitting the floor with a thud. You might say I made a grand entrance.

Other home visits also presented surprises. I once was greeted by a flock of "watch geese" who snapped and hissed and chased me back to my car in record time. In other homes, I met up with a variety of dogs, goats, and sheep, all wandering around the yard, waiting for a fresh face to harass. Mind you, these animals were not deliberately set out to deny access to visiting social workers. They were simply living at the residence and had the ultimate freedom, the ability to wander at will. I learned very quickly to wear clothing that was easily washed, boots that could be hosed down, and to bring nothing that I could not do without, in the event it was eaten.

Small towns present unusual problems relative to confidentiality. Since everyone knows everyone else and is probably related to them in some way, it is not unlikely that one would be accosted in the grocery store by a well meaning neighbor or relative wanting to know how so-and-so is doing. I developed a number of pat responses to this question, all the way from: " I am sorry but I cannot talk about my clients," to "You will have to ask their parents," to "Isn't the weather awful today?" Although this dilemma followed me constantly, I was not annoyed, because I really believed that the people who lived here were interested in their community, and not merely interested in the latest gossip.

At times, however, it was scary how fast word got around. One night, my friend became lost in the woods while preparing his deer blind. It was quite late by the time he was found. The next morning, at 9 a.m., the local bank teller asked me how my friend was doing after his adventure the previous night. I once had a UPS delivery person leave a package for me in my agency vehicle, which was parked outside a local school. How the driver knew that I was the ISD employee who was inside the building at the time is beyond me! Several of us drove the school car at different times, but somehow he knew that it was *me* who drove it on that day. We have a better communication system here than the Internet will ever be, but it certainly makes confidentiality a challenging issue.

There are many factors that allowed me to work effectively with the rural population in my area. The first of these was a social work education that taught a systems approach to social work practice. There were many occasions when I was called upon to work with individuals, groups of parents, staff or administrators, agencies, and communities. Without a problem-focused approach to social work practice, I would have been unable to do the job. The flexibility to be able to flow from one skill to another is critical to working in an area where YOU ARE THE ONLY SOCIAL WORKER. Social workers who are stuck in casework or group work or community practice and do not have the ability to move into different systems effectively are very handicapped in this setting.

The other major necessity in school social work practice in rural areas is that one has to become a trusted member of the community. This means respecting local values and traditions, and being a part of the community during non-working hours. There are times when advocacy is necessary and runs in the face of local practices, but if one has gained the confidence and trust of the community, it will accept your intervention, even though it may not agree with it. I remember having to report a beloved teacher to protective services because she punished a child who had decorated the bathroom with toilet paper by wrapping him in toilet paper and parading him through the halls.

The school district wished that I hadn't reported the incident but understood that I had certain responsibilities in my job which I could not avoid. I learned to pick my battles but do what was ethically responsible, even if it meant the entire community would know.

It was extremely important to be able to efficiently network with other agencies in the area. We were all on a first-name basis and when I called an agency with a concern or a question, I was always treated like royalty. One's reputation is extremely important in rural school social work because word of mouth is the method most often used to evaluate people. If the word passed about you is that you are professional and competent, but also understanding, compassionate, and respectful of the community in which you practice, you will be given the best that other agencies and professionals have available to give. How you handle your personal and professional life is a major component in how successfully you can practice rural school social work. You are very visible.

The difficulties that hampered my professional performance most were the lack of other professional social workers from whom to learn and the ability to obtain continuing education without great commitments of travel time and money. At one time, we tried to form a peer review group consisting of the six professional social workers in the area. We found that we were all in need of new input, and without it we were just trading old, stale material. This meant making continuing education a major priority. Some of the individuals were not committed to that end. For this reason, the group disbanded and those of us who could, made the long journeys to new professional learning opportunities. Those who could not or did not want to make this commitment remained in a static position relative to their professional knowledge and practice.

Practicing rural school social work has been, for me, a good professional decision. I have become very close to the population I serve, and I feel as though I am a respected member of the community. This has enhanced my ability to practice without sacrificing ethics or values. Being nonjudgmental about the differences between my personal beliefs and those of the community is a priority but then, it is in any social work practice. It is just more important in rural school social work, because EVERYONE KNOWS your personal beliefs.

My husband and I have indeed "smelled the flowers" for more than twenty years now and have never regretted our decision to leave the urban area. We have felt personally and professionally satisfied and have learned that people everywhere are just people and need to be respected for the individuals that they are.

PART 4:
CHILDREN, YOUTH, AND FAMILIES

Chapter 13
Urban Child Protective Services

by Susan Dodd Gaylor, MSW, ACSW

I was experiencing one of the "goods"—and I knew it was one of those that would last a long time—and I took the time to savor it.

I learned early in my career as an inner-city social worker working in child protective services that I would see more than my share of the bad that life has to offer. I learned to work in an environment of broken families, extreme poverty, violence, and rampant substance abuse—where there was little quality of life for those who existed there. There is no way to work in this environment if you don't have the "goods." The "goods" are what make working in an inner-city environment a rewarding experience—the things that you carry with you for when the going is tough. You have to be able to recognize a "good." It may be a child's smile or a caller that says, "It has only been a month, but I'm still clean!" The inner-city environment is tough; but the rewards are many—if you recognize them. You can truly be an instrument of change in this place. My advice to someone who wants to work in the inner-city or to work anywhere in child protective services is an always and a never—ALWAYS recognize and hold onto the "goods" and NEVER lose your sense of humor!

There were baby clothes and toys scattered all over the room—we had walked into a baby shower! Minutes earlier, I was the one who placed a baby in the arms of the man and woman, who became her new parents in that instant. Definitely one of the "goods!"

As the baby began a new life with adoptive parents, I thought about the baby's mother, Karen—now an adult "street person." Karen came into the state foster care system as a teenager. She was mentally ill, had mild brain damage, and had suffered severe physical and sexual abuse. I worked with Karen—sometimes on a daily basis—and I constantly fought for funding to insure that Karen received the care and help that she needed. But funding was scarce and Karen ran away every time she was placed in a new program. Karen was a chronic runaway, often months at a time. With the help of a benevolent police detective, I retrieved Karen many times from other cities, other states. She always questioned how we were able to find her, and never suspected that it was from the return address that she always (inadvertently?) put on letters she mailed to me.

Placing the baby in the adoptive home would have been a great way to end a day; however, on the way back to the city, the beeper signaled that my on-call weekend had begun.

One-year-old Tanika had been taken to a local hospital with third-degree burns covering from the middle of her back down to the backs of her knees. She had been transferred to a regional burn center. These types of burns are indicative of a child being dipped in scalding water, and this was in direct contradiction to her father's story of the child having accidentally injured herself. Tanika's father was known to our agency and had a history of substance abuse and psychiatric problems. He was also a suspected drug dealer and had a long history of violence. Her mother was in jail on drug and prostitution charges. Tanika was safe at the hospital, but there were two other small children in the home.

I was asked to accompany another social worker to remove the two other children for placement in foster care. Police officers accompanied us to the home, which was located in a federal housing project. When we arrived, we found 2-year-old Renata and 4-year-old James alone with their elderly grandmother, who was in poor health and could not care for the children. As we were preparing to leave with the children, we heard loud crashing noises. The father had crashed through the back door of the house and was screaming curses. He grabbed James, who appeared terrified of his father; and the police officers wrestled the child away from him. As he grabbed me and threw me against a wall, Laura picked up Renata and ran for the agency vehicle. As the police subdued the father, I took a screaming James to the car. Following our agency procedures, we took the children for pre-placement physicals, which had to occur through the emergency room of a large, public hospital. When you sit with children for hours in emergency rooms, it teaches you to be very creative! We played games with the children and kept them comfortable. They were very dirty and hungry, but were in general good health. At the end of our time together, James looked at me and asked, "Do you have any little boys at home?" I did not back then, and when I told him "no," he said in a hopeful voice, "I could go home with you and be your little boy!" It still amazes me how many times children said that to me over the years. I did as I always did—I hoped he wouldn't see the tears well up in my eyes as I explained to him about the foster home picked especially for him because he is such a special little boy.

As we were finishing another "good"—talking with James' and Renata's new foster parent—a spiritually strong woman devoted to children and to bettering her community—the beeper went off again.

The car clock read 9:45 p.m. when our agency vehicle followed four police cars onto a street known as "Crack Alley." The neighborhood had earned this name because of the abandoned houses turned "crack houses," the ever-present drug deals, and the violence that is part of that package. Our report stated that two children were being kept in one of the "crack houses." I was accompanied by Liz, a brand new social worker, who was making her first "beeper call." She stared at the dark house and said, "We're not actually going to go in there, are we?" Actually, Liz didn't go too far into the house. She was so overwhelmed by what she saw inside that she and a rookie police officer (also making his first call) repeatedly bumped into each other attempting to be the one closest to the door! The floors were covered with old clothes, trash, and debris piled waist high—barely enough for tiny paths through the house. There was no electricity, so there was no heat (this was a cold November night), but more importantly, there were NO LIGHTS!

The dark made this an extremely dangerous place. Initially, it was impossible to determine how many people were in the house and what weapons might pose a threat. The police searched everyone who could be found. Ever the social worker—trying to establish rapport—I found myself (amidst this utter chaos) going up to the person who appeared to be in charge in this house (at least he was the biggest, meanest-looking person there), introducing myself, shaking his hand, explaining what we were doing there, and asking for his help in this situation. The man appeared so stunned by my gesture that he actually began showing us around inside the house. With only the aid of police flashlights to navigate the tiny paths through the debris, we discovered that there was no running water (no bathroom facilities) and there was human waste strewn about the house. Old food in the refrigerator laid under mold that grew out of the refrigerator and up the wall.

The man led us to where 8-year-old William and 2-year-old Darius were asleep on an old couch under a pile of clothes. The children seemed sluggish and were difficult to awaken— I knew it was important to get them to a hospital as soon as possible. As we started to leave with the children, Liz finally found her voice and yelled, "There's a crowd outside!" There was a hostile crowd of about 50 people outside the house. Everything happened very fast—shielded by the police officers, we carried the children, literally through a gauntlet to the agency vehicle. Liz clutched the 2-year-old in the car and kept repeating, "I'll never get used to this," as we made a speedy exit from the neighborhood. It turns out Liz was right—she never did get used to it—and she left the agency several months later. We took the two unwashed, malnourished little boys to the public hospital, where lab tests revealed traces of drugs in their blood. We stayed overnight at the hospital with the little boys, because there had to be someone with them to offer security and comfort.

As this day was ending and a new day beginning, 8-year-old William asked me, "Do you have a little boy at home?"

Chapter 14
A Neighborhood Youth Center

by Amber Daniels, MSW

7 a.m. Wake up from a fitful sleep. I'm ready to loosen up with a run. Ring, ring. "Amber, David's school is closed because the power is out. I can't come to work."

Mary runs the day treatment program for adolescent drop outs, Survival School. She picks them up in the van and then starts the program. I have to find a van driver and a program facilitator.

"I'm going to use today to find David a new day care. He got kicked out of his old one last week. They said he was being too violent." David is a special needs child. He's been kicked out of four other day care programs.

"Okay, Mary, thanks for calling." I get another van driver to come in two hours early. Today it works out. My morning run is preserved. My morning run is necessary. My morning run is sacred.

One and a half hours later, I arrive at Latino Family Services. The receptionist informs me we are having an impromptu management team meeting. In ten minutes. Cancel your appointments with clients; the executive director has important things to discuss.

It's not fair to imply that my director is placing her needs over those of the clients. I am the supervisor of a youth center in Southwest Detroit and I also happen to have an MSW. I love the client interaction, seeing them in a group or one-on-one setting. Therefore, I have given myself the privilege and difficulty of trying to manage a department of a middle-sized human services agency, while still trying to maintain a small caseload. The agency is in a low-income neighborhood with historically high crime rates and low pay, so not many social workers want to work here. That means we are in short supply, so seeing clients is a necessity. But so are the administrative tasks. Today the administrative tasks win.

Latino Family Services is a "neighborhood" human service organization. Most of the Latinos in Detroit city live in a 5-census track area, the small southwestern corner. We work toward meeting the advocacy and mental health needs of the broad Latino community that is located here. We employ approximately 45 folks, mostly from the community. We serve approximately 2,000-3,000 clients a month through outpatient substance abuse treatment, HIV/AIDS counseling, testing and outreach, English as a Second Language classes, developmental disabilities case management, senior outreach, and youth programming. The Youth Center serves approximately 70 youth a day in afterschool programs and through our Survival School.

My job consists mostly of managing the staff, interns, and volunteers, and supervising the programming. I also maintain a small caseload of adolescents in need of individual therapy. I have about 12 staff during the school year and about 20 during the summer. We also have between 20 and 40 interns and volunteers who come to the agency weekly from the University of Michigan and Wayne State University. The staff and volunteers are very diverse. They range in age from 15-65, their educational level varies from GED to Master's level, and their socioeconomic background varies from working poor to upper middle class.

The most amazing, challenging part of the work is managing the staff. I'm young (28) and my mistakes far outweigh my successes at this point. Many decisions are educated guesses. That makes guiding other people somewhat of a challenge. Sometimes I get lucky, and if I just listen hard enough, people bring me the answers.

"So, the thing is that when we went to pick up Michael and Manuel today, the next door neighbor told us that they were going to be evicted by the end of the week." Michael and

Manuel's mom is slightly impaired and has difficulty keeping the family out of financial difficulty. Their gas and water has been shut off for months. Manuel is on probation. Neither of the boys has consistently been to school since they were in kindergarten. They are now 15 and 16 years old.

"Well, I suppose the only thing we can do is just ask Michael and Manuel how they are doing. Make sure mom knows about our next parent group meeting."

"But shouldn't we do something? The family is going to be homeless." But what can we do? Mom hasn't told us about her financial difficulties herself.

"Just keep picking them up everyday and offering consistent services. That is all we have to offer."

After the management team meeting, I head out for a city-wide meeting. I have been working in youth development for four years in Detroit, so I know many folks at other youth service agencies.

As I walk in, I wonder to myself if I am somehow invisible or have some sort of obvious ailment. I feel faceless, without identity.

"Hey, hi, how are you?" I walk up to the first person I recognize. She struggles between faint knowledge of who I am and ignoring my presence altogether. She chooses to acknowledge me.

"Blessed. I have been trying to get to your parent involvement meetings." She knows where she knows me from.

"I know, I appreciate your efforts. This initiative requires so many meetings. I've been at four already this week."

I put on my nametag and I can see her relief as she finally has access to my name.

Conversation remains polite, introducing me to her colleagues. It is genuine and warm. We serve on a volunteer council that is attempting to reform the public school system. It is hard work, long term, but good in quality, and has created many strong, honest relationships.

It is uncomfortable, meetings like this. People I know very well will sit down and chat. But acquaintances either pretend they don't know me or that they barely know me. At least until some good friend validates my existence. It is a phenomenon I'm not resentful of. This is something I probably perpetuate. I sometimes feel safer in the role of inside outsider, knowing it is much easier to watch than participate. Lonely, sometimes ineffective. But easier.

The instant distrust that says, "What gives you the right to be here?" or the anxiety, "You're not going to *teach* me or *help* me are you?" or the out and out hate, "What are you doing here, white girl?" All those unspoken questions are exhausting for me. It has to be tiring for everyone else, as well. I understand that I represent my race, gender, socioeconomic status, and profession, regardless of people's best efforts not to stereotype. It is just exhausting to always be surprised back into reality. The surprise gets me every time.

It's a lonely world, sometimes. There is a window of truth that is opened by having honest, real relationships with communities who are different from me. It feels as if I am the only one with that perspective and that there are no words to describe what I see. Besides, very few are listening, anyhow. People don't really want to think about how their choices affect others.

I make more than double what some of my staff make. A portion of that differential is because I have two advanced degrees. But I have those degrees in part because of the many privileges that come with being from a middle-class suburban white family who is able to value education. Some of it is my own ambition and dedication. And some of it is just luck. Given my background, I often feel honored to be allowed into the intimate spaces of other cultures.

Yes, it's lonely because the insight I have gained forces me out of the community I come from. Yet, I don't really belong with the people I work with. Sometimes I'm able to find other double dwellers. And for a moment or two, it is a relief to speak the same language. Could be called something like suburban urbanesque. When we speak it together, it feels wonderful to not have to be an advocate or to have to be careful of offending someone. We share and, for a moment, it is wonderful to belong. And I vaguely understand how communities isolate from each other in an attempt to buffer themselves.

After the meeting, back at L.F.S., I settle myself in for a long day. The maintenance man is on vacation, so I need to stay until 7:00 so I can lock up the building when the afterschool program is over. We run programs from 9:00 a.m. until 7:00 p.m. It's not every day that I need to stay all day long, but my schedule must be flexible enough to be able to fill in, should someone call in sick.

I walk into another office to talk with my intern. She's graduating and she's having many mixed feelings about leaving. In the middle of the discussion, as if to prove her point that it's a crazy place to leave, another staff member comes in.

"Amber, you have to deal with John. I can't get him to do anything. I'm about to lose it."

"Send him in."

John comes in with his whole posture screaming that he's on the defense. He is wearing his best gangster garb, name brand coat, stocking cap, baggy jeans, headphones on his ears.

"Why do you have on your headphones?"

"Don't ask me to give them up, man. Can't nobody take them from me. You'd have to kill me first. Nobody." The tears are creeping up in his eyes. He's bursting at the seams. A time bomb, one staff said.

We talk more about the headphones, his desire to go back to school, his refusal to look at alternatives to violent outbursts and substance abuse.

"John, I'm worried you are going to die."

Jerks the hat down, purses his lips in a stoic gangster grimace, knits his eyebrows. "So what man, so what?" His hands gesture in a calculated fashion, scooping the air with pointed fingers. "Everybody gotta die sometime."

The little boy is just below the surface, pounding to get out. He screams without words, "Grab me, it's a big hole and I'm slipping." His out loud words go on, "My homeys keep dying and that didn't change anything. So what?"

"John, didn't it change your life?"

Silence. "Yeah, right."

John came to us wanting to be an artist and go back to school after being kicked out of three of them. He designed and painted two murals for the agency, and he spoke at a conference about his turn-around.

But with more intensive counseling, staff has discovered a badly beaten past. Everyone in his life has either abandoned or tried to kill him. Asking him to dip below the carefully crafted, albeit fragile exterior of flat affect has resurrected an unfathomable rage. He's beating up "crackheads and neighborhood drunks."

"I don't care what happens. I gotta do what I gotta do when they get up in my face and start talking about my mom...or my sister...or take my bike. I just got to go to a school where I don't know anyone. I just need to start again."

The Survival School youth leave and the staff depressurizes.

"Has anyone seen my keys?"

"Did you ask Don Herman?" Don Herman has a long-standing tradition of hiding stray keys and denying any knowledge of their whereabouts.

"Don Herman?"

"I don't know anything, but I saw some keys in the trashcan...." He laughs and shrugs his shoulders.

"Argh." The owner has again been foiled by Don Herman's key retrieval antics.

"You shouldn't leave your keys just lying around. You never know who might pick them up."

Although sometimes to the detriment of the kids, the Youth Center staff has a frisky sense of humor. They pull pranks, laugh at themselves, and bring each other goofy gifts. They pick play fights with one another as the youth gleefully join in.

But the best part of the humor is the fact that we all get to screw around and screw up once in awhile. I'm relatively new to the community and often say or do things that I shouldn't. But the youth staff is there to check me with humor and push me to grow.

At 3:15, we get an all-call telling staff to leave the building by 4:00 because the roads are covered in snow. We were just about to leave to pick up the elementary school children to bring them to the program. The coordinator of the elementary school program and I hop in my little car to make sure they can find alternative transportation. The van driver takes home the kids who have already arrived at the agency.

It's 10 degrees outside and as my car swerves into a spot near the school, we see that some of the children are already waiting for us.

"What are you doing here, Ms. Amber...isn't there *Latino* today? You sent us a letter. Didn't you send us a letter?" We've already been closed for a week because of heavy snow.

My staff member ducks into the building to talk to the principal and call parents.

"Okay, who can walk?" I check to make sure everyone has on thick coats and gloves.

"Is there ever going to be *Latino* again?"

"I hope so...be careful."

I'm left with three 8-year-old girls. My staff member waits at the school with the others while I take the girls home. We squeeze into my little Civic.

"How was your snow week?"

"Cold. I froze my fingers off." Pause "We just got our heat turned back on the other day." I swallow hard. It has been subzero temperatures for a week.

"Yeah, us too—our heat was off for two or three days."

"How did you stay warm?"

"Went to my grandma's."

"Not me. We just waited for them to turn it back on. It was only a couple of days." It's a wonder they still have fingers.

Their streets are completely unplowed. Even though they've declared a snow emergency, many cars are still under a foot of snow.

The girls are giggling about their pets.

"My pit bull ripped the head off my best Christmas gift—my big teddy bear."

"Well, it better not have been your chihuahua."

"Did you have a nice Christmas?"

"It was okay. Most gifts were old and opened. But I got a nice basketball and clothes from *Latino*." I wonder about the wisdom of being able to outdo their parents so they can have Christmas gifts.

All these difficult discussions don't appear to affect their energy. They laugh and play the whole way home. As I pull up to their old and broken houses, their mothers, brothers, and families greet them worriedly at the door.

"See you tomorrow, Amber. Thanks."

I, however, am left to contemplate the contrasting scenario they've left me with. Childhood discussions of pets and toys, adult thoughts on staying warm and getting what they need. The young people who grow up here in our program need to be children. But in this neighborhood, they are required to be adults from the day they are born.

Working with the littlest children is often the best and hardest part. Their innocent questions, their poking and prodding for attention. Their desire for gifts and treasures of any kind. I had to equally divide up a few handfuls of glittering confetti the other day. I wish I could fulfill everyone's wishes with a bit of shiny paper.

With the little guys, it's also hard to know how much to focus on their brokenness, how much on their strengths. The other day I had the 5- to 8-year-olds paint pictures of their families. It was a tougher project than I thought: only one of eight could draw parents, only three could draw siblings. The children were lost when it came to figuring out who or what was in their "family." But they all needed support for the work they had done...whether they drew mom, dad, a blank field, or three rocks. Their pictures were a far cry from the mom, dad, and two children with a dog, but it was their understanding of family and it was important to them that I validate what they created.

After I return to L.F.S., I take a few minutes to open my mail. There are endless stacks of healthy-people propaganda. I invest daily in the hope that there will be some news of new money: a grant granted, new requests for proposals, unrestricted generous gifts to urban youth who just need a chance.

No such luck today—a few meeting notices, some drug-free pamphlets, and a fabulous new nonprofit management training for only $500 a person. And a packet containing a small glossy booklet in black and white. The end product of a teen summer project. 20 poems and pictures.

Coughing back tears, I read the bleak hopeful pain-become-words of these nine African American Detroit young people. The project is sponsored by a poet we worked with last year. I am struck by their insightful grasp of the local found-art installment, their self-strong discussion of their home. I hope fervently that they get a chance to keep giving voice to their all-too-often ignored world.

At the end of the day, a 14-year-old young man comes into my office in search of the canceled afterschool program. I know him well. We've been involved together in leadership development projects for the last two years. He comes to us just to "see how we are." He tells me he's going to court in the morning because his parents have declared him incorrigible. After some discussion, I realize he's trying to tell me that his dad has threatened him and beat him up. It is a startling realization for me. Good heavens, I almost missed it. We call the local runaway shelter, and they request that he go to the police.

We're driving down the Boulevard at 9:00 p.m. We reminisce about other youth leaders. I want to talk about different times.

"Remember David...how is David?"

"David...he's fine. Annoying, but fine." Quiet laugh. Sobering pause. "He's annoying because he's got a right to be annoying. (Pause.) He's been through some stuff." The Christmas lights are gorgeous.

"I like that." I don't know how else to respond to his gentle wisdom.

At the police station, they don't believe he's been beaten up by his father. They call his parents and send him back home.

He calls me after he gets home, whispering into the receiver, "Could you come to court with me and just sit?"

"I can't hear you."

"I know, I'm trying to be quiet...on the low down. I'm home."

"Are you safe for now?"

"Yeah, whatever...I'll see you at court. 8:15, right?"

Chapter 15
Working with Gay and Lesbian Youth

by Andrew J. Peters, CSW, MSW

I work at a small, not-for-profit, community-based organization that operates a project for lesbian and gay youth. Since I began working at this agency as a second-year graduate school intern, I have risen up in the ranks to Project Director, in charge of a small staff of social workers, health educators, adolescent peer educators, and social work interns.

What I like most about my job is that I have the ability to combine administrative work (program development, grant writing, supervision) with direct client services—individual, family, and group counseling. I would not give up the latter for anything in the world! Each week, I look forward the most to the times that I meet with the kids, either individually, through my weekly group, or at our Friday night Drop-in Center program called "The Coffeehouse."

I knew that I wanted to do this work even before I started graduate school to become a social worker. As a young gay man, I felt a desire to help young people who were struggling to come out. I knew that coming out to myself and others was a painful struggle—the most difficult thing that I had ever done in my life. At the same time, I was lucky—having a largely supportive family and group of friends who helped me through this time. I knew that there were many teenagers who did not or would not have it so easy. I learned from the social work literature about the high rates of suicide, substance abuse, and HIV among lesbian and gay youth. In school, I devoured any books or articles I could find about lesbian and gay adolescents, keeping my copies of journal articles neatly organized in a filing cabinet.

My personal experience and research provided a foundation for understanding and helping young people through the complicated process of coming out. But it is the experience of actually working with these young people that teaches me new lessons practically every week. It is very easy from reading the literature and analyzing the tremendous stigma attached to being gay to view lesbian and gay adolescents as passive victims, coping with isolation, violence, and rejection from family members and peers. I find it also important to acknowledge that growing up gay can be a very positive experience for many young people. Amidst the self-doubt, confusion, and sometimes anguish, there exists exceptional resilience, excitement, and creativity in the youth with whom I work. These are the qualities that keep me motivated for doing this work—the opportunities in the face of very difficult circumstances.

My biggest day of the week is Friday, when my work starts at 1:00 p.m. and ends at ten or eleven at night. Arriving at the office, my first task is to sort through an overflowing mail box, full of envelopes, intra-agency memos, and phone messages. After prioritizing the heap, I return a couple of calls—a request for a sensitivity training for high school faculty and a call from a psychologist looking for referrals for his 15-year-old client who has recently come out as gay.

My intercom buzzes and a counselor tells me she has a young man on our hotline who is interested in joining my Wednesday night support group. She wonders if I am available to talk to him about the group. I pick up my phone and speak with a 16-year-old young man who just came out to his mother last night. He is feeling relieved about having "finally" told her and happy that she told him she still loves him. He wants to meet other teenagers who are gay and get some help with figuring out how to tell his dad. I tell him about the group—six to eight teenagers between 15 and 18 years old who are each gay, bisexual, or questioning. The group helps members work on problems around coming out, and I tell him that it is important that he comes into the group as both a person needing help and a person able to provide help to others. I ask him if he has time to answer some questions for my group screening. In addition to identifying information, I ask him about his mental health history, risk factors like suicide and substance abuse, and his coming out experience. I deem him appropriate for the group, so I give him the time and location of the meetings.

After the call, I am joined in my office by my Drop-in Center Coordinator. In addition to overseeing the "Coffeehouse" program, she carries a caseload of youth and families. She is looking for last minute guidance around working with a young woman and her mother. Her appointment is in 30 minutes, and she has been telling me about her anxiety around engaging the mother, who has pronounced her 18-year-old lesbian daughter: an "abomination." I validate her fears, sharing my past experience working with a fundamentalist Christian mother and her gay son. I talk about what seemed to work for me—validating the mother's sense of disappointment and loss and searching for the strengths in her relationship with her son. We talk about how to engage the mother while supporting the daughter's brave decision to come out and be honest with the people around her. Armed with a little more confidence, she leaves the office to face this difficult pair.

At two o'clock, it is time to meet with my Executive Director to discuss grant-getting leads. We have put together a list of private foundations that support services to lesbian and gay youth. We go over the application guidelines and create a time-line for applying to a small array of local and national groups. My Executive Director will help me construct a budget for these proposals, and I will write the need statement, organizational history, and description of services to be funded. During my history at this agency, we have been fortunate to secure both public and private support for this work. State grants comprise the bulk of my project's budget, and annual grants from private foundations allow us to provide services like client transportation and a summer recreation group.

At three o'clock, I am meeting with one of my interns, reviewing her weekly process recording and talking about her work with a young gay man who is also hearing impaired. We talk about the dual stigma of growing up gay and growing up deaf. We brainstorm ways to communicate better with this young man. I attend to her own feelings about working with this client, listening to how she has joined with him in his frequent sense of hopelessness, feeling like he will never "fit in." I offer some suggestions around validating these feelings at this beginning stage of their work together. I caution her about moving too quickly into problem solving, challenging her to make greater use of silence and reflecting his feelings.

One hour later, I have my staff together for our weekly meeting. We start out with "Appreciations," giving each staff member an opportunity to thank co-workers for something they have done during the week. After an initial awkward silence, several thoughts are shared, appreciating each other for helping with various projects or taking the time to listen to each other. We cover a packed agenda, starting with plans to collaborate with a local hospital to provide HIV testing and counseling to our program participants. The social worker reports back from a conference he attended on harm reduction counseling. We talk about a new group that the social work interns are starting and share leads on recruiting group members. The Drop-in Center Coordinator gives an update on upcoming programs at the Coffeehouse—a speaker from the local chapter of Parents and Friends of Lesbians and Gays (P.F.L.A.G.) is coming next week, two young people have volunteered to Dee-Jay for our monthly Club Night, and we will be having an Open Mic/Poetry Reading Night.

Last, we move into my favorite part of the agenda—the "Participant Round-Up," where we share significant news about Drop-in Center participants. We review an incident from last week when three young women were smoking pot in the parking lot. I share that one young participant contacted me during the week to tell me that his mother had died. We talk about how to approach this young man, offering support but trying not to draw attention to his grief, per his wishes. We engage in a lengthy discussion about how to socialize into the Drop-in Center group a socially awkward young man who has recently started attending. I suggest that we try to wean him away from spending all of his time with staff members when he could be socializing with people his own age.

At the end of the meeting, staff members are scrambling to get things together for the opening of the Coffeehouse. While they busily collect their things to trek over to the site in a nearby town, I have a brief quiet moment when I can microwave a bowl of lentil soup that one of the agency's volunteers has graciously brought in for me. Used to working through most of my breaks, I find myself reading mail and studying my appointment book while I drink the soup.

I make the drive over to the Coffeehouse and carry my briefcase and an assortment of items up the stairs to a narrow hallway. My arms are full with a box of cookies, light bulbs, and copies of flyers to post on our community awareness bulletin board. Even though the place has not officially opened, there are already a half dozen young people wandering around the site, helping staff move tables and chairs, and anxiously awaiting the arrival of others. I brightly greet each of them, happy to see them after spending most of the week in front of my computer, in meetings with adults, or on the phone.

I am particularly happy to see Richard, an 18-year-old man who seems to pop in and out of our program. Richard is a handsome young man, short and slight of frame, who dropped out of school a year ago and has been working from time to time as a drag queen at a local gay nightclub. He has been participating at the Drop-in Center almost as long as I have been working there, but there are times when I don't see him for months. I tell him that I'm glad to see him and ask him what he's been doing. He tells me that he got a new job working at a fast food restaurant and says that he sometimes has to work Friday nights. I ask him if he ever followed through with the suggestions that I gave him for G.E.D. programs. He says "Not yet," and looks a little annoyed. I resist giving him a lecture about the importance of getting a high school diploma, but tell him that I would love to help him get back into school if he is interested in returning.

I settle into an office that staff members use for counseling and groups. Well worn by the dozens of young people who use it each week, the room has a pair of small couches, some comfortable chairs, and a tiny desk that we rarely use. This will be my headquarters for most of the evening—meeting with three clients back to back before I have the opportunity to join the rest of the gang in our large meeting room.

My first client is a 19-year-old named Carl with whom I just started working. A recent immigrant to the U.S., Carl has a limited command of English, but this handicap hardly subdues him from telling me the details of his week. I break up his excited telling of a new boy he met at a nightclub last weekend to clarify what he is saying. Carl is living in an emergency shelter for youth, on the waiting list for a longer-term placement in an independent living home for boys. He came to this country about six months ago, escaping his father, who threatened to kill him after he revealed that he is gay.

Carl enjoys the freedom of living in the U.S., explaining how difficult it was to live as a young gay man in his country. It is strange for me to imagine suburban New York as a liberating place for young gay people to live, but his tales of persecution and violence from his home country help put things in perspective.

He is barely out of my office when my next client arrives, a 20-year-old young woman who also has had instability in her living situation. Jeanette is a bright young woman who seems to have become considerably more comfortable with me since we started working together six months ago. Originally coming into my program homeless, she presented an array of concrete needs—finding shelter, applying for Medicaid, getting a full-time job. She also revealed a complicated history of physical and sexual abuse by family members. Presently, neither parent appears to want to have anything to do with her. Her mother recently told her that she was not welcome in her house if she "continues" being a lesbian. We have just started talking about her deep despair and rage at her father and mother. Hardened by three years of living on the edge of homelessness at various friends' homes, Jeanette is guarded when talking about these feelings. We have also slowly started talking about her own stereotypes about lesbians and gay men, a conversation that began when I reflected on her frequent criticism of "butch" lesbians. This exploration of the young person's internalized homophobia is an almost universal component of working with lesbian and gay kids.

I have a short break before Barbara arrives. She has been late for her last two appointments, having difficulty tearing herself away from her friends at the Coffeehouse. She bounces into the office about ten minutes late. Sixteen years old, Barbara is a tall, somewhat awkward-looking girl. She came out as bisexual nine months ago and is presently dating a young man. Full of nervous energy, she smiles and laughs a lot, enjoying her frequent success at making me laugh at her funny faces and jokes. We have been using her poetry as a way to explore her feelings around being bisexual and the recent death of her mother. Each week, Barbara proudly produces a new poem and we read it together. The poems express her fears about not being accepted by others and her worries about important people in her life disappearing, like her mother.

Once settled in, it is difficult to get Barbara out of the office at the end of our appointment, but I slowly coax her back to the Coffeehouse room. Now I have a moment to breathe before venturing out to see how things are going in the big room. I scribble a few notes about my sessions on a pad.

Loud pop music, laughter, and voices fill the large room of about forty young people. At least a dozen others have gone out to the parking lot to smoke cigarettes and hang out in this quieter space. I check in with the other staff—most are engaged in conversation with the kids. The Drop-in Center Coordinator filters through the crowd with a clipboard trying to take a census. Several of our regulars say hello to me as I enter the room. I have to work on establishing a rapport with the new kids and the shyer ones. There's a 15-year-old boy who nervously runs by me every time we are in the same space. I always make a point of saying hello to him, hoping one day to have the breakthrough of his returning my greeting. Jesse, a stout 18-year-old boy, rushes over to me and dramatically breathes out, "I have to talk to you!" Before I can even suggest that we go somewhere more private, he rattles off his latest dilemma—he has a crush on his best friend and can't tell if his feelings are returned.

I help the staff gather the group to watch our Peer Educators perform their monthly educational skit on a small stage at the end of the room. Under the direction of our health educator, they have put together an improvisational piece about getting tested for HIV. Assembling a group of about fifty kids and quieting them down (it takes five of us to do it!), we sit and stand in the audience as the youth on stage depict a story about a young woman deciding to get the test.

Afterwards, a pair of peer educators facilitate a short discussion about their performance, asking how people felt watching it and if they have any questions about testing. One young man complains that he is sick of hearing about AIDS and already knows everything he needs to know about it. Another young woman tells the group that she has a close friend who is HIV-positive and thinks it is important that others realize it can happen to them. Proud of the peer educators' progress in putting together skits, I clap loudly during their second round of applause. I go over to congratulate the group, beaming at their success.

The remainder of the evening passes quickly—following up with a former client who was in crisis last week because his father angrily confronted him about being gay, a brief consultation with a staff member who just finished screening a young woman with a drug abuse history, hanging out with a group of kids who each came into the program separately but have since become close friends. Looking at my watch, it's now eleven o'clock. The Coffeehouse will close in a half hour, but I have the freedom to go home early, leaving my staff in charge of closing up. My good-byes stretch out all the way to the parking lot, where some kids are still hanging out, furtively smoking cigarettes and joking around.

I experience a sense of satisfaction, thinking about how the Coffeehouse provides a safe place for so many young people to gather and make friends. They may be going home at the end of the night to families who demand that they hide being gay and returning to schools where they are targets of taunts and verbal intimidation, but they have at least one place where they know they can be who they are.

Chapter 16
Child Welfare Ombudsman

by Kenneth Cohen, BSW

Building Fourteen, the administration building, is unlocked, coffee is started, and I can already hear my phone ringing. It's twenty minutes before eight—twenty minutes before I intend to answer it. I know there is someone on the other end seeking justice—revenge for something a social worker or supervisor has or has not done. On adrenaline alone, this unknown caller has risen hours before regular routine—unaccustomed to how low the sun can be on the Eastern horizon. Today's light is still soft. Except for the persistent, clamoring phone, the air is still. Awakening song birds reinforce how early it is. The quiet glides me through morning's minutia. I'm not answering that phone until eight—this time is mine!

In what has now become one fluid routine, doors, file cabinets, and lights are beckoned to perform. Life comes to my outer office. In 90 minutes, it will house one of my students and my assistant. It will be filled with the noise of printers hammering out pages, keyboards clicking away in response to conversations with other expectant customers over the phone—for now, it's still. My briefcase finally reaches its second home. With the push of a plastic button, a reassuring flurry of tiny, electric, mechanical sounds begins. Like the impatient and persistent caller, it's all getting ready.

The phone begins to ring again as I leave the room for more preparatory trivia. I unlock the back door, anticipating the morning's first cigarette, now tepid coffee, and what the day portends. Letters to be sent out to complainants explaining why Agency staff have done the things they have, final disposition on a case into its 60th day, and retrieving information from administrators who feel their right to work with families, the way they see fit, is sacred. The cigarette gone, the cup almost empty, the phone waiting to be answered, it is time to begin.

One minute after eight and again the caller reaches for a sympathetic ear. Headset on, fingers at the keys of my electronic memory, a blank screen, the rhapsody begins, the caller hits pay dirt. She's reached someone in the administration building, someone with the capacity to make change. I don't attempt to alter the image as she tells me about her two children in a foster home.

She saw her kids at a visit last night, and she thought they looked ill. She feels guilty, although she doesn't come out and tell me that. She is paying more attention to their appearance and affect now than she did when they were home. She feels guilty about them being taken away—away to a stranger's house—but she doesn't come out and tell me that. She feels guilty and she can't escape the pain. The social worker offers her no receptive tone, no reassuring words. She says the social worker stopped returning her calls, suggesting the social worker is sick of hearing from her. I suggest too many responsibilities, with too little time to tend to them, is the answer, but I know there is truth to what my caller says. The social worker is sick of talking to her. Someone who answered the Agency's 24-hour hot line, where you can call in allegations of child abuse and neglect, told her she had to talk with her social worker, but her social worker won't return her calls. My caller tells me the disinterested voice on the other end of that line told her, "You can call the ombudsman. He's there to fix things."

"Help me," my caller pleads, but I know before I start that time is the answer. She will have to grow used to the quiet in her life. She's never had such quiet before. Another computer screen reveals my caller as a second generation "Agency Brat," with involvement in Children Services ever since she reached adolescence, five years ago. The social worker was assigned to the case only six weeks ago, and has less than a year under his belt. My caller tells me she has tried to talk with the supervisor, who tells her she has to talk to the social worker. Everyone wants mother to talk to the social worker, but mother says the worker ain't talking. I can hear the slight relief talking to me has given her. Perhaps she'll get some peace. Perhaps she'll get too comfortable.

The lower light on my telephone begins to flash. A secretary has "parked" another call on the line. Another set of expectations in line, waiting. After collecting some data, explaining the procedure I'll follow to resolve the mother's concerns, I'm on to my second caller.

The school principal can't understand why the social worker hasn't removed the children of a mother who can't keep the children from repeatedly getting head lice. Her angry words meld together to form a recognizable tone that causes me to wait. I have learned to let it come without response or judgment. Like the tears from the loss of a loved one, she needs to let it out. When the time is right and some of her tension is gone, I offer several explanations in soft and thoughtful tones. I tell her how the social worker's supervisor needs an opportunity to hear what she has to say. I tell her the supervisor needs an opportunity to address these concerns before I'll intervene. I invite my caller to call back if there is no response to her call, or the response is unsatisfactory. She tells me it's nice just to have someone who listens without judging, who hears what you're saying without signaling you're running out of time. She says she'll call the worker's supervisor. For now, it's okay.

As I finish my first caller's characterization, a yearning for nicotine and caffeine reemerges. I finish typing the brief narrative and data that turns my first caller's plea into a complaint. The computer prints a copy for the social worker, supervisor, associate director, and region director and sends our request for response within 5 business days to its destination. Before the phone can sound another alarm, I slink through the back door of my smoke-free building for quiet. Before the third puff is exhaled, a secretary leans out telling me there is someone calling from a pay phone who has an "emergency." A final drag and I'm off.

An hour has passed, and my student is busy screening someone else's emergency. This is an opportunity to assemble a response to the adoptive couple. They are sick and tired of being accused of abusing their sexually abusive teen boy. The technology allows me to fill in a template as an opening to my written response. "Dear...I am writing in response to the contact made with my office on....concern for the Agency's misbehavior was voiced." The letter goes on to explain how the Agency is mandated to respond to allegations and how no one is protected from this intrusive process. I suggest she consider allowing a protective service case opening. The Agency's involvement could assist in getting services for their troubled teen, and ongoing involvement would allow a familiarity that could help avoid repeated visits from an Intake investigator.

I'm on a roll, 60 words per minute, when the executive director's assistant asks me to come to the executive's office. The anxiety of being summoned to his office 10 months earlier returns. I freshen my coffee, walk towards his door, and the recollection of turning gray while he told me the end of my twenty-two-year career with Children Services was ending, overwhelms me. I was numbed. I remember that feeling in my stomach. You read about it all the time—it's the subject of fiction and fact, and you're glad it's not your stomach. Well, here it was for me, as he threw these words at me. Half of my life was spent in child welfare. I sleep, eat, and breathe these issues. I advocate for the innocents. I will never forget him telling me he had to show others he was willing to make sacrifices in the Executive Office. How dare he do this to me.

Later, the County Commissioner's office made a deal to keep the Office of the Ombudsman alive. They found some bucks to keep a few pet projects going. They like having someone to send disgruntled constituents to. They like knowing there is someone there to listen and respond. I'm still here, the office is busier than ever—almost 1500 calls last year— but the anxiety of being summoned in this way now shares my space. It sits in one of my chairs, always, like an uninvited guest.

I enter his dark wood decor and he invites me to sit. He tells me of a situation in which a woman claims we allowed her birth daughter to find her. Thirty-two years back, the woman relinquished her child for adoption. She signed no consent to have her child know where and who she was. She's angry, and the executive wants to know what, where, who, and when. I commit to query staff who were involved, imagining the wording that will go into this complaint. I leave his office with a small sigh of relief.

Letters—callers—a staffing to determine the best resolution for a foster parent who suffered $10,000 in damages to her home from a fire a foster child started—all blend together to speed the day closer to an end. A call from my wife becomes an oasis with a friendly voice. The first activity of the day in which nothing is asked of me. The respite ends too soon, as the day grows old.

My best writing is done in the morning hours, so I reserve the afternoons for reviewing case documents, if time allows. This afternoon's prize is a 40-page investigation. The handwritten record of activities is barely legible. My complainants are grandparents who have been accused of molesting their grandson. The investigator concluded they had done what they were accused of. Having found significant omissions in the work, I draft a memo to the director of Intake requesting consideration for another finding. I ask him to respond within 5 working days.

It goes on like this until it's time to close shop. I back up the digital files that have collected the day's activity, clean the coffee pot, and lock the back door.

While on auto-pilot, I relish the activity that has allowed me to have an impact. I remember cases, too rare, in which I was able to shape the way this huge child protection agency deals with people. I recall having created a safety net for some, and how antagonistic a dolt I appear to others. I envision the Agency as a large ship, cruising steadily in an ocean to its unknown destination. Every once in a while, I am able to alter its course, ever so slightly, in a direction that offers children a better way. Every now and then, I am able to make it a better world for the innocents.

Those recollections fuel the desire to keep at it, to try and make the difference. This is the best child protection agency and the first Ombudsman exclusive to a child welfare agency in the state—maybe in the country. I help make it happen.

Chapter 17
Family Advocacy in the Military

by Carol Hendler, MSW, LCSW-C, LICSW, LCSW

I t's 5:30 a.m. I stick my arm out of the covers to turn off the strident beeping of the alarm clock. Oh, how I would love to turn over and sleep for another couple of hours! Wouldn't it be nice to have a "normal" job with people who don't think the day begins before the birds waken? What in the world is a former flower child type like me doing working for the Army, anyhow?

I force myself out of bed, turning on the bedroom light to help begin the transition from sleeping beauty to Ms. Hendler, Clinical Social Worker. A quick shower, tending to the cat's needs for fresh water and food, my own breakfast, and I'm in the car, thankful to be going to the military hospital at which I work in the Family Advocacy Program of the Department of Social Work.

It took something of a circuitous route for me to enter civil service. I worked for two years in the Family Advocacy Program at a nearby Army installation under a contract with a private firm, which filled social work positions at the various military bases around the country. It was in this position that I learned about the unique military culture. Confidentiality in the military regarding a soldier's personal affairs is applicable for soldiers who seek assistance. Even then, if commanders wish information about their soldiers, they have the right to ask, but the clinician is only required to surrender the information when directed by a military lawyer. This release of information to a commander is on a "need to know" basis, which allows the clinician to stick to the minimum and "nothing but the essential facts."

The Family Advocacy Program was designed to assist commanders in dealing with the distractions their soldiers experience when there is a child or spouse abuse situation. In fact,

F.A.P. (in the military, if anything can be reduced to an acronym, it will be) is called a commander's program. The function of the Armed Services is to defend our country. When a person enters the service, it is made quite clear that he or she is now a military asset. Being victims of familial abuse not only deters the soldiers from their mission; it also might harm government property, the soldier's body. Being perpetrators interferes with soldiers' ability to do their job and brings into question their judgment. I've been told by many soldiers that they have been told they are expected to control their families. Therefore, it seems the violence is sometimes the result of a soldier's felt impotence in that endeavor, because, as those outside the military community recognize, it is not within the scope of healthy human relationships to control others. As soon as a report of family abuse is received at F.A.P., the commander of the sponsor is notified. The sponsor is the military member of the family who is responsible for his or her family members, also known as dependents.

Despite doing the same work as Federal employees, while working for the contractor, I was paid 10 percent less and had much poorer benefits than my equivalent civil service colleagues. I also felt like Cinderella in the home of her stepmother. I entered the civil service system by taking a job at the commuting distance Department of Veterans Affairs in a long-term drug and alcohol treatment program. I stayed a year and missed being in Washington, so I applied for a civil service social work position in the Family Advocacy Program at the hospital where I am now employed. The experience with substance abuse was invaluable, as a high percentage of F.A.P. cases involve addictions.

I definitely am NOT grateful for the parking situation at my hospital. By 0700 (7:00 a.m.), the main lot is already filling up fast, despite the fact that work, even for most military personnel, doesn't begin until 0730. There is a frantic scramble, like ants at their hole, as civilian employees and soldiers try to secure the quickly evaporating spaces before they will all be gone. The process is generally completed in another 2-3 minutes. The smaller lots closer to the main hospital and main buildings on the installation have filled up at least a half hour before. No sense in even looking for a place there, wasting precious time while the big lot fills up. My car joins the row, front bumpers all lined up at attention.

I walk the equivalent of a couple of city streets to the mental health building, our new quarters as of this past September. It's a nice feeling, walking into the clean, modern edifice. Our old quarters were next door in an ancient, patch painted building with inadequate ventilation and a broken water fountain. When we moved into our new building, we all received individual offices with new computers and maroon and tan color-coordinated furniture. Within the sanctuary of my office, there's enough room to accommodate four adults and one child. Because the furniture was part of the contract for the construction of the building, we were faced with another of the strange thought processes which occur in the military. Despite the fact that the mental health building houses the Department of Psychiatry, the Department of Psychology, and the Department of Social Work, chairs in the offices look ideal for people applying for bank loans. Comfortable, relaxing therapy chairs they are not. "I must find some second hand cushy seats to replace these as soon as I can," I think to myself as I enter my office.

After locking my purse in the cabinet over my desk and disengaging the call forwarding from the front reception desk, I check the e-mail for any important bits of information. Today there is a reminder about the in-service presentation to be held after the Case Review Committee (C.R.C.) meeting. I pull out yesterday's statistics form, which itemizes my time in 15-minute increments, and add up the figures. My door is open, and as I conduct these activities, colleagues are filtering down the corridor to their offices, stopping to wish me and each other a good morning, filling coffee pots with water and exchanging a few pleasantries.

My phone rings. "Good morning, Carol Hendler here." "Good morning, Ms. Hendler. This is Alice. Do you have a few minutes?" she asks, hesitatingly, soft spoken, sounding timid, frightened. Alice is typical of several civilian wives in my spouse abuse case load. They tend to be polite, passive, and unhappy, and hope their husbands will someday have a sudden awakening to how their inconsiderate behavior is hurting their wives. At the time of this realization, the husbands will change their behavior and become loving, involved spouses. Many of these wives say they endure continuing abuse, in addition to the documented dynamics of abuse, because they were told during their indoctrination as military wives that their husbands' careers depend on maintaining a "good" family. Family problems could lead to demotions with their attendant reduction in pay, bars to reenlistment, discharge, or in extreme cases, Courts Martial. They are often fearful their husbands will take out their rage about being disciplined on their wives. A reduction in pay also affects the entire family, so most of the women keep silent. To counteract this situation, the Congress has passed legislation called the Transitional Assistance Program. This law provides the families of soldiers discharged because of abusive behavior with twelve to thirty-six months' salary.

When a commander is called and informed that his or her soldier is involved in an act of family violence, the case manager can make the recommendation that the commander place his or her soldier in the barracks for a few days, providing a cool-down period. Commanders have no authority over civilian family members. In the case where a female soldier, living in military housing, is being abused by her civilian husband, it is the wife who can be ordered out of the home. When there are children in the home, these judgments seem to require the return of King Solomon.

Alice's situation came to the attention of the Family Advocacy staff when the unit's administrative coordinator received a call from the on-call social worker. All the civilian social workers take a week's worth of turns providing after hours and weekend coverage. The turns occur two to three times per year. On the previous evening, the on-call social worker received a call from the emergency room reporting a possible Family Advocacy case of a wife who had a scratch on her neck and a bruise on her upper right arm, which the wife stated had occurred during a fight with her husband. Her husband had come home at 0100. They argued. It became physical when he grabbed her by the arm and pushed her against the wall. She can't remember how she got the scratch on her neck. She did know she didn't have it before the fight. At this point, the wife was able to reach the front door and run to her neighbor's. The couple lives in Army supplied quarters a couple of miles from the Army hospital installation in a community setting.

The on-call social worker checked to be sure there were no children in need of supervision, then called the soldier's commander, who went out to the home and ordered the soldier into the barracks for a few days for a cool-down period. The social worker spoke with the wife who said her neighbor was with her and could drive her home. The wife was informed that someone from the F. A. P. would be calling her to set up an appointment. The F.A.P. supervisor referred the case to my co-worker who, as part of her standard operating procedure, called the Provost Marshall's (P.M.) Office and the Criminal Investigation Division (C.I.D.) to report the cases. I am providing individual therapy to the wife. The case manager has enrolled the husband in the anger management group, which F.A.P. pays an independent contract clinical social worker to lead. As the couple shows they are ready for conjoint sessions, they will be given that opportunity. Had this been a child abuse or neglect case, the Child Protection Service in the appropriate county would be notified immediately.

The case manager has written a synopsis of the case for presentation to the C.R.C. As 0800 approaches, the F.A.P. staff and a multidisciplinary team from various hospital agencies assembles. New cases and cases up for review are presented with only a number to identify them. Reviews are generally on a three-month basis, but can be scheduled sooner depending on individual circumstances. The commanders related to each case have been invited to attend and are generally present. Following the case presentation and any questions asked and answered, a vote whether to substantiate or unsubstantiate abuse or neglect is taken on new cases. Most votes follow the recommendation of the case manager, but that is not always the case. The C.R.C. determination carries. This is not a court of law. The goal is to provide treatment for the family to prevent violence from occurring again. Therefore, only a preponderance of information that an incident occurred is required to substantiate a case. On rare occasions, a C.R.C. has recommended to a Commander that she or he initiate administrative action against a soldier. In such cases, it is usually when the soldier is noncompliant with the treatment plan or is declared a treatment failure or has had other incidents of abuse.

Following the C.R.C. is the 1½-hour in-service presentation, at the main hospital building, about a city block away. One of my social work colleagues is presenting a case study of a client dealing with bulimia. Following this is lunch at the hospital cafeteria and a return to my office to spend the afternoon in two individual sessions and one conjoint couple session. It's now 1600 (4:00 p.m.) and time to return to what feels like a very different world.

Chapter 18
Employee Assistance Programs

by Glenda Dewberry Rooney, MSW, Ph.D.

Employee assistance programs (EAPs) are often described as humanizing the workplace, because they are a mechanism for providing human services to employees and their family members. Employee assistance is a short-term, cost-effective intervention strategy considered to be of benefit to the employee and the employer. A program may be sponsored by an employer or a union. Perhaps the most important contribution of the employee assistance program is that it serves as an alternative to the termination of an employee who is experiencing problems that alter productivity. Services are also available to employee family members. The following hypothetical account is a composite of some of my own experiences as a former EAP professional and those of my colleagues currently in the field.

Let's say that I work for a family service agency that is a member of a national network of employee assistance program contract providers. I am a licensed clinical social worker, a certified employee assistance professional, and a certified chemical dependency counselor. There are many other health and helping professionals involved in occupational settings. While there are other corporate social work roles, most social workers in occupational settings work in employee assistance programs.

I consider myself a workplace expert. My primary role is to help employees take their personal problems out of the workplace and into the employee assistance program. Hopefully, this occurs before their job performance becomes impaired.

Being an employee assistance social worker is quite different from my previous position as a clinical social worker in a mental health organization. My job involved seeing clients in my office over a longer period of time. The specialized nature of that work meant that I was rarely involved in other service activities. By comparison, as an employee assistance professional, emphasis is on the immediate problem, in particular, concerns that have an impact on job performance. The position also involves a number of roles and functions, both in and out of the office. On any given day, I deal with an array of organizational and employee concerns. The range of social work roles I engage in include being a counselor, mediator, broker, advocate, and organizer. I also function as a trainer, information specialist, account manager, and contract negotiator. Variety is one of the features I like most about my position as an employee assistance professional.

To help you understand the role and function of the employee assistance professional, I invite you to follow me through a day of work (actually a composite of EAP experiences). While the day begins in the office, my work in the afternoon is out of the office. I begin the day at 8 a.m., meeting with a family who has self-referred. Their specific concern according to Intake is parent/child conflict—specifically, a teenager who is involved with friends that the parents consider to be unsuitable. The contact with the EAP was initiated by Mariana, the teenager's mother. The primary concern of both parents is that hanging out with certain groups of youth will lead to involvement with drugs. They trust their daughter, but they feel that the other youth lack appropriate parental supervision. This is a typical family issue that is presented to the EAP.

The next office appointment is with Paul, an African-American male who has been referred by the supervisor for inability to get along with co-workers. This is a difficult situation, because the supervisor did not indicate that Paul's job performance was an issue. Although EAP professionals emphasize using the program as a supervisory tool, utilization for non-performance related issues or as a form of punishment is inappropriate.

This situation is particularly problematic to me for several reasons. First, the referral appears to single out one individual, and I do not have the benefit of observing group dynamics. Paul can provide me with his perspective; I will also need to discuss the matter with the supervisor. Second, "inability to get along with co-workers" is quite vague. Third, it is unclear what outcome the supervisor expects from my contact with Paul.

And finally, the situation is troublesome, because I have noticed an increase in the number of African-American and Hispanic employees being referred by supervisors for similar reasons. This fact suggests to me that an overriding concern may be organizational, in which case the intervention strategy may involve Paul and the work group.

Matters related to diversity are still common, even in those organizations that actively seek and support a diverse workforce. Tensions tend to emerge from the fact that while the organization may embrace diversity, there is the unspoken expectation that the employee who is different will not act differently.

In this situation, I will need to help Paul find ways of coping, so that job performance does not become an issue. I will also mediate between the employee, the work group, and the supervisor. If the situation warrants, one of my co-workers or I may offer to provide diversity training for the organization.

The final appointment for me in the office is a chemical dependency assessment. John has been referred by the supervisor for poor job performance. According to his supervisor, John has been absent from work 15 days over the past three months and has been found several times asleep on the job, smelling of alcohol. The assessment involves a standardized questionnaire that explores chemical use.

During the assessment, John admits to smoking marijuana and drinking beer. He asserts that he does not smoke or drink while at work and does not see job performance as an issue. In the course of our discussion, he gives several reasons for being absent from work. He also reluctantly admits that his drinking may at times interfere with his work.

The supervisor has indicated in the referral and has told John that he is on the verge of losing his job because of poor performance. The referral is an opportunity for John to use the employee assistance program as a resource. John has the option to not use the EAP, at which point the supervisor may take action based on his performance, which may include termination.

Although substance use may be the focus, the supervisor's main concern is job performance. John's contact with me is a coerced choice. In this initial contact, it is important that I acknowledge this fact and that he and I reach an agreement about our work together.

The assessment with John will explore his substance use and also the extent to which his use impairs his ability to function on the job. After the assessment in my office, John has the option of accepting a referral for an additional assessment and treatment at an outpatient facility. In addition, it is important that he and I work out a plan that will enable him to maintain an acceptable level of productivity at work, and also reduce the number of times he is absent.

Helping employees with issues of alcohol and substance abuse was at one time the primary focus of human services programs in the workplace. The employee assistance program evolved from the Occupational Alcoholism Programs (OAPs). One of the things you should have noticed about my schedule is that contemporary EAP services are responsive to a broader array of issues.

Much of the afternoon will be spent conducting training for managers and supervisors about how to manage employee situations. I stress to the group that they should not become involved in the personal affairs of employees, as this involvement tends to complicate and confuse the situation. Part of the session with managers and supervisors is devoted to identifying performance issues—for example, excessive absenteeism, work slow down or stoppage, arriving late or leaving early, excessive personal phone calls while at work, or emotional issues. I also help supervisors become aware of the stressors experienced by employees. Most of all, I want them to understand and utilize the EAP as a resource, and as an alternative to terminating employment.

Later in the week, I will hold employee orientation sessions for employees at the same organization. These sessions are a form of outreach, in that the focus is on ensuring that employees are aware of the EAP. I tell them how they or a family member may access services, and I explain the confidential nature of their contact with the program.

Before I leave the office, I have several phone calls to make. A portion of my job involves information and referral, follow-up evaluations, and locating provider services for employees in other states. This function requires that I stay abreast of community resources in the local community and also those resources available through the provider network.

The first call is to a local child care resource center to obtain information about affordable day care for an employee who is a single parent. I also call an EAP network provider in Connecticut to refer an employee who needs assistance for an elderly parent there. The final call is to a couple I referred to a local agency for marital counseling. I want to follow up on their success with accessing services provided by the agency. As I am walking out the door, Intake puts a call through to me from an individual who is seeking vocational/career counseling. Because the caller is anxious not to miss or be late for work, the appointment is made for 7:30 a.m. the following day. At 6 p.m. today, I will return to the office to meet with a couple experiencing marital conflict.

Following me through this hypothetical day has hopefully given you a glimpse of employee assistance work. I used a number of social work skills. I have found that assessment skills are very important at both the individual and organizational levels. Knowledge of effective, short-term models of practice is important, as is an understanding of the dynamics of relationship building and working with involuntary clients. Remember, John and Paul did not seek help from the employee assistance program on their own—they were referred by their supervisors.

It is also important to adhere to the ethics required of a social worker and to balance the needs of both the employer and the employee. An EAP professional is the neutral party whose job it is to help the employee and the supervisor stay focused on and resolve issues surrounding productivity and job performance. Equally important is understanding that the workplace may also be a source of stress and strain for employees and that all performance issues may not be solely related to employee personal problems.

Over the course of the week, I am scheduled to conduct a series of informational/educational seminars related to work and family balance, parenting, strategies regarding the management and reduction of stress, and elder care. In addition to conducting workshops, my colleagues and I distribute informational materials in the workplace.

One new aspect of employee assistance is critical incident stress debriefing. My most recent session was the result of an employee being assaulted at the worksite. When a situation of this type occurs, assistance is needed not only by the individual affected, but also by co-workers who fear for their own safety.

One challenge for employee assistance professionals involves helping work organizations understand and deal with issues that will accompany a more feminized and diverse workforce. Work and family balance and quality, affordable child care will remain prominent issues. The demand for elder care assistance is expected to increase. Health conditions, AIDS in particular, and those problems associated with an aging population may also be expected to be central concerns. Because of their proximity to employees and their concerns, employee assistance professionals may be strategically positioned to articulate these concerns and influence organizational benefit policies.

PART 5: DISABILITIES

Chapter 19
Developmental Disabilities

by Toni Murphy, MSSW, CCSW

Developmental disabilities was not an area I was particularly interested in, or knew much about, when I took the position of Director of Social Services for a non-profit agency that provided services for children and adults with disabilities. At that time, I was working as a case manager with older adults, and seized the opportunity to once again work with children and families. Little did I know how limited my knowledge was about disability-related issues. My true "education" was yet to begin.

During the first six to eight months, as I learned more about the unique issues of our clients, and as I slowly became familiar with and knowledgeable about specific resources available, I wondered why on earth I was ever hired for the job! In response, my supervisor told me that very few qualified applicants had even applied. I was shocked! The requirements were not especially strict or unusual: MSW, experience in working with young children and families, basic case management skills and experience, and only a couple of years' post-graduate experience. It seemed the social workers who fit this broad description must number in the zillions. The salary was somewhat competitive, certainly average, and it was a supervisory/department head position—something that looks great on a résumé. The agency also had a long successful history and was well positioned within the community. Why the dearth in applicants? I surmised that the area of developmental disabilities within the social work profession was not widely publicized or acknowledged.

Now to describe a "typical" day in the life of a social worker in the rehabilitation setting. Upon arrival to our 50+ year-old building, which is cold in the winter and hot in the summer, and leaks year-round, I am greeted by a stack of phone messages, which I take to my little office in the basement to sort through and prioritize. Typical requests are for diapers to be sent home with "Johnny" on the bus following his therapy session, information about our program or community resources, referrals for services, and not uncommonly, requests for help in advocating for a child with special needs to obtain necessary services from other public or private agencies. And there is one client who calls several times a week for various reasons. She has physical and cognitive disabilities and demonstrates extraordinary insight about these limitations and a tenacious determination to overcome them. She is an inspiration to me, and one of the strongest women I've ever known. Our receptionist doesn't bother to write down her name and number for me on a formal phone message pad. She just lets me know T has called, and smiles.

After my triage treatment of returning calls, it is time to find the city map and look up the address for an intake and assessment scheduled for 9:30. Upon locating the address on the map, I realize it is an area with which I am familiar. No problemo. I know my way well. Of course, actually bundling up all of my paperwork, signing out on the board upstairs, asking the receptionist to please take a message (I'm going to be late!), and being detained in the hall by a perturbed occupational therapist who demands to know why one of my clients has missed her last two therapy sessions, are all hurdles I must clear before I escape to my car and make for a clean getaway!

As I attempt a safe merge onto the freeway, I muse about the unique position in which I find myself as a social worker on an interdisciplinary team with physical therapists, occupational therapists, speech therapists, and special education teachers. These professionals are not social workers, and they have different sets of priorities influencing and guiding their work with clients. Specifically with regard to the therapists, a medical model perspective primarily directs their intervention choices and treatment planning. Some conflict between us is inevitable. Later, when I meet with the occupational therapist who stopped me before I left, I will explain to her that the client in question was recently evicted, and that although their daughter clearly needs therapy, the family is struggling to meet the very basic needs of all their children.

I arrive just in time, and the interpreter with whom we contract is already there. Since this client moved to the States from Mexico, Spanish is her primary language. The little house is very dark inside as she tries to keep it cool during the hot summer months. An electric box fan blows across the tiny living room to facilitate air circulation. The mother, A, greets us warmly and somewhat cautiously. The television is tuned to a channel that offers programming in Spanish. The interpreter and I sit down together on a small sofa covered with blankets. A sits in a chair near a child's crib. As we begin introductions, A motions for us to approach the crib and meet her 13-month-old son, B. He is beautiful with smooth light brown skin and big dark eyes. He looks exceptionally small for his age and seems to have some spasticity in his muscles. Little B is the reason for our visit.

As we begin gathering information about the child's and family's needs, I find myself feeling increasingly frustrated with my inability to communicate directly with A. (Why didn't I stick with those "Community School" Spanish classes?) The intake is taking twice the time it normally takes, because of the time involved in interpreting information back and forth. Halfway through the intake, A breaks down in tears. She explains that all of her family is still in Mexico and she has no friends here. Furthermore, her husband takes the only family vehicle to work, which leaves her more isolated. Since the family lives outside of town, public transportation is not an option.

She continues to describe her frustrations and challenges, particularly with regard to locating and accessing services for her son. Her most immediate concern is that he has been congested for several days, but she has been unsuccessful in securing him an appointment with the doctor. I definitely feel overwhelmed by the end of our visit, and cannot imagine how this young mother must feel. I wonder where I can get a good deal on a magic wand.

Before we leave, we assist A in making an appointment for
B with the doctor, and in contacting some other agencies to
address various needs. I make a mental note to place this
family on my list of high priorities, which will inevitably juggle
another family to a lower spot. Some of these decisions are
not easy!

It is well into the lunch hour by the time I arrive back at
the office. I decide to eat in my office and try to complete my
paperwork for this case. At our agency, the social work staff
schedule the interdisciplinary team assessments for new clients. I look at the "Evaluation Calendar" and add B in the
first available slot. I scurry up the stairs from the basement to
check my messages—a manageable stack. I run back downstairs and return a call from a former client labeled "important."

C is a former client whose child transitioned out of our
program about six months ago. While enrolled in our program, D received physical therapy to address his gross motor
needs. D is currently in the preschool program at a local public school. C, his mom, is a single mother with two young
sons. She is unemployed, receives public assistance and financial support from the children's father, and utilizes the
bus system for transportation. During the two years her son
was in our program, I got to know C as a strong, loving, determined advocate for both of her children.

When C answers the phone, she is in tears. It is difficult
to understand what she is trying to say, because she is crying
so hard. Apparently, D has been ill with an ear infection, and
C has taken him to the clinic on two separate occasions this
week. Today, when she walked to his school to pick him up,
her son's teacher accused C of being a "bad mother" because
she let her son go to school when he really needed to see a
doctor. C adds that she has felt for weeks that his teacher did
not adequately address his needs in the classroom. I feel angry at the teacher's insensitivity to this parent, who struggles
to meet the needs of her children, in spite of her limited resources. I also feel frustrated that because of funding and
"rules," this is not something I should be spending time on,
since the family is no longer a client of our agency.

Fortunately, our city has a support program within the public school system, specifically for parents of young children with special needs. Since I have met with representatives from this program on a number of occasions in working with families transitioning from our program to the public school, I call one of my contacts and explain the situation. Ultimately, a representative from this support program arranges a meeting with herself, C, D's teacher, and the school principal. Much to C's relief, D is placed in another classroom with another teacher. Advocacy is a big part of this job.

As an MSW with this agency, part of my job is to supervise the BSWs on staff. This afternoon, I am scheduled to meet with one of them to discuss a new case involving a diagnosis he has not encountered previously. My supervisee wants to learn more about the diagnosis before his initial meeting with the family. We review the medical information together to identify symptoms and assess what impact this diagnosis may have on the child and family. We consult with a therapist on staff who is able to provide us with more information and resource material for my supervisee to read prior to his intake. One of the many positive aspects of working within an interdisciplinary team is the opportunity to learn from other staff, who collectively and individually possess a wealth of knowledge and experience.

OOPS! I glance at my calendar and realize I almost forgot my Community Task Force meeting! It is a task force comprised of representatives from various agencies in the community who work with parents of young children with disabilities. A local resource was not funded this year, which has caused a gap in services for our clients. Members of the task force combined efforts and successfully accessed grant money to provide these needed services. We now face the challenge of hiring a coordinator for the program and assisting that person with developing a program that effectively meets the needs of families. How will we determine eligibility? How many families can we realistically serve? How much money should be allocated for each family? How will we recruit and train staff? How will we ensure quality services? This is cutting edge social work! The opportunity to create a program that will effectively meet the real needs of clients is exciting! It is also a significant time commitment, and I am fortunate that my agency has allowed me to shift some of my responsibilities in order to participate on the task force.

After I return to my office, I check my messages, gather up my things, and head out to another home visit on my way home. ("On the road again.") The family I am visiting was recently informed that their 18-month-old girl will need extensive heart surgery. Little E was born with a serious heart condition and receives therapy at our agency for mild developmental delays. Mr. and Mrs. F also have two older daughters, 6 years and 8 years old, who truly look like princesses. They greet me at the door with drawings in hand. Mrs. F invites me in, thanks me for coming, and begins to cry. I listen and offer support. She tells me what the doctors explained to her about E's condition, and what to expect following surgery. It sounds quite risky and very scary. Mr. and Mrs. F are involved with their church, which has been their main support since E was born. Mrs. F hasn't needed to cook or clean for the past week! And someone from the church will be with the family at the hospital during surgery.

We say good-bye and I head home. As I pull out of their driveway, I am struck by the difference between this family's access to support and the lack of support A has available to her. Support is a key issue in working with families who have children with special needs. Some of the most effective programs for this client population are "Parent to Parent" programs that "match" trained support parents with parents in crisis. These programs are available across the country and represent one of many resources available. There are also many organizations that offer information and support for persons with a specific disability. Our agency offers a Parent Support group and provides transportation as needed, so that everyone has access and can take advantage of the opportunity to share with other parents. I find this aspect of our program particularly rewarding, because clients often establish relationships that continue long after the group has ended.

There are several characteristics that are essential for any social worker considering practice in the area of developmental disabilities. A social worker must be comfortable with people who have abilities different from their own, and understand that everyone has the right to be an individual. Someone who cannot handle seeing children with significant medical involvement may need to seriously consider another area of practice. Families of children with special needs encounter so many people who are uncomfortable with their children. They should not have to deal with professionals who have similar attitudes and behaviors.

Additionally, social workers working with this population must allow parents to make their own decisions regarding their children and families. Simply put, parents observe and interact with their child in the child's own environment on a daily basis—we don't. It is equally important to allow parents to be where they are in the grieving process. Parents who have children with special needs face incredible challenges every day, yet find a way to make their lives work. Social workers need to demonstrate empathy, offer support, advocate as necessary, and provide information. These special moms, dads, and caregivers deserve special praise!

Finally, it will be necessary to communicate effectively with professionals from other disciplines within your own agency, professionals from other agencies, and a wide variety of people in general. Anyone can have a child with special needs, regardless of race, ethnicity, age, lifestyle, or socioeconomic status.

Working in the area of developmental disabilities provides a rare opportunity to share the joys, personal triumphs, and sometimes sorrows of everyday heroes. As professionals, we may touch their lives in some way, but the truly most meaningful connection is their lives touching ours.

Chapter 20
"Us" Becoming "Them"

by Roberta (Rusty) VanSickle, MSW

My story is that of a disabilities worker—one of "us," the social workers—who became one of "them," the disabled. Although I doubted for a while that the field could adapt to this upheaval in one of its own, I found it could. So this chapter includes two related fields and a big, big transition.

I loved the field of Supported Employment (SE). Finding resources that enabled our clients to work and live independently in the community was immensely rewarding. I supervised 13 employment specialists (job coaches), who worked directly with each client to find a job with necessary accommodations according to individual needs. With training and on-the-job support, most of our clients could succeed in a community job, even some who were severely impaired. I loved the position because it involved quick thinking and close teamwork—two qualities I always took pride in. We were a tightly bonded team. We were proud of our professional dedication and our goal of gainful and meaningful employment for persons with disabilities. We had confidence in ourselves and each other.

The pay was sufficient for supervisory-middle management, between $30,000 and $40,000. I had come up "through the ranks" and had about eight years' experience as a line worker before qualifying for the supervisory role. Much of this line work included 24-hour availability, flexible hours, a lot of driving and taxi-work with clients who had all degrees and types of disabilities. We worked constantly with employers and prospective employers. We sold the supported employment concept and helped them to tailor jobs and understand our clients while still getting their work done and selling their merchandise. As a supervisor, then, I spent my time in team leadership and supervision, and coordination with other agency and community resources. The job hadn't changed much—it had broadened and taken on new variety. I loved it and intended to continue in this branch of social work.

As I worked full time, I was completing an MSW program at Rutgers University. I served an internship at my agency, which included writing policies and employment standards for my department. I became a CARF (Commission for Accreditation of Rehabilitation Facilities) surveyor as part of the internship. These experiences helped me gain management expertise, which I had hoped to use to create mobility in my future within the agency. It was all neatly laid out in my mind.

What I did not expect was that this path would suddenly change as I faced my own personal disability. Getting ready at home to attend a morning meeting, I suffered a sudden stroke. A neighbor and co-worker found me and called an ambulance. I was hospitalized. A few days later, a second stroke nearly ended my life. When the crisis was past, I had lost the use of my entire left side.

My initial reaction was anger, fear, and confusion. How could I maintain my commitment to my graduate work and my job? My life goals now seemed forever out of reach. Friends, family, and co-workers tried to be supportive, but couldn't seem to identify with the thwarted drive and the intense frustrations I felt, trapped in my semi-functional body. Still hospitalized, I let my primary social work instincts kick in, and I began to share my disability resources and knowledge. I passed my time helping other patients and demanding that doctors understand the viewpoints that came from sudden major life change. I was lucky. I had the language to describe what I—and others—were going through. Using it again helped me a lot. Getting listened to helped even more. As I continued my slow adjustment to my "new" self, self-pity diminished in proportion to growing ability to compensate for the functions I had lost.

I tried to return to my old position as supervisor. I had changed, and those around me adapted poorly to these changes. Our team, once bonded, suffered as interactions, once predictable, became uncertain. We had been well people caring for needy people. Now one of the team had disability needs, too. A supervisor looked too much like one of the clients. Within the agency, my needs were resented. The changes in me were too much to tolerate. For this reason, and to accommodate continuing medical needs, I had to move on. I had to reevaluate my job potential, priorities, changed abilities, new strengths and weaknesses, and I had to do it quickly.

First priority was to complete my MSW. With the help of my Rutgers professors and an aggressive policy of disability accommodation within the School of Social Work, I was able to finish all course work and graduate in December 1995. Then my husband's work took him to Florida. I was glad to be away from the New Jersey winters.

For two years, just before and after my stroke, I had been sharing practical knowledge of the Supported Employment field through a professional publication, *Job Training and Placement Report*. When the editor, a fellow social worker, wanted to leave, she approached me about replacing her. She convinced me that my social work knowledge, vocational rehabilitation experience, writing skills, and new "disABILITY" would bring a needed perspective to the publication. The publisher agreed, and I was hired.

Most of the accommodations that I needed were natural to the position: flexible hours to accommodate needed therapy, tele-commuting privileges, and a layout editor who double checked my submitted copy. I already had a computer with "bells and whistles" to help me edit copy despite some remaining perceptual difficulty. I invested in a scanner and text-converter to complete my office.

My years of maintaining good professional files and my nationwide list of professional contacts paid off. I couldn't do the running any more. But I had done it long enough that I could now provide a service to those still on the road.

There were new skills to acquire in a hurry as I became an editor. It's surprising how quickly I became proficient in one-handed typing. It was a crash course to learn the ins and outs of computer and modem management. It took a while to get acquainted with "Fat Boy," the new fax/scanner/copier. Those details had always been for others, and now friends and family were teaching me fast. My mother, a retired social worker/psychologist/writer/editor, assisted me in learning how to operate all my equipment, as well as organize my new one-handed office.

Setting up a "one-handed" office where everything is accessible from a wheelchair was a challenge, but it was possible after all. Low shelves and lots of table space were important. Most important of all, though, was the inclusion of professional and personal mementos, family photos, the old poster collection—the things that make a happy place to work. I have it and I love it.

My office has a mailing center where material is logged in and sent out. It took planning and ingenuity to make this center a one-handed operation. Some things—like stamps—want two hands on them before they'll cooperate. Letters, samples of the publication, copy, clippings, and floppy disks come in and go out in a steady stream. A rolling wooden file stays handy for keeping the papers manageable. Permanent storage means big notebooks and a hole-puncher operated on the floor with a heavy foot.

Each day now is an exciting new adventure. Office hours apply at home, just as they did at the agency. I have three phone lines—personal, office/computer, and fax. They all stay busy.

The first part of the day I'm online, managing the e-mail. Faxes may have come in overnight, and they need attention. Then I answer urgent mail, following up with the routine stuff. Phone calls go out and come in frequently during this process.

Monthly editorial planning sheets organize my copy for the entire year. My computer files are set up to save old copy for reference and the new contributions for future editions. I have my computer set up to remind me of daily "must-do's" as I turn it on first thing every morning.

A lot of my time is spent contacting potential new authors, including persons with disabilities who have reentered the workforce with success. My resources include the professional publications I monitor, my old professional friends who suggest new ones, and the whole big Internet. New resources and networking opportunities show up daily. When a potential contributor appears in print or in the news, I make a contact by phone, fax, or e-mail.

Copy that comes in must be put into a form that's suitable to the space needs and style of the publication. Since I can't retype a large volume of material, I scan it, turn it electronically into editable text, and process it with fewer and easier keystrokes. I recopy it to a floppy or onto e-mail and ship it out to the publisher. If something doesn't scan well, I fax it on and the layout editor in Minnesota helps me out with her fast retyping.

My greatest victory has been to expand my vision of social work from what it was before—fast-paced and mobile—into a home-based position modified to fit my new disability. As "one of them" now, I am immensely aware of the untapped abilities that I saw before in our clients, a little vaguely then. I also see the tremendous resources available within the system, if we'll take the trouble to learn and tap them. I fit this type of publication work precisely because of my years in and love for the Supported Employment field. My goals are still there and still attainable. I'm still a social worker specializing in disabilities, just as I planned to be. I just experience it from both sides now.

I'm regaining some mobility with intensive therapy and practice. I'm driving again, with a specially-equipped car. This year I will represent my publication and my employer at a professional association conference in New Orleans. I will also begin consulting for agencies seeking CARF accreditation for their disability programs. This is a real milestone. I've missed my CARF surveyor duties. With broadening networking supports, I'll be able to expand my position as I become more mobile. I can take on more editing, writing, consulting, and special jobs. Pay and challenges will change with each job and with my own ever-changing needs. I'll still be helping people with disabilities to improve their lives, as I keep on improving my own.

It's not so bad, being "one of them."

PART 6:
MENTAL HEALTH

Chapter 21
Involuntary Admission: A New Worker's Introduction to the "603"

by Beth Boyett, MFA, CMSW

I had scarcely learned the term "603" when, on the second day of my final field placement, I found myself hurtling down a hospital alley in a security van, trying to calm the first adult client I had ever seen in therapy, all the while garnering sympathetic stares by four burly security guards who kept my client pinned to the van's bench.

The attending psychiatrist's last words to me as my client was being carried out of the therapy room—two guards at her feet, one guard on each arm—a strange, yet stunningly graceful ballet—"You made the right call. No doubt about it."

But, as I made my way behind my struggling, 100-pound patient, now being ported in pig-on-a-spit fashion—as if she were a wild beast carried off to slaughter—I doubted plenty.

How could this *be right?* Yet, I had tried every option available to me. The client had presented intoxicated, still swigging rum from an Icee cup, all attitude, yet plaintive.

"You got to help me," she said.

"You got to help *me*," I said. "We can't have a session when you're drinking. Let's schedule some time tomorrow."

"Don't matter. I got a piece in my truck, and I'm gonna blow my f---ing head off. F--- therapy!" She slumped down on the therapy room's couch and gave me a curious smile. "I'm gonna do it," she said again, softly this time.

I had witnessed some great histrionic performances with former adolescent clients, but her resolve frightened me: she supposedly had the means and she had a definite plan. She was drunk. She had driven herself to the appointment, so she was a danger of harming self, not to mention other motorists, if she were to insist on leaving. I decided to set some limits, yet give her the choices. I asked for some phone numbers of friends or relatives to call to pick her up.

I was surprised when she lifted her head and recited five names and numbers, as if it were rote to her. Five calls later, three people had refused to help her, and two lines had been disconnected. I had, however, gotten her to give me the keys to her truck—perhaps the only confident decision I had made all day.

"I want to call my mama," she said.

I handed her the phone.

I watched her transform from a hard-talking, 33-year-old woman to a child in mere seconds. The salutation was a torrent of whines:

"Hey, it's Jesse. I messed up again and—" She began to wail. "I don't want a damn thing from you! Just—hey!" She let the receiver drop beside the chair. "My own mama won't help me. My own *mama*..."

She looked up at me. "I got to go. Ain't no more use trying."

I wanted to slow her down a bit, see if I could learn more and buy time to figure out how to insure she wouldn't harm herself or put anyone else in danger. I was in way over my head. The kids at the residential treatment center where I had interned the previous year were monitored 24 hours a day, so when I left them at night, I knew they were protected as well as anyone could be. But this was a strong-willed adult who had a history of threatening others at gunpoint, and I was scared but simultaneously intrigued. According to the intake form, this client had requested counseling because she had been raped four months previously; that was all I knew. I decided to play it safe.

"Jesse, since I think we're going to be here past five (it was now 4:55, and everyone in the office was due to leave), I need to let my supervisor know we'll need this room for a while longer."

Jesse slumped down on the couch and closed her eyes, either passing out or ignoring me.

I left the door ajar and stepped next door to let the secretary know to notify the psychiatrist on call that I might need him and to please check in with me when he arrived from the hospital.

I went back in and pulled my chair a little closer to the couch.

"So, Jesse, you've been trying?"

"I been trying all my life since the day I was born!" Her eyes snapped open. "And I ain't gonna try no more!"

In rapid fire, she spoke of a family lost to her, a series of abusive men, three instances of rape, the constant struggle to avoid killing herself with a gun she either kept at her bedside at home or in her truck.

"That truck's paid for. Don't nobody love me, and I don't love nobody but my truck, my gun, and my drink, you know?"

I didn't know. I didn't know anything. Dumbly, I nodded, and just let her talk. *I'm not supposed to know,* I reasoned with myself, *I just have to make sure she does not harm herself. How could I have known my first adult client was going to come in drunk and talking suicide? How can one prepare for this? One can't.* I recalled the oft-repeated advice by instructors at the University of Tennessee School of Social Work, "Start where the client is!" *The client is DRUNK, damn it, and I'd like to be at this point!* My sarcastic inner monologue kept me sane a few more seconds. Then I heard myself say, "This is the first time we've met, so I need to ask you something. What are you hoping to get from therapy?"

"Not a damn thing." She snorted.

"You sure went through a lot of trouble to get here today. Didn't you want something?"

She locked eyes with me a few seconds. I knew I was failing miserably. "I'm so tired. I'm so damned tired of this sh--. I know I'm going to do it. I done it once already. Only, I didn't do it right." She pulled at her collar, and showed me a long, violet scar at the base of her throat. "I just want to do it right."

"So, you're telling me you plan to injure or kill yourself, and maybe you're telling me so that I'll stop you?"

"I'm tired," she said, and closed her eyes again.

There was a rap at the door—my mentor, my savior. I glanced back at my client who appeared to have passed out again. Tom, my mentor, was still in his white coat, and I felt oddly comforted by its brightness, imagined it could cut through the darkness of my ignorance.

"I screwed up," I greeted him.

The elder, Tom, peered around me. "Is she dead?" he asked, mocking my serious tone.

"No."

"Then you didn't screw up. What's her name?"

"Jesse."

I was angry now. Didn't Tom realize I didn't know what I was doing?

Tom squatted beside the couch. "Jesse, I'm Dr. C—, and I need to ask you a question."

Jesse opened her eyes and scowled.

"I don't need no f---ing doctor. I hate the bastards."

Tom grinned broadly. "Then I'll make this as quick as possible. I want you to tell me something. Is it true you told Beth you were thinking about killing yourself and that you have a gun in your truck?"

"I ain't thinking 'bout, I'm *gonna*," she whispered.

Tom cocked his ear closer to her. "You're gonna what? Tell me."

"I ain't telling you sh--!" She sprang to her feet, and was suddenly in my face. "Gimme my damn keys!"

Tom stepped in front of me, and Jesse backed up.

"Will you sign yourself in or let us arrange for someone to pick you up? You need some time to let the whiskey wear off. Then we can talk." He managed to keep a pleasant, yet firm tone of voice.

"Gimme my keys!" She raised a fist to him, but he just stepped back.

"Is there anybody we can call for you?"

Jesse shook her head.

"Go call the emergency number on her chart," he told me. As I dialed, they shadowed each other, Tom blocking the door.

"It's Jesse's answering machine." I put the receiver down.

"Jesse, I'm going to sign you in at the hospital for obser-vation until I am sure you are sober. Then we'll talk." Tom eased around the door. "Jack, 603."

An older guard from downstairs entered. "Miss, I'll just see that you get over to the hospital safely." He offered her his arm as if to escort her.

"I ain't going!"

"Yes, you are," Tom said quietly and he took her other arm. Three other guards entered the room, and she began screaming at me:

"I trusted you, bitch!"

Within seconds, four security men, Jesse, and I were mov-ing in a huddle toward the elevator.

"You don't have to go with them!" Tom called after me.

But I did. She was my first adult client; this was our first therapy session, and if I had made this decision to detain her, I had to see and be responsible for it. I had to know what happened after attempts toward reason failed and blurred into the irony of "the unreasonable," being forced into restraints in order to prevent her from harming herself.

"I trusted you," she said to me as we pulled up to the hospital.

You'll live and perhaps trust me again, I thought, but held my words; this was *her* pain; she needed the last word.

When Jesse refused to leave the van, the guards pulled her hands from the armrest and carried her through the door.

"We'll send the doc out to you. It's pretty tight in there!" One of the guards called to me. Even after they were through the door, I could hear Jesse's curses.

A more experienced therapist could have prevented such drastic measures, I berated myself as I waited in the alley. I had no concept of what lay beyond the door in front of me.

An intern clad in seafoam scrubs burst through the door, took one look at me, and grabbed my arm. "Looks like your first 603," he said as he propelled me down a brightly lighted hall. "You brought us a wild one. She almost bit one of the techs! Looks like she did some crack with her vodka, and God knows what else. It'll take awhile for her to sober up, and then we'll assess the suicidal intent." We stopped at a security door, and he punched numbers into a key pad. "Exclusive club you've joined." He smiled. "We'll make sure she's safe. The place looks bad, but the staff's good."

He led me to a cinder-block room the size of a closet. Jesse lay on a stretcher, trussed up and florid. When she saw me, she began struggling.

"What kind of therapist are you?" she screamed.

I wondered myself, but became momentarily distracted by a pale line moving down the wall. I watched it travel all the way down until it faintly tapped the floor's cotton matting.

"The last guy just peed," the intern said. "We had to hustle him out to make room for her. Housekeeping will be by in a minute to clean it up."

He talked as if it all made sense, and without commenting or understanding, I followed him to the entry desk to complete the paperwork—all that was required was a signature under Tom's—*my* signature—indicating that Jesse was a "harm to self." It was, on the surface, such an ordinary action, like signing for an overnight letter. I made my mark, stepped back, and that was that.

As I made my way out, Jesse said, "Hey, Bitch!" She forced up one fettered wrist, giving me the finger. Then she smiled a strange smile, as if indicating we shared some funny secret. I felt strangely victorious as we locked eyes, and that repulsed me. *Had I enjoyed being a part of this mad dash toward "sanity"?* No. But I knew that she was not likely to kill herself this night, and maybe there was a chance to begin again tomorrow.

When I returned to the office, the older security guard led me over to Jesse's truck. He pointed to the handgun, lying in full view, on the front seat. On the driver's side, there were pills and prescription bottles scattered about.

"I reckon we done her and somebody else a favor," he said, and left me, truck-side, staring at the mess, contemplating the myriad of messes that fuel and sustain human suffering.

The fact was, there was no *right* choice that day or any day. Six hours later, Jesse would be transported by ambulance to a public mental hospital, where she would remain, against her will, for five days. As I had no privileges at the public hospital, and since I was not yet her primary therapist, I was not permitted to call her or to receive any information about her progress.

Much to my surprise, upon discharge from the hospital, she returned to my office and requested that we resume individual outpatient therapy. Jesse and I were to work together for seven months, and our last meeting was no less surprising than our first.

At our last meeting, I waited to see if Jesse would talk about her decision regarding my recommendation that she enter a drug and alcohol program (as she had recently acknowledged that she wanted to stop using). She began to tell me about her intake appointment with the director of the drug and alcohol prevention center:

"I asked that woman what would she do if I ever said I was low and I was gonna kill myself: would she put me in the dirtiest, meanest, crazy bin in the state?" Jesse snorted and took a long drag of her cigarette. "And that woman, she said to me, 'If it was the only other option between having you alive or dead, then yes!' " And I said, 'Well then, I reckon you'll do.' "

I suppose my bewildered look prompted her to add, "You was the only one who stopped me. All them other times, I'd tell 'em I wouldn't promise not to do it, and they'd pack me off home in a cab or even call the cops on me. They sure never rode with me! It's easy to send somebody off when you don't have to see that place, but you seen it! You keep on bein' a bitch when you have to, Beth!"

The decision to admit a client involuntarily is not an easy one. Jesse is the only suicidal client with whom I have worked who refused inpatient admission. Through her sacrifice, she taught me plenty. As Jesse once put it, "You can get over mad, but you can't get over dead."

You make the hard decision when you have to.

Chapter 22
Partial Hospitalization

by Kenneth G. Smith, MSW, LCSW

I am an experienced clinical social worker who enjoys doing accelerated therapy work with clients over a succinct period of time. Inpatient psychiatric hospital work—which I did for several years—has limited appeal to me now, especially with ever-decreasing lengths of stays and quicker patient turnover. I am not now attracted to being in private practice, something I've also done in the past. I am stimulated by doing groups, and though I have skills in psychodynamically-oriented therapy, I am most comfortable in the cognitive-behavioral arena.

Is there a place for someone like myself in today's clinical social work?

You bet! I have found it!

It's called Partial Hospitalization, which is a fancy word for day treatment.

The partial hospitalization model is based on the fact that numerous mental health clients do not need 24-hour, locked inpatient treatment, but do need more than the traditional one-hour-per-week outpatient appointment. The partial hospitalization mode of treatment began to take shape in the 1960s, when a small group of clinicians in the northeast United States became frustrated at what they saw as a lack of alternatives for mental health clients. These clinicians believed that psychiatric clients could recover more quickly if they could pursue their treatment in concert with their existing community and family ties. With the increase of community mental health and deinstitutionalization movements in the 1970s, partial hospitalization programs began to build their strength and effectiveness on core values of group therapy, psychological rehabilitation, and the use of therapeutic milieus. The discovery of new psychiatric medications, which reduced client hospital stays, also helped. By the 1980s, partial hospitalization programs were widespread, particularly as third-party payors began to realize the cost effectiveness of day treatment, as opposed to 24-hour inpatient care.

I am the coordinator and primary therapist for a Partial Hospitalization Program (PHP) in St. Petersburg, Florida. The program is housed at a mid-sized, not-for-profit medical hospital. The basic requirements for someone in my position are being licensed in my state and having at least five years' postgraduate clinical experience.

Since I wear both administrative and therapy hats, a typical workday begins with my assessing the upcoming day in both areas. My staff—consisting of psychiatric nurses and mental health technicians—meets each morning to receive assignments from me. Within their core job descriptions, each day is varied as to specifically what duties my staff may perform. For example, the nurse could focus on technical obligations (charting, taking orders from physicians, checking clients' vital signs), or clinical work (doing assessments and leading groups), depending on where the greater need exists that day. The staff and I then work on facilitating any admissions or discharges planned for that day, and work on updating clients' treatment plans. A treatment plan is a formal document found in the client's chart, detailing the client's problems, specific goals for each problem, discharge criteria, and expected length of stay in PHP. When the staff meeting ends, I make my own appraisal as to what kind of interface I may need to have with peers, supervisors, physicians, or persons outside the hospital during that day.

Clinically, with staff input, I ask myself several questions in pondering over clients' needs for that day: Which clients are presenting for treatment today? How are they progressing (or not) in their treatment? What might be some leftover issues from the previous day's therapy? What patterns of group dynamics are surfacing? What mental health topics do my clients need to focus on today? This assessment phase usually takes about an hour.

I typically lead two morning groups of an hour and fifteen minutes each with the clients. The first group is the community meeting, which has a several-fold purpose: (a) for clients to report to each other how they are feeling and functioning, (b) for clients to share any victories and struggles they have experienced since the last group they attended, (c) for clients to set daily, specific treatment goals, and (d) for clients to give each other support, feedback, or confrontation. I view my primary therapeutic role in the community as creating a warm, accepting milieu where clients feel safe enough to describe honestly what they are experiencing. Most, if not all, of my clients need to learn how to be honest with themselves and others. Some have been taught that their feelings and thoughts don't matter. Others have been locked in a pattern of shaming relationships, devoid of honesty. For all the aforementioned reasons, I consider the morning community meeting to be the most crucial group of the day for clients. In essence, I believe the community meeting most accurately reflects the reality of the client's current life.

After a break, clients then attend the psycho-educational group. During this group, I lecture to the clients on various mental health topics of interest to them. I have compiled lectures on over 30 different topics. Examples include family dynamics, communication skills, anxiety and anger management, overcoming depression, and self-esteem. Addiction topics such as relapse prevention, 12-step work, and co-dependency education are taught if I have clients who have those needs. Clients are strongly encouraged to take notes during the lecture, and to ask questions. Handouts accompany many of the lectures, and written assignments are sometimes given to the clients to complete during group. Psycho-education is the group that I most enjoy doing, because if I hadn't become a social worker, I probably would have chosen teaching as a career!

I am an energetic speaker who likes to use humor. When appropriate (and I, like other therapists, must be careful about this), I will share vignettes from my life as they pertain to the topic. Therefore, this group allows me to integrate facets of my interests and personality with my clients. Clients seem to benefit from the practical, life-skill based information they receive.

The next scheduled event of the day is lunch, which is provided to PHP clients at no charge. At first glance, it's tempting to view lunch time as a trivial part of the program. However, I find this time of the day to be clinically important, as I can learn much about clients by observing their lunch time behaviors. For example, does the client eat alone, or with peers? Which peers? What types of food, and in what amounts does the client eat? How is free time spent after the meal is finished? The lunch period affords me the opportunity to be with my clients in a relaxed, informal manner. Then there are days when I choose to be away from my clients during lunch!

Following lunch, the clients attend two more groups before their day is over. Medicare and other third-party payors stipulate that PHP clients receive at least four separate groups per day. The afternoon time is geared toward exposing the clients to other hospital or outside therapists. These sessions are intended to be process and metaphorically-oriented, utilizing various forms of self expression. Art, recreation, music, dance/movement, and psychodrama are examples of modalities used.

After clients are dismissed for the day (the hospital provides transportation for clients who need it), my time is spent on charting, reviewing the day with my staff, meetings, phone calls, and other activities. Clinical documentation is crucial. The client's medical record presents a picture of who the client is, why he is in treatment, what his goals are, and how he is progressing toward those goals. PHP documentation is done on a group by group basis, using a focus-outcome approach. I strive to document the specific clinical focus of the group the client attended, and what the outcome was for the client, i.e. how that client responded verbally or behaviorally to the intervention presented in the group. Documentation should also reflect why the client needed to be in the particular group, and how the group dovetailed with the client's treatment plan goals. An example group note: "Client attended psycho-educational which focused on learning a set of assertive communication skills. Client verbally indicated that she understood the material presented. Client agreed to practice the skill with a certain family member, and will report back to peers as to whether she reached this goal. Client clearly needs to learn these skills, as she is currently experiencing conflict with family members, which is causing anxiety."

This typical day involves my spending at least ten hours per week with PHP clients. Family therapy theorists have spoken of the therapist's need to join the client's system while doing therapy. Certainly, if nothing else, the amount of time I have with my PHP clients each week allows me to join them directly and become an integral part of their lives. I don't mind saying I enjoy playing this role with my clients for the time they are in the program. Hopefully, each client can benefit in some manner from their time with me. I know I certainly learn much from them!

My typical PHP client is an adult with a psychiatric and/ or chemical dependent history, who is referred because of acute and/or severe impairment of daily functioning. Their psychiatric or addictive symptoms are such that PHP is needed as an alternative to, and prevention of, inpatient treatment. PHP clients are under the order and care of a staff psychiatrist who has made a formal assessment and diagnosis of their condition. PHP clients carry a diagnosis found in the Diagnostic and Statistical Manual of Mental Disorders (DSM-IV). The task of the PHP therapy staff is to generally focus on the acute Axis I DSM diagnosis, which is the class of information used to describe the client's clinical symptoms. Major depression (i.e. sad moods, crying spells, sleep or eating dysfunction, lack of energy, and so on), anxiety and substance abuse are among the most common classes of symptoms presented by PHP clients.

Many of my clients are transferring into PHP from an inpatient hospitalization stay. Thus, these clients can continue to receive daily treatment, yet are able to return home for the evening. Other clients enter PHP as a less-restrictive alternative to being hospitalized. According to the accepted national standards, PHP clients attend the program five days per week, for a total of 20 hours of treatment per week. PHP is generally intended to be a one- to three-week program, depending on the severity of the client's need. As clients progress in their treatment and become more stabilized, they can step down to an even less restrictive model of outpatient care, commonly known as Intensive Outpatient Treatment (IOP). In this level of programming, clients attend treatment at least two or three days per week for a minimum of three to four hours per day.

Besides addressing the client's core symptoms, the PHP takes into consideration the personality factors of each client. I am seasoned enough as a therapist to realize that the goal is not to alter or change a person's personality (as personality is usually well-ingrained in childhood), but to respond to a client's character in such a manner as to accentuate the client's strength. For example, let's say I'm working with a client who exhibits dependent personality traits. According to Gorski in a 1996 workshop I attended, this type of client's life stance is "I'm here to serve others, because others are more important than me." I want this client not to give up helping others in appropriate ways, but instead to learn to help him/herself, as well as others. Thus, in PHP groups, this client can set goals involving realistic and practical skills for self care. The client's peers can support the client's progress, or can explore with the client resistance to meeting goals. Attempts by the client to inappropriately rescue a peer, which inevitably occurs in the PHP milieu, can also be directly dealt with in the group process, or in an individual session if needed.

I provide individual, marital, and family therapy, if necessary. Obviously, client mental health issues affect family members and vice-versa. A few PHP clients also engage in outside therapy and/or support groups simultaneously with their PHP treatment. I welcome this, and clients usually have no objection to my consulting with their outside therapist.

Another clinical issue that I must contend with is the client's attitude toward being in PHP. Some clients, particularly those with dependent traits, cling to PHP tightly, and resist being weaned off the program. These clients are often isolated, or are in chaotic environments, and they view PHP as a safe haven. Other clients seem to begin treatment with fairly high motivation, but quickly lose interest and drop out. Still others attend out of some level of duress, having to satisfy an outside force such as the court system or an employer. Regardless of the client's motivation level, I keep my therapeutic focus on the purpose of PHP. That is, I constantly remind clients that PHP is a short-term program designed to assist them in returning to maximum functioning in the community. The setting of goals, then, becomes crucial, as the client is challenged to set concrete, specific, and practical treatment goals.

In the end, a successful PHP client will have achieved a level of little or no impairment of daily life, will have demonstrated the ability to form and maintain relationships outside of treatment, and will have committed to a specific discharge plan of continuing care. We hold a graduation group for clients on their final day of PHP. During this group, peers affirm the client's work done in treatment and offer best wishes for the future. The graduating client returns affirmation back to peers, and says good-byes.

Not all PHP clients graduate. Some drop out prematurely, clients with addictions relapse, and others may decompensate and end up re-hospitalized. While client resistance and sabotage clearly exists, I find immeasurable value in learning how I (and my staff) could have intervened with a client differently in such a way as to prevent an unsuccessful outcome. Like all therapists, I make mistakes with my clients every day!! I choose not to brood over my mistakes, but to learn from them.

The stressors I face on my job generally fall into three broad categories: (a) clinical stressors, which all therapists face, such as burnout, responding to client transferences, dealing with my own countertransferences, and frustrations with clients who choose to sabotage their or others' treatment; (b) programmatic stressors, involving staff relations and management of staff, satisfying psychiatrists' expectations, satisfying third-party payors' expectations, monitoring program quality and effectiveness, and abiding properly with state mental health laws and requirements; and (c) industry stressors, mainly keeping current with the trends and changes in mental health care and nationally accepted standards of PHP care.

To assist me with industry stressors, I have joined my state association for Ambulatory Behavioral Healthcare. My state group is patterned closely after a national organization known as the Association for Ambulatory Behavioral Healthcare (AABH), which was founded in 1985. The phrase ambulatory behavioral healthcare is the accepted jargon for a continuum of outpatient mental health services ranging from PHP to less structured aftercare programs. In 1996, AABH changed its name from the American Association of Partial

Hospitalization—the name change reflects the fact that a wide variety of outpatient programs, in addition to PHP, are now available nationally. In addition to annual training conferences, AABH offers numerous publications and newsletters designed to keep its members informed of ambulatory issues. My state's organization offers an annual conference, as well as quarterly meetings, during which members can network and exchange practical ideas for improving their PHP outpatient programs.

What is the future of partial hospitalization? I believe the coming years will find a continual need for quality PHPs to assist clients who are experiencing acute crisis. However, I foresee an increasing emphasis on IOPs and other intermediate-type outpatient programs that are less intensive than PHP. The broadening of outpatient ambulatory behavioral mental health will be necessitated by such factors as increasingly rigid reimbursements for inpatient and PHP care insisted upon by managed care companies, groundbreaking medications through which clients can achieve a higher level of psychiatric stability with fewer side effects, and the explosive growth of community support groups, whereby clients can receive free and structured support on a daily basis.

I do not know what the future holds for me as a clinical social worker, but for right now, I have found my niche in PHP. I look forward to continuing to serve my clients in this exciting model of mental health care. As one of my clients recently remarked to me, "Ken, you were made for this job!"

Chapter 23
Social Work in a Clubhouse

by Jack Yatsko, MSW, LSW

I work in a psychosocial rehabilitation program called Friendship House. I work with adults who have a mental illness, and our program follows the Clubhouse Model of rehabilitation. The Clubhouse Model is nontraditional in that it embodies a side-by-side relationship between staff and members, rather than the traditional medical model in which the members are treated as patients in a day care or partial hospitalization program. A good clubhouse is an energetic, vibrant, alive place, with a variety of opportunities available for members to participate in as they work toward their individual goals.

There are four guaranteed rights in the Clubhouse: the guaranteed right to a place to come to, the guaranteed right to meaningful work, the guaranteed right to meaningful relationships, and the guaranteed right to a place to return. The successful operation of a good club rests on the members and staff working together. Our club has four prevocational work unit areas; Thrift Shop, Communications Unit, Food Service, and Snack Shop.

Friendship House offers members opportunities to return to competitive work through its Transitional Employment Program. Friendship House also offers members assistance with their educational goals through a Supportive Education Program. Work should also be combined with a fair amount of play, and Friendship House has an evening social program in which we participate in a variety of community activities and fun.

Friendship House is located on the island of Kauai, Hawaii. The members and staff who make up Friendship House represent a multi-cultural mixture of populations. Our membership is comprised of Filipino, Chinese, Hawaiian, Japanese, Caucasian, Puerto Rican, and a variety of other ethnicities. The uniqueness that each individual brings to the club is emphasized and supported as we focus on strengths, not weaknesses, on what the members can do, not what they can't do.

In the clubhouse, it is difficult to define a typical day. There are so many variables that can occur, that as much as I plan and try to organize my day, I also need to be flexible enough to adjust if none of these plans work out. At Friendship House, I may be called to work on a transitional employment placement, I may need to fill in a different work unit, I may need to just be there to listen when I have ninety other things waiting to be done. In the clubhouse model, my coworkers and I need to juggle many things, and we absolutely need the membership in order to make it work.

On a recent day, my schedule looked like this:

6:30 a.m.-7:45 a.m. We are scheduled to start work at 7:45. However, there is so much to do in the clubhouse that I like to come in early most of the time. Today I'm trying to figure out how to duplicate our chart note form on the computer, so that staff and members can use the computers to complete these notes more efficiently, and so they can be read more easily. I think I finally have it figured out and, more important, can now explain to others how to use it.

7:45-9:00 Transitional Employment Site Visit at the YWCA. I am the Placement Manager for the two TE jobs I am visiting this morning. Kalani works in an outdoor maintenance job, and Mark works in an indoor maintenance job. I check with both members and the staff to monitor their progress and use the YWCA truck to make a trip to the recycling center to turn in some cans and glass. There are lots of tangerines ready for picking, so I show Kalani how to cut them so they stay ripe for a longer period. I also assist Mark with reviewing the procedures to fill out his time sheet.

9:00-11:00 Meet with Sarah, a member who is taking courses at our local community college. She called yesterday requesting assistance with her keyboarding course. She is majoring in hotel management and having a difficult time trying to keep up in this course.

Friendship House offers a Supportive Education component in which we provide members with support in their educational goals, similarly to how the Transitional Employment program operates. Kauai Community College has been amenable to our involvement, and in the past I've been in French class, a ceramics class, and a typing course. I have assisted members with various realities that have involved paranoid thoughts, hallucinations that make it difficult to concentrate, and in managing anxiety effectively.

Today, Sarah is experiencing difficulty figuring out the computer bar codes and subsequently is having anxiety and problems with completing her assignments. We practice for an hour with the computer and then go outside so she can have a cigarette. We process some of her feelings about potentially failing the class and what alternatives she can try when feeling overwhelmed in the class. Sarah is so determined to graduate that she has difficulty recognizing her limitations and becomes easily frustrated and defensive in discussing these issues. I am torn in that I want to support Sarah in her goals, but also need to provide some reality checking to her. She needs to type at least 35 words per minute to pass the class, and she is only at 18 words a minute. It doesn't seem possible that she will improve that quickly over the next four weeks. However, Sarah is the type of person who has to experience things for herself in order to truly believe them, so I see her go through tremendous stress and anxiety and am both inspired by her gritty determination and saddened by her difficulty in hearing others' concerns. She goes to class today with a purpose to forge on.

11:00-12:00 Stop by a local vegetable market that has a hiring sign. Unemployment is currently 12% on Kauai and job development has become exceedingly difficult. To see a "For Hire" sign is something I have to jump on. The employer appears open to possible transitional employment placements in stocking and packaging work. He asks for a brochure and discusses potential opportunities. Many times I have to keep making subsequent contacts with employers to develop an opening, so to get an audience with the owner on a cold call on the first try is a bonus. We close the meeting by agreeing to assess the specific job duties next week. Everything looks good so far....hurray!

12:00-1:30 Arrive back to Friendship House and meet with members to discuss a voter registration drive and a Medicaid Reform Proposal project. We also finish up participant forms for the Supported Employment Conference coming up later this year.

1:30-2:00 Meet with Keoki, who is experiencing some difficulties with adjusting to some medication changes. He is currently exhibiting hypomanic symptoms and is having difficulty concentrating. We follow up by calling the local mental health center and scheduling an appointment for the following day. We also contact his care home operator regarding this issue. We talk about what Keoki feels he can do today to cope with his heightened energy, and he returns to the prevocational work unit to help with preparations for a barbecue we are having tomorrow.

2:00-2:30 Back into the communications work unit to assist various members with typing projects and outreach calls to absent members. In the clubhouse we try to create an atmosphere of "ohana," which means family. Frequently contacting absent members helps develop a family feeling of being wanted and needed. Today, we make several calls and agree to transport a sofa to an apartment a member has just moved into.

2:30-3:00 Take a break to go swimming in the ocean. The clubhouse tends to pull me in a variety of directions, and it is easy to just forget about taking any kind of break and just keep going on. Today, though, I think of all the snow on the east coast and look outside at the beautiful 85 degree sunny day and ask myself, "Why am I even debating this?" Off I go into the blue Pacific, and thirty minutes later I feel revitalized and ready to go!

3:00-3:30 Meet with our next door neighbor, who has been complaining that the poison under our building is attracting rodents that are dying in his yard and leaving a horrible smell. I crawl under our building and don't smell anything and fortunately don't find any rodents, dead or alive! I agree to convey his concerns to my boss and the vector control person.

3:30-4:30 Work on a financial project for our nonprofit application. Review expenditures with several club members and we work together on breaking down the previous year's finances. I sometimes struggle with this area, as it would take me less time to work on this by myself, but in the clubhouse the process is as important as the outcome. To deny the membership the opportunity to work on this with me would deny someone else's talents and abilities from developing further. Doing this together will make our club stronger in the future, and I need to remind myself of this at times.

4:30-5:00 Call Sarah back to see how her class went today. She received help from the instructor today but remains confused about the computer bar codes. Sarah plans to finish out the semester. We talk about what she will do this weekend, and one of my concerns is that she will cope with her frustration by drinking. In addition to a mental illness, Sarah has a dual diagnosis of alcohol dependence. She is at a high risk time now and we process various alternatives. Sarah decides to go shopping and to an AA meeting tonight. She thanks me for my help and plans to come to the club next week to go over the typing tutorial with me again.

5:00 No one else here at the club. I think of my wife, pregnant and probably home from work by now, and I think of my dogs and cats waiting to be fed and exercised. Time for me to put the brakes on and head home.

Every day, my job brings with it new challenges and sur-prises. To work in the clubhouse model requires a high de-gree of flexibility and the ability to work with a wide variety of people. I move in and out of many roles, which include side-by-side work with the members, meeting with various em-ployers in the community, administrative tasks, and dealing periodically with neighbors concerned about "our" rodents. I literally have four sets of clothes at work each day and usu-ally change into at least three of them, depending on what I am doing on that particular day. When I wear long pants, a certain member always asks me, "Where are you going to-day?" I love when he asks me that, because he really is say-ing, "I know you would be much more comfortable in shorts, just like the rest of us. But you need to put on your various costumes to communicate with a wide range of people and to do your job effectively. Just when you're done, don't forget where your roots are." I tell him not to worry, I won't, and I hope that I never do.

Working in a clubhouse rehabilitation program is clearly not the job for a social worker looking to conduct private prac-tice or work in a clinically-based setting. However, if you en-joy developing and using your social work skills in a variety of capacities and can handle a high degree of flexibility, club-house work may be worth looking into. You will meet people who happen to have a severe mental illness but who are still people who have similar needs, wants, and desires as anyone else. To work in a clubhouse and help people improve the quality of their lives is a wonderful opportunity for a social worker to share, learn, and grow, both professionally and per-sonally.

Chapter 24
Life as a Group Home Manager

by Angela Marie Brinton, BSW

Patience, tolerance and a sense of humor—the three virtues for working with the mentally ill population. I say this because in the past year, I have been called every name in the book, spit on, hit and, on occasion, threatened by clients who were decompensating, mad, or just having a bad day. It's all part of the territory, but I love my job as the Manager/Director of a group home for young adults, ages 17-25. The first time I assisted in moving a high risk client out into his own apartment, and three months later he was baking me cookies, I was hooked. I have forgiven (not forgotten) a lot of actions. This is not to say that clients should get by with murder, but clients can change their behaviors. They just have to be taught how to act appropriately in the community, and they have to feel secure. In our program, we preach natural consequences as often as possible. I've been told that our staff work miracles, but it's really our clients.

I received my BSW in May 1992 and started my first "real" post-graduation job in the big city (Kansas City) that same year, as an outpatient case manager for the State of Missouri. I later transferred to my current position within the same organization. I had worked many fill-in shifts, and was therefore familiar with the clients and the program.

The Young Adult Program is very successful and I am part of a wonderful team of group home staff, case managers, community members, and family members. Our program is located in the inner city, but we serve clients from all over Missouri. We are completely community-based. Our clients live in the group home, their own apartments, community residential settings, or with their families. The clients living in the group home have curfews but are able to go out in the community by themselves.

As a part of my job, I am on call to my staff 24 hours a day, 7 days a week. I am responsible for ongoing tasks such as staff training, budgeting, charting, and scheduling. There are two things that I hate about my job. Those are politicking so that our clients can receive the services they should be automatically receiving and dealing with lazy employees who hate their jobs.

It's 5:30 a.m., well before my usual start time of 9:00, as I trudge into work. I was paged at 1:30 a.m. to talk with Tiffany, who had just trashed her room. We talked about her behavior and why she broke some of her own personal items until about 2:30 a.m., when she finally retired to bed. Her family had promised to visit for about the thirtieth time and didn't show up. One of the staff called me at 5:00 a.m. to inform me that Tiffany wouldn't get out of bed for school and that he needed reinforcements. One of the requirements is that clients go to work or to school every day unless they are dying. Since we adhere to natural consequences, it also means that sometimes we have to have extra staff on very short notice, which explains why Tiffany's case manager and I are here at 5:30 this morning. Tiffany is in her senior year of high school. She will be the only child of 16 in her family to graduate from high school, and she is the only one diagnosed with a mental illness.

When Tiffany came to our program, she wouldn't talk to anyone for about the first three weeks, and refused to get out of bed most days. She had spent most of the last six years living in an inpatient facility. Her solution to every stressor was to cut on herself. She had poor hygiene and low self-esteem. Today she is a clothes hound, hasn't missed a full day of school for two months, and hasn't cut on herself in over a year. She has also not spent one day in the hospital since she came to our program. At 6:30, she is finally ready, and since she missed the school bus, she has to take the city bus, which another client taught her to ride. (We refuse to drive any of our clients to their programs.)

My next task of the day is to work with J.T., who is diagnosed with schizophrenia. This is always a challenge, since he frequently cannot tell you what day it is. He has been ousted from every outpatient program in the city, so we have tried to create our own program for him within our group home. He has been at the group home for four years, but for two separate stays. We have taught J.T. how to ride the bus to the mall approximately 75 times. He would frequently forget how to get home once he got there, lose his bus tokens, and show up a couple of hours late. Once the police brought him home, because he couldn't remember his telephone number. After driving about 25 minutes each way to pick him up from the mall one day, with him yelling at me because he thought he had missed dinner, I told myself that it just wasn't going to happen. I was so frustrated that he couldn't figure this one simple task out, but I gave him a bus token again a few days later. After an eternity, J.T. can take the bus about four places. It really can happen, but it has to happen within the client's time frame.

Today, we are making pancakes. J.T. likes to eat, so he's motivated. I have to explain each task thoroughly, from what kind of pan to use to how to turn the stove off when he's finished. We have been trying to teach J.T. how to cook one meal a week, rotating three or four different items. When he first started, he wouldn't stay in the kitchen, but now he'll stay until it comes time to clean up. He's no fool. Before J.T. had his first hospitalization, he was at the top of his class making straight A's and excelled in several sports. He has a near genius IQ.

It's now about ten o'clock, and I have to partake in the scheduling nightmare. We are two staff short and I have a lot of empty shifts to cover, but a budget ceiling that will only allow full coverage for certain shifts. One major downside to the mental health field is that entry level positions pay very little, which makes it difficult to retain really good staff. I have worked very hard to find other ways to compensate employees who go above and beyond the basic expectations.

Unfortunately, completing paperwork is easier said than done, because I always have an array of visitors in my office. Our program is very community-based, so we have a lot of clients who visit. Today, my first visitor is Howard. He has come to tell me about his latest life mishap. He "left his $10,000 paycheck lying on the back porch and someone stole it." Considering that he has no job, one can quickly conclude that there is no paycheck. I ask him if he would like to report it to the police, but he tells me that it's not necessary, because he'll get paid again next week. I ask him what employment he has these days. He relates that he has been working as an undercover agent for the FBI. I tell him that if he ever gets sick of the undercover work, I have a really good program that he can sign up for that pays $4.50 an hour. He thanks me and leaves, only to come back in about a half hour to sign up for the program. I am really excited about this, because I have asked him about 100 times, and this is the first time that he would make the necessary phone calls. I like working with Howard, because he is very challenging. Since I have known him, he's been shot about 50 times, robbed 100 times, and "beat up" more times than I can count, although there is never a scratch on his body. He used to visit the Emergency Room via ambulance about two or three times per week. The staff worked intensively with him, and now he uses the ambulance about once a month.

I am finally back to my scheduling for about 20 minutes before my next interruption from one of our more humorous clients. She meets me at my car every morning to tell me that I look beautiful and that she missed me. It's a great ego boost to hear that every day. Today, Marie is upset because she cannot carry her own spending money. She receives $15 per week. The first time we let her have all of it, she went to the beauty salon and had her head shaved, which is not necessarily a crime, but she then begged me for about a month to buy her a wig. Her reasoning for shaving her head was that she wanted to look like her favorite staff person, Charles. Charles is African-American and wears his hair very short. Marie is Caucasian and female. Marie and I reach an agreement that she can keep five dollars of her spending money per week and that she can buy things with the rest of the money if she will let one of the staff help her with her shopping.

Today is my favorite day of my work week, Wednesday, because we have social night. Any of our clients, old and new, can come. The only requirements are that they have to wear clean clothes, bathe before arriving, and follow the rules. We had to make the prerequisites very specific, because some of the clients would bathe, but then wear dirty clothes they hadn't washed for three weeks. It is a great time. We usually have about 20-25 clients show up, from very high functioning to very low functioning. Today we are going out for dinner to a nice restaurant, a treat for most of the clients. They have to pay for their own meals. I have been asked at least 50 times today when we are leaving. It's about 4:30, and we are trying to get everyone gathered up. Tiffany has just arrived home from school in a really good mood and cleaned up her room without being asked. That's what it's really all about, and programs like this can work.

Most of our clients have been in and out of hospitals most of their lives. Our goals have changed a lot since the program first started. Originally, our goal was for everyone to have their own apartments when they left our program, but through trial and error, we realized that wasn't going to happen. We currently place about 90% of our clients in their own apartments when they leave the program. Approximately 80% of them are still in their apartments after six months. It is difficult to predict how a client will do in an apartment. It is frequently the lower functioning, persistent mentally ill clients who do better in apartments. They will usually take our advice. If we tell them not to go out past 11:00 because they can get killed or robbed, they usually will stay home.

You have to measure success in small increments in working with the mentally ill. What you see as successful may not be to your client. You can't put your values and goals on their treatment plan and have any success.

Chapter 25
Disaster Mental Health Services

by John D. Weaver, ACSW, LSW

As I write this, it is very early in the morning and I am in the Everglades, near Miami, Florida, on an American Red Cross disaster assignment at the site of an air crash. Our team is working at the crash site, to help the recovery crews (and the other relief workers) cope with the slow and difficult process of gathering the human remains and the pieces of the plane. I don't get paid for this work (in fact, I often use my vacation time and I lose private practice income to make these trips), but it is very much a part of my professional life as a social worker.

My full-time job is Casework Supervisor for a county mental health clinic in Pennsylvania. I generally am in my office by 6:30 or 7:00 a.m. The day there officially begins at 8:30, so while I'm not yet on the clock, I make the coffee, do paperwork, and set things up for the day to come. I also will frequently use this quiet time to write (I've authored several articles and two books), update my Internet home page, or work on some of my private consulting projects.

On Monday mornings, the early time is often used to finish writing emergency sheets and to phone in reports from weekend on-call shifts. I've always enjoyed providing crisis intervention services, so as one of my part-time jobs, I frequently take five or six emergency shifts per month. Depending upon the types of shifts I take, the work involves phone counseling, information and referral, site counseling (with our mobile crisis team), arranging voluntary hospitalizations, and delegating involuntary commitments.

Once my regular 8:30 to 4:30 day begins, one might find me supervising one of seven case managers, overseeing treatment plan writing and reviews, handling complaints, doing utilization reviews, backing up my workers when they are out of the office, writing discharge summaries, answering corre-spondence (especially requests for records), attending meet-ings, or assisting with wraparound planning for children at risk for out-of-home placements. I am also involved with an-nual license reviews, planning, and public speaking on be-half of our program.

Three days a week, when my day ends at that job, I head across town to my part-time job at Concern. There I see indi-viduals, families, and some foster children (Concern is also a foster care provider agency) for therapy. I'll usually see two to four clients each night I'm there. Most of the private clients are middle class, highly motivated, and privately insured. They are usually paying for their services up front and seeking re-imbursement, if any, from their insurance. We tend to use cognitive-behavioral approaches and see people for a brief course of treatment (five to seven sessions). Concern uses several part-time therapists and offers no benefits; most of us have day jobs to cover our insurance needs.

Far more personally and professionally rewarding to me than any of the jobs already mentioned is my volunteer ca-reer. After graduate school, I served on the board of directors of the local and state chapters of the Mental Health Associa-tion. I eventually served for two years as the president of each of those organizations. This kept me at the forefront of con-sumer advocacy, offered me many opportunities for public speaking, and provided me with a lot of administrative expe-riences, all at a time when I was working in an entry level paid position at the clinic.

More recently, my volunteer interests have swung to the Disaster Mental Health Services (DMHS) component of the American Red Cross (ARC). ARC offers free training to anyone who qualifies and is interested in helping out with DMHS, or any of its other relief services (e.g., mass care, damage as-sessment, family services, health services, logistics, liaison functions, staffing, and computers). I took my first class in 1993 and went out on my first two disasters that year (one on administrative leave time and the other on vacation time). I immediately was hooked.

Many social workers, psychologists, nurses, counselors, and psychiatrists are finding their caseloads (patient loads) are too high. The mere mention of managed care makes their necks stiffen. They're fed up with treatment plans, progress notes, and forms of all sorts, and they're tired of the same old blend of bureaucracy, politics, paperwork, and pathology. Upon finding that the magic has gone out of their careers, they've made a change by becoming DMHS volunteers.

Once they've qualified and completed free training (which also offers no-cost continuing education units), they too are able to "travel to exotic and not-so-exotic places, meet people whose lives have been struck by disasters—and help them," with ARC covering all disaster-related expenses. Participants in ARC training learn all about the Red Cross DMHS program's requirements and opportunities to serve locally, nationally, and internationally.

To date, I have served as a DMHS volunteer on seven major, national disasters and many more local events. Most memorable were my visit to Iowa during the summer-long Midwest flooding of 1993 and my service as coordinator of DMHS services for the morgue workers in the wake of the 1994 Pittsburgh air crash that killed 132 passengers and crew. Going out on one or two disaster assignments (and several teaching assignments to teach the DMHS course all over the country) each year provides me with some much needed respite from my regular full-time and part-time job duties.

So, today, I find myself in Florida amid the remains of an air crash where 110 people were killed. The days are long, starting at about 6:30 a.m. and ending around 6:00 p.m. We work in shifts at the command post and the forward base of operations, which is about 11 miles deeper into the glades, where the plane went down. We offer defusing and debriefing interviews and support. In these situations, we work closely with the other professionals assigned to the operation, such as police psychologists and critical incident stress management (CISM or CISD) team members.

We get on the road from our hotel by 6:30 a.m. for the trip into the Everglades. We arrive at the site, our I.D. is checked, and we get to work. We all have Red Cross and Salvation Army mass care meals with the police, fire rescue, and recovery personnel at the sites. In fact, part of our work is to help serve meals and snacks at times when we are short on mass care workers. In a job like this, we wear buttons that identify us as mental health team members, and we make ourselves available to anyone needing to talk.

We avoid asking "How do you feel?" and we try not to be too aggressive in our approaches to the other workers, who tend to seek us out as needed. Some services are provided by experienced disaster mental health workers, but we also try to include new, local people. We'll orient the new folks at the start of their first shifts and supervise them more closely. This use of brand new staff members is important for capacity building in the local area.

Disaster victims are generally normal people who are experiencing very typical reactions to the abnormally stressful situations they face in the aftermath of the event. DMHS workers use techniques like psychoeducation, crisis intervention, defusing, and debriefing, to help the victims become survivors and help the helpers (the other relief workers) manage their stress. In this assignment, we are working to keep the rescue workers from becoming secondary victims. We provide stress inoculation to incoming workers, preparing them for the sights, sounds, smells, thoughts, and memories they will face. Workers are always changed by involvement in disaster relief activities, but they need not be damaged by it.

Here, as with the 1994 crash near Pittsburgh, dealing with the body parts is generally less stressful than dealing with personal effects (photos, toys, clothing). Workers' defenses can be quickly broken down when something reminds them of their own lives and families. Then they need to find one of us and talk it out. Sometimes, we'll ask them to take a little time off or switch to a less stressful assignment for a while. Most of the recovery workers here are paid, highly-trained police and fire/rescue personnel who have faced mass-casualty situations before. They are having a much easier time of it than did many of the recovery volunteers we used in Pittsburgh, who had little knowledge of what they were getting themselves into. Consequently, our job here is less stressful.

Many of the folks I've spoken with over the past several days are talking about their memories of 1992's Hurricane Andrew. The influx of Red Cross and Salvation Army trucks and relief workers has reminded them how tough things were for them the last time they had to rely on outside help in a time of disaster. That rekindling of both positive and painful memories is another element disaster mental health workers commonly address during relief efforts.

At day's end, which has sometimes been moved up an hour or two by the Florida phenomena of late afternoon thunderstorms, we head back to our hotel, get cleaned up, and go to a late dinner. On this kind of assignment, teams quickly form tight friendships. This is important for stress management and peer support. A typical DMHS assignment will be 10-14 days for workers flown in from other areas. Local volunteers can plug into the operation as their schedules permit.

No other moments in my career have come close to providing me the personal and professional rewards that I have experienced as a Red Cross volunteer. I urge you to contact ARC and see what it is all about. Calling the disaster relief component of your local ARC chapter (or the next larger regional or state office) is the best way to get started. If your local chapter does not yet have a DMHS component, you can help get one organized.

Once back home in Pennsylvania, my days are spent at my three jobs, or in my additional work as a private consultant, where I have worked on such projects as developing a training program for volunteer coordinators who want to better understand the role of mentally ill persons who wish to volunteer in their agencies.

Interspersed with my day-to-day work, I take every opportunity I can to use the new skills I've learned in my volunteer work and to share my new knowledge with others through speaking engagements; presentations at national conferences such as NASW, APA, and ACA; and writing. And, of course, I'm always ready to answer the call for help when another disaster strikes.

Note from John Weaver: In the wake of the ValuJet crash and, later that same year, the crash of TWA Flight 800, Congress held hearings on the problems surviving family members face in the aftermath of these tragic events. In response to the testimony they received, the members of Congress quickly enacted the Aviation Disaster Family Assistance Act of 1996. Subsequently, and in recognition of the fine work Red Cross volunteers had done following several airline accidents, the National Transportation Safety Board has designated ARC the "independent nonprofit organization with experience in disasters and posttrauma communications with families." ARC has now formed a special Aviation Incident Response (AIR) Team, a rapid-response group that quickly provides assistance to families and to other personnel involved in the relief operations following aviation accidents and other major transportation accidents.

ARC continues to seek help from persons interested in volunteering in future relief efforts. ARC especially needs more licensed mental health professionals to expand the ranks of the DMHS team. The goal is to train a pool of 10,000 people who will have the skills needed to assist locally and nationally with all types of disasters.

I'm proud to report that social workers now comprise 40% of the volunteers assisting in this function and our numbers appear to be expanding somewhat more rapidly than the other mental health disciplines. Please join us. Call your local Red Cross chapter and get involved.

PART 7:
SUBSTANCE ABUSE

Chapter 26
Dual Diagnosis: Substance Abuse and Mental Health in an Inpatient Setting

by Catherine Lau Crisp, MSW

I am a clinical social worker on an inpatient psychiatry unit at a large teaching hospital in the southeast. I work with the "dual diagnosis service," a part of the inpatient psychiatry department whose job it is to treat people with both a substance abuse problem and a mental health issue.

Seventy percent of the people I treat have a substance induced mood disorder; that is, their depression is due to their addiction. Eighty-five percent of my clients have no insurance and little resources to pay for treatment. Many clients have reached rock bottom in their lives. They have reached the point where they feel a desire to end their lives because they have tried, and usually failed, to triumph over their drug problems. Many clients have been through several treatment programs in the past and are trapped in the web of addiction. With its commitment to the indigent, the hospital where I work is the only option for some people in this area.

My day starts at 7:30 in the morning when I arrive on the unit. Immediately upon arrival, I look over the list of patients assigned to my team. This list tells me who has been admitted since I left the unit and who has left. At any given time, I work with a maximum of nine clients. Additional clients presenting with a mental health and substance abuse issue are placed on one of the five other psychiatry services.

The majority of my morning is spent meeting with my team and the clients that we serve. My team consists of a part-time attending psychiatrist, a first-year or second-year psychiatry resident (who has completed medical school, is now training for four years before becoming a full fledged psychiatrist, and spends thirty days on the dual diagnosis service), a third-year medical student (who spends six weeks on my team), and a nurse. We generally meet as a team and then make "rounds" to see each of the clients. In working with each of our clients, our goals are two-fold: 1) assess and diagnose the mental health issue and 2) address the addiction. Neither of these is easy. The average length of stay on our service is nine days. Many clients come in with exceptionally high alcohol levels (a blood alcohol level of 0.35 is not uncommon) and/or are in acute withdrawal from the effects of heroin. In a very short time, we are faced with the tasks of decreasing their suicidality and/or hallucinations, detoxifying them from their substances, motivating them for treatment of their substance abuse and mental health issues, meeting with their families, and arranging follow-up treatment for them upon discharge from the hospital. As a social worker, I am involved in each of these aspects, although the psychiatrist and resident will ultimately decide on the diagnosis. I hold primary responsibility for meeting with the families, conducting individual and group therapy with the clients, and arranging the discharge plan.

In addition to my work with the clients, one of the most enjoyable aspects of my job is the education I do with both the resident and the medical student about the interplay between substance abuse and mental illness. On several occasions, our team has had lengthy debates about the diagnosis of a particular client. Is he/she depressed because he/she can't get off drugs? Did the depression precede the drug use? If the depression preceded the drug use, at what point did they start to use drugs and how did that affect their depression? What is their diagnosis? Is it substance-induced mood disorder or is it a major depression with a coexisting substance dependence problem? Is the client's irritability due to: 1) a component of their mental illness, 2) the effects of withdrawing from their drug of choice (irritability is particularly common among people who are addicted to crack cocaine), 3) a component of a personality disorder, or 4) just a part of their personality style? Many times, each of the team members has a very different opinion about the diagnosis and the recommended course of treatment. It seems like a miracle when we can all agree. At other times, it is clear that we will not reach a consensus. When this happens, the attending psychiatrist ultimately makes the final call about the diagnosis and treatment that we will provide. Although I am surrounded by people with a clear medical model bias, I feel that my opinions and the bio-psycho-social-spiritual perspective I bring to the team are respected and valued by those I work with.

My afternoon consists of individual and group therapy and begins with the group I do each day at 1 o'clock. The group is "required" for all clients on the dual diagnosis unit, but I consider it to be a good day when I have a 75% turn-out. The group focuses on substance abuse issues and is a combination of psycho-education and therapy; the content and focus of the group depends largely on the group of clients. There are some weeks when the client population appears insightful, motivated, verbal, and bond together as a group. When this happens, I have fantastic groups. I come in with a topic for discussion and the clients have so many questions and comments that I, as facilitator, play a very minimal role.

In one recent group, we discussed "Consequences of My Addiction." The group members felt close to one another, comfortable with the group setting, and were able to open up and share the pain and losses they had experienced in their own lives and created for other people as a result of their addictions. People cried and shared and comforted one another. I felt I could have left the room and the clients would have continued with the topic without me. My role was to clarify confusion people had, not to direct them in the discussion. It was a powerful group and one that the clients felt was among the more meaningful groups they attended during their hospitalization.

Unfortunately, groups like the one mentioned above are very rare. Clients are often unwilling to attend groups and need much more individual treatment. Addressing clients' refusal to attend groups frequently presents philosophical dilemmas for the team. Much of the substance abuse theory would advocate a hard-lined approach: attend the group or leave treatment. Mental illness theory would advocate a softer approach: nurture the client and treat the underlying mental illness and the client will be able and willing to attend groups. My team does not have any set rules about how we approach each client; instead we treat each client as an individual and try to understand the client's objections to attending group.

Much of the work I do with clients individually is based on a strengths perspective and motivational therapy techniques. As noted before, many clients have tried and failed many times in their sobriety and have little hope in their ability to recover from their addiction. I attempt to educate them about the process of relapse, help them identify individual strengths and resources that may be helpful in their recovery, confront them on their denial, and assist them in understanding elements of their substance abuse and their mental illness or depression. The most valuable thing I think I offer clients is a belief that if they are willing to do the work, they can recover. I let them know that they have the abilities to recover but, ultimately, must complete the tasks themselves.

When not meeting with the team or clients, my attention turns to discharge planning. I remember quite well the message I received as a student. "Discharge planning begins the day you start treatment with a client." I have never seen this more true than in my work with the dually diagnosed. In considering discharge planning for clients, most of my focus entails connecting the clients with mental health and substance abuse agencies. For clients without insurance, this entails a referral to the mental health center that serves the area where they live. Many agencies here require that clients contact the agency themselves; my work in this area consists primarily of giving the clients the telephone number of the appropriate agency for them to contact. After the client has made contact with the agency, I send information regarding diagnosis, medications, and course of treatment to the agency. If the client has been referred by a mental health center, I maintain contact with the referring clinician from the date of admission to the date of discharge. Frequently, clinicians have specific goals that they want their clients to accomplish with the hospitalization, such as decreasing suicidality, decreasing hallucinations, reevaluating medications, detoxifying from drugs and/ or alcohol, and providing a more conclusive diagnosis. In addition, the clinician frequently has a plan for the client upon discharge, such as entering residential treatment or beginning intensive outpatient treatment. My role in working with the outpatient clinician is to coordinate services among the mental health center, the client, and the treatment team at the hospital to provide the highest level of care for the client.

In addition to making referrals for mental health and substance abuse treatment, I also assist approximately ten percent of clients with addressing their homelessness. As noted earlier, many of the people I treat are depressed and have hit bottom. Much of this is due to the losses they have experienced as a result of their addiction. It is not uncommon for my team to treat people who have lost their jobs, homes, transportation, and families to their addiction. Many clients report living "with friends, on the street, by the river, wherever I can find a place." Despite such seeming desperation, referrals to homeless shelters are often rejected. Clients are frequently familiar with the shelter system and prefer the streets to the shelters. Others report that the shelter system is filled with drugs and not conducive to sobriety. These reports are very frustrating to hear as the shelters are often the only public resource for homeless individuals. One of the hardest things to accept is that clients may leave the hospital and decide not to change any of the circumstances that led to their hospitalization.

In the course of discharge planning, I also attempt to meet with clients' families. While there is much disagreement about specific approaches to treatment with dually diagnosed individuals, there is consensus that the family is a valuable source of information. Many clients are cut off from their families. They may have stolen from and lied to their families to the point that their families no longer want any contact with them. When I am able to meet with family members, I have two basic goals: 1) obtain information about events in the client's life that precipitated the hospitalization and 2) educate the family about addiction and mental illness. Families are generally relieved when they realize that my goal is not to convince them to assist the client with money or housing, although I freely acknowledge that were the family to do so, my job with discharge planning would be much easier.

I reinforce to families that it is important to set consequences for the negative behaviors of the addict and in doing
so, to validate the limits that they have or want to set for the
addict. After meeting with the family members, I invite the
client in to join the meeting. This is a useful time for both the
family member and the client, because they have a safe space
with a mediator to express certain issues. The intensity of the
emotions can get quite high, but by and large, these meetings
are productive for the client (who hears previously unspoken
feelings and thoughts from the family member), for the family
member (who has been given a chance to be a part of the
client's treatment and has obtained information about the
treatment), and for myself and the treatment team (who now
have a more complete picture of the client's life and history,
thus enabling us to provide better treatment to the client).

As you can see, theoretical dilemmas are common in working with dually diagnosed individuals. Anyone who wishes to
work with this population must have a good understanding
of theory regarding both substance abuse and mental illness.
In addition, one must be able to handle both the theoretical
and the direct practice conflicts. These conflicts fascinate me.
The potential for a variety of approaches in work with this
population is enormous.

I never know what to expect from moment to moment.
The client population is as diverse as any group of clients; I
have treated angry alcoholic men who lost $100,000 jobs and
depressed women who were addicted to prescription pain kill-
ers. The range of psychiatric diagnoses varies from the more
common substance-induced mood disorder to the less common somatoform disorder. The common denominator is the
substance abuse issue and the common ground that clients
share as addicts.

Chapter 27
Social Work in the Alaskan Bush

by Taylor Burns, LCSW

I don't think there's anything "typical" about my days as the Director of the Northern Lights Recovery Center in Nome, Alaska. But it is social work, and I love what I do. It's difficult to comprehend from the lower 48, but our Recovery Center is the sole alcohol and drug treatment center for the neighboring 26,000 square miles, known as the Norton Sound Region. Nome is the hub of the region with a population of about 4,000. There is a total population of about 8,000 in the region. You cannot drive to Nome. You must come in by plane or boat. The cars and trucks that are here come by barge. Barges run from late May to late September. They say it doesn't get cold here until November. That's when the Bering Sea freezes. I came to Nome in August of 1994. During my first 12 weeks here, we had eight suicides. Mostly males under the age of 25. Most jumped into the Bering Sea off the jetty. When the Bering Sea froze, I was very happy. It meant they wouldn't be jumping off the jetty for another nine months. I had already learned the meaning of the black helicopter hovering over the jetty. I didn't like seeing it.

My first meeting of the day is at the Federal Building on Front Street. It's a sunny day and it reminds me of my first sunny day in Nome. I remember sitting in Dr. Jackman's office as part of my interview for the job. She took a phone call near the end of our time, and I got up to look out her window at the Bering Sea. I saw a whale breach. I thought my eyes were fooling me. I called Dr. Jackman to the window to confirm his continued breaches. She confirmed it. That was a sign to me that I should come to Nome.

My meeting is with the Injury Prevention committee. This year's state report showed suicide to be the number one cause of death in our region. The committee was formed to address the problem in a more coordinated effort. Again, I remember my first 12 weeks on the job, and the seriousness of the problems here. It is a harsh reality that my job here is more serious than anywhere else I have worked. I believe there's a spiritual calling to work in Nome. People either love it or hate it. It's such an odd combination. The beauty of the land and the Sea, and the harshness of the climate. But even more so, the harshness of the trauma (both past and present) that continues to assault the families of the region.

I've watched people come and go, and I've only been here two years. The population of the region is predominantly Eskimo—Yupik, Siberian Yupik, and Inupiat. Here in Nome, the population is about 50% Eskimo. The other 50% is predominantly Caucasian, with a lesser population of Asian, Hispanic, and African American.

The meeting is well attended. But there's a concern expressed about the lack of input from the villages. There is talk that we should set up a teleconference with persons in the villages to have input on this problem. We discuss the Suicide Prevention staff in the villages, and their need for training and support. There's a high turnover in the village positions as well. Unlike the lower 48, we cannot drive to these villages. We must travel by small airplane. And if the weather is bad, there's no getting in or out. I've learned to appreciate the depth and breadth of the problems of the bush. There are no easy and quick solutions. Solutions are "long-term." The solutions include and require community "evolution," individuals' sobriety, cultural sensitivity, and healing.

My next meeting is a teleconference with the State Director's Association. We have monthly teleconferences to discuss statewide issues. Now that I've been here for two years, I know more about the politics and the struggles between the bush communities and the communities on a "road system." Bush communities have a higher cost of living. We have minimal services, and almost no referral services. We have nowhere to refer the clients who come through the treatment center with a history of battering. We have no place to refer the women and men who have been sexually abused and now need a long-term group to continue their recovery work. I stay on the teleconference and remind them of the continued needs for a continuum of care that reaches out to the villages and doesn't stop in Nome. I remind them of the lack of services here, so there will be an understanding of the needs in our region. I'm still angry about the Medicaid funding. There is a cost of living adjustment for Alaska, but no cost of living adjustment for the disparity in the cost of living between Anchorage and some of the villages. People balk at the prices in our grocery stores, but they won't allow a cost of living adjustment for people who live in the villages.

I take my role as an advocate very seriously. I know it is my job to assist the State office, the State legislators, and the Commissioner to understand the extent to which we have to go to provide even minimal services. As I work on the budget, I am reminded of the time and resources necessary to provide basic services.

Last year I went with a staff member to a nearby village. I went in order to train this staff on how to work with families. We had been working with this family in response to a father's request for help regarding his son's inhalant abuse. We flew out in a small plane, stopping at other villages to drop off mail. Most villages had agents on snow machines with sleds to pick up passengers and the mail. Once we arrived at the village, we met with the family. I had requested the "extended family" be present to gain the most information about the situation as possible. As it turned out, we had 23 persons sitting around a pot bellied stove in a three-room house. In most of the villages there is no running water in the homes. A "honeybucket" is used for bathroom facilities, and a local washateria has both a shower facility and a washer and dryer. Ice chipped out of the river is stacked outside the house to be melted for drinking water. I was offered pickled herring as an afternoon snack. The family session was educational for us all. The family agreed to send their adolescent boy to treatment in Anchorage. I learned how much families care for their children. I learned how much effort it takes to reach out and perform quality services. I learned that our budget is nowhere near large enough to provide the quality of care needed in the region. I learned to realize that what Anchorage could provide would be a stark contrast to the world in which this young adolescent really lives.

I finish my day with a phone conversation with the grantwriter for the corporation. We're in search of federal and private foundation money to assist us in an outdoor adventure-based program for adolescents and young adult males, ages 19-25. We're looking for ways to do effective and cost-effective services in a region of 26,000 square miles with no roads other than the three gravel roads (70 miles each) outside of Nome. I'm searching for ways to gain dollars at a time when the rest of the country is shutting down services, and cutting funding right and left. I smile thinking about the juvenile justice grant we got this year, and the group of adolescents who are leaving to go kayaking on the Sound as part of our new pilot project. I think about the grizzly bear I saw from the road two days ago, less than 15 miles from town. I say a prayer that our group will be safe while they're out this week.

On my way home, I go by the grocery store and pick up a *Nome Nugget* newspaper. There's a memorial service for someone who had been missing since last November. His body was found after the thaw. No one has put in print that it was an alcohol-related death, but the deceased had a reputation for driving a snow machine under the influence. I realize I'm starting to recognize the names and faces of the deceased. I'm part of the story, and I'm experiencing the grief and trauma of the region.

I feel grateful that my therapist taught me how to let go of pain and not hold it in my body. I head for home to do my own body work, knowing I have a purpose in being here. I feel grateful to be alive today.

Chapter 28
Adventure-Based Practice

by Christian Itin, BSW, MSW, Ph.D.

I awake, it's bitterly cold outside, the sun has barely risen. It's about 6 a.m. I roll over to light the stove and start the water for some hot tea. Now comes the hardest part of the day—getting out of my warm sleeping bag and starting the day. You see, I'm a social worker whose area of practice is adventure therapy. "Adventure therapy," you say. "What is that? Is that a form of practice that social workers engage in?" We certainly do, and for the last 14 years or so, this has been my primary area of practice. I'd like to tell you about a day in the life of a social worker engaged in adventure-based practice. This particular program is a four-day course run by the Colorado Outward Bound School as an adjunct to inpatient substance abuse treatment.

As I greet the morning, the only thing I know for certain is that the day will be uncertain. Regardless of the population I'm working with, or the length of the course, the beauty of adventure-based practice, and particularly wilderness-based practice, is that each day is a new adventure for me and the clients. The day brings with it all the unpredictability of life, with its moments of joy and elation, and despair and frustration. Though I might have a sense of what the activity of the day will be, I cannot know how the participants (I prefer this to clients, because it clearly reflects the participatory nature of the experience) will respond, what the weather will provide in terms of challenge, or what other unforeseen forces will be at play. Flexibility on my part is a critical skill in effectively using the lessons that the day will present.

The day starts with making sure the participants are up and beginning breakfast. You see, we have become a community, dependent upon each other for our survival. If each member of the community does not contribute to the tasks that need to be accomplished, the entire group suffers. Since much of my work is with individuals and families in recovery from some form of addiction, understanding the mutuality of support is critical. It is one thing to talk about relying on the support of others, and being responsible to (as opposed to responsible for) others; and quite another to get up in the cold morning air to start the stoves, fetch water, and begin breakfast as a critical contribution to the community. The nature of living together, participant and social worker, facing the same obstacles, opens up new frontiers for exploration.

After breakfast, the group cleans up, packs up, and prepares for the day's activity. Today it is rock climbing. Yesterday we engaged in some problem-solving activities, some trust building activities, and a high ropes course. Tomorrow we have a peak climb planned. On a longer course, there may be many days of backpacking, including climbing high passes, fording rivers, and traveling off trail. However, on a four-day course, we often engage the participants in rock climbing on the second day, because of the dramatic nature of the activity.

There are two major components to rock climbing—the technical skills and the process. Therapeutically, I am interested in both. The technical skills enable participants to become fully involved in the activity. They must learn how to "belay," a term that means to hold. Each participant will be asked to belay another, to literally hold another person's life in his hands. Participants learn the skills of belaying and practice on the ground before they have to use the skills on the rock. This is a perfect metaphor for the course and therapy in general. The participant is provided an opportunity to practice new behaviors and new ways of approaching old problems in the relative safety of our program. By learning belaying, participants are also able to feel a sense of mastery and accomplishment in learning a new skill that will be directly relevant to their lives. Though this relevance is short-term (most will not continue to rock climb), it provides an excellent example of mastering a task, just like tasks in recovery must be mastered.

Once the skills of belaying are mastered, we head to the rock face. But before we climb, we set the stage, or frame the

event, and help establish an isomorphic link for the participants between the climbing and their recovery. This is the
process of the activity. I share with the participants that climbing is not so much about getting to the top, but is more about
how you get to the top. The rock is waiting to provide you
with lessons about how you approach obstacles in your life.
Do you hug the rock, limiting your vision, your options, your
choices; or do you attempt to lean back and increase your
vision? Do you engage in the activity in isolation, by yourself,
seeking to get it done as quickly as possible; or do you ask for
support from others, enjoying the experience? The rock, like
life, does not care what you do, and how you do it; but your
experience of the rock will be different depending on how you
approach it and work with it. The participants' experiences of
the rock usually have implications for their recovery, in reflecting how they are approaching their recovery.

As the participants climb, each has lessons to learn,
struggles to encounter. Some participants rely on others, others battle the rock; some are hesitant to try, others are more
eager. My job is to help them process the experience and explore the opportunities fully. For those reluctant to try, I work
with them, attempting to help them make choices that are
actual choices, rather than ones based on default. For example, one person is refusing to climb because he is afraid. In
exploring the fear, we discover it is not a fear of height or a
fear of falling, but rather a fear of not succeeding. For this
person, it is better not to try than to try and not succeed. We
talk about the implications for recovery, about the implica-
tion of this choice, and about what the worst thing that could
happen would be. After some discussion, soul searching, and
consultation with fellow participants, the participant decides
to attempt a climb. It's not really important if they summit or
not, but it is important that they discover something new about
approaching fear.

The day is long, and what started out as a cold day has
turned into a blistering hot afternoon. I run around the cliff
checking the safety systems, watching the participants belay, consulting with other staff, and not least of all paying
attention to participants' therapeutic goals. Every part of the
day holds potential lessons for the participants. As the
belayers, what do they experience holding another person's

life in their hands? As the climbers, what can they learn about dealing with challenge, with obstacles, with unforeseen circumstances? As some not "actively" involved, what do they do to support others, what do they do when they are not the center of attention? My job is to provide the opportunity for each participant to be conscious of the lessons presented throughout the day and to relate their personal treatment goals to the day's activity, or to help them stay alert to the opportunities to work on a treatment goal.

Often, participants come with treatment goals related to asking for help, focusing on their own goals and not others, dealing with anger appropriately, or any number of other goals. The true power of adventure-based practice is helping participants work on these goals through the activities, not through simply talking about them. In recovery work and Outward Bound, we are fond of the expression "walking your talk," which is really about doing what you say you want to or are doing. The experiential nature of adventure-based practice challenges clients to walk their talk, to follow through with what they have said they want to or need to do. Treatment goals become concrete experiences that clients can take with them in their recovery.

After the day we head to camp, but the day is far from over. There is dinner to prepare. It takes effort to accomplish those things necessary for the community when everyone is tired and would simply like to sleep. The effort required is not like the effort required for recovery; making dinner is a necessity. The challenge for participants becomes how to use this experience as a beneficial part of recovery. Some of the most profound conversations between participants happen while cooking dinner or doing the dishes afterwards. As some participants prepare dinner, the staff members gather to plan the evening group. Group will be a formal time to integrate the lessons from the day, to give participants a chance to share and work through concerns from the day, and for the group to plan for tomorrow's adventure.

After dinner and clean-up, we gather for group. The participants share their experiences, their frustrations, the lessons they are taking away from the day, and what they hope for tomorrow. Some of the participants express satisfaction with the day; others wish they had done something different. Some make clear connections to their recovery; others see no relevance. The group is challenged to work with the material that comes up in the group and to help each other make connections with recovery. I also work to help the participants make connections and engage with each other. Often, I challenge participants with an observation from the day or a comment they made earlier, or invite a fellow participant to challenge a peer. Group is an opportunity to take care of the business of the community as well. Who will cook breakfast? Who will get water?

As the group winds down, it is nearing 10 p.m. I still have progress notes to write and sleep to catch before the sun rises again tomorrow. It's not like other work where you get to go home in the evening, to family and friends. You are with the clients 24 hours a day. It's been a full day; one with unexpected surprises in the lessons learned by both participants and staff. I've seen participants challenge themselves and their perceptions of themselves. I've seen acts of courage and compassion as members have worked to help each other. I've also seen participants shirk away from responsibility, choose not to be honest, fall into old negative patterns of behavior. Part of the beauty of this work is that there is always tomorrow.

I was first attracted to this type of work by an article by Janice Kaplan, which suggested that Outward Bound was a treatment modality unexplored by the social work profession. I later came to the Colorado Outward Bound School in part because of another article written by a social worker, Nelson Chase, who had founded the Health Services Program at the Colorado Outward Bound School. In the 14 years I've worked in adventure-based programs, I've met numerous social workers doing this type of work. One of the professional associations I'm active in, the Association for Experiential Education, has a professional group called Therapeutic Adventure, to which social workers belong. In a recent search of the social work abstracts, I identified 36 citations related to adventure-based practice in the social work professional literature. Social workers have considered adventure-based practice, though it probably remains relatively unknown as a specific area of practice.

Outward Bound is the most well-known adventure-based program, but not all adventure-based programs are Outward Bound. In fact, most adventure-based programs now are less wilderness-based and actually often occur in an urban environment. The most common form of adventure-based practice usually involves what is termed a ropes course (a series of obstacles suspended by cables in the air), problem solving initiatives, and trust activities on the ground. This form of adventure-based practice can be conducted at a treatment center, a school, or local community center. The advantage of this type of adventure-based practice is that the social worker can return home after work, and usually is paid a salary commensurate with other standard treatment personnel in the agency. In wilderness programs, staff are often paid a much lower salary than others with similar responsibilities in a treatment context.

The social worker looking to get involved in adventure-based practice can often work in conjunction with someone who has the technical skills to conduct the activities (though I strongly encourage social workers to develop the skills necessary to conduct the activities, as it makes the practice more integrated). There are numerous avenues for gaining the training necessary to facilitate the process of adventure-based practice. Unfortunately, most are not formally recognized within social work education.

I invite social workers to consider adventure-based practice. It is a form of practice I've found invaluable in working with adults and adolescents, men and women, those dealing with addictions, and those who are survivors of violence, as a means of bringing communities together and as a means of organizational change. I have found my professional education in social work to be invaluable in conceptualizing adventure-based practice. Adventure-based practice requires a blending of individual and group practice skills, an understanding of community and organizations, and an ability to act as a manager and administrator. My education focused on an advanced generalist perspective with an emphasis on integrated practice. This base has served me well as I have developed professional competency in adventure-based practice.

PART 8:
PRIVATE PRACTICE

Chapter 29
Private Practice and the Eclectic Social Worker

by Diane Rullo-Cooney, MA, MSW, LCSW, CADC

Private practice in social work creates an array of emotion from excitement to fear. An understanding of the week of a private practitioner takes you from seeing individual patients in a private office to standing in front of sixty students teaching the ideals of social work practice. This story is a journey through thirty years of accomplishing the dream to be a SOCIAL WORKER.

In identifying my role as a social worker today, I must start over twenty-five years ago. Somehow, in my early adolescence, I knew the phrase "social worker" but had no concept of the meaning of that role. When I was thirteen and someone asked what my future goals were in life, I would respond, "I want to be a social worker," not understanding exactly what that meant. I held onto my dream many years before it came to fruition.

Life, as tumultuous as it is, did not take me directly onto an educational track. Like so many others in my family and social circle, I went to work full time after my high school graduation. At nineteen, I was promoted to a manager's position, but I wasn't fulfilled. I might have had a strong future in business, but I knew this was not a perfect fit. I enrolled in evening classes at a local college. Surprising myself, I did well. I became even less satisfied in my employment and changed jobs to become a sales representative, thinking this was the answer to my happiness.

It wasn't. I envied my colleagues at sales meetings who appeared more sophisticated and confident. I decided that one major difference between myself and the rest of the sales force was a college degree. I made one of the biggest decisions of my life, quit work, and returned to school full time.

I was naïve about the educational system, and unaware there were specific programs for social workers, so I entered a psychology program. Perseverance paid off. I received my undergraduate degree in psychology in two and one half years. During this time, I was required to do field work, which led me into the working world of being a clinician. I volunteered as a peer counselor and later in a grass roots community counseling center that had recently opened. My supervisor at the community counseling center was attending school for her master's degree in social work, which awakened me to the specialization of social work.

Still, I returned to school and obtained my master of arts in counseling. I was employed as a mental health clinician, substance abuse counselor, and a clinical supervisor in addiction services. I worked for years in the mental health field, not fulfilling my original goal of becoming a "social worker."

Twelve years after I originally returned to college, I entered an MSW program. Working full time, I entered a full-time Saturday program, and completed my second master's degree. I had finally achieved my goal. I was now officially a SOCIAL WORKER.

Over the years, I worked in hospitals, community agencies, family agencies, and free standing programs. Looking for autonomy, I decided to venture out into private practice. I am a clinical social worker. Conducting individual, group, and family therapy is my love, my destiny. I consider my work fun, not torturous. When I wake up in the morning, I do not dread the work day. The excitement persists because I have managed to make my job eclectic. I assume many different functions in one week. The following is a composite of the roles I undertake during a week's time.

My major role is that of a private practitioner. Having a private practice is a double-edged sword. I have autonomy. I do not have a supervisor or administrator monitoring me. My evaluations are based upon the return of my patients to my practice, and the ongoing referrals. (NOTE: The field of social work identifies individuals as 'clients.' I use the word 'patient' to emphasize the importance of the situation [as one is viewed when seeking treatment from a physician] and to establish the validity of mental health treatment. I believe 'patient' eliminates a moralistic and value laden focus on the individual.) It is exciting to be able to, as I put it, "run my own show." All decisions are mine alone. I schedule appointments when I choose. I decide when I want to work or relax. Flexibility is my nature. I keep my work week open seven days. This gives me the advantage to block off time any day of the week and still be available for patients.

Looking at the other side, private practice is frightening. The economy and health care benefits play a role in the income I receive. If the economy is experiencing a recession, mental health treatment is not a priority. Individuals will not spend money on a "luxury" such as therapy unless they are completely decompensated. Managed care companies and insurance companies determine fees. As a private practitioner who accepts insurance, I am at the mercy of the health care system to determine my income. There are no employer-paid benefits in private practice. I do not get paid vacations, sick days, health insurance, or a retirement plan. When I choose to go on vacation, I need to make sure I have covered myself financially for the month.

My day starts by checking to see if I received any messages. I return emergency calls from home. I have an additional telephone line in my home, on which I keep the ringer off. This line is solely to return calls, protecting myself from caller IDs and anyone getting my personal number. As I drive to the office, I think about my schedule and the patients I am to see today. This includes reviewing last week's session for each patient and assessing the therapeutic treatment plan. I try to make an effort to identify any transference and counter-transference issues that may have arisen.

Private practice is a business as well as a community service. While my goal as a social worker is to help patients change unwanted behavior, I must be aware of the need to keep the business financially stable. There is always a concern about patients canceling appointments, which reduces my weekly income. Some private practitioners choose to charge for missed

appointments. I have a theory about cancellations and patients not showing up for their scheduled appointments. When
individuals have a mental illness, it affects all parts of their
lives. I do not believe in penalizing a patient for his or her
pathology. Missed or canceled appointments are a result of
the person's pathology and as a clinician I need to resolve
this with the patient. Balancing the fear of reduced income
and understanding the patient's pathology is a process I have
successfully undertaken.

The element of worry about cancellations subsides quickly
as I pull into my office complex. Upon entering my office, I
once again check to see if I have messages. Private practitioners must continuously review calls for patient emergencies
and new referrals. The core of our business is new referrals.
When a call comes in, the successful clinician returns the
call as soon as possible. This is how to build a business. Additionally, as a sole proprietor, I don't have someone else covering emergencies, so the telephone system becomes an important tool. Some added expenses to being in private practice are having a pager and a cellular phone. When my patients have emergencies, I am available. Luckily, emergencies
do not happen very often.

I wait for my first appointment. My appointments are
scheduled for fifty minutes. This leaves ten minutes to re-
group for the next patient. My fees are on a sliding scale basis, and I accept insurance. Establishing fees and collecting
money are two of the hardest things for me to do. Social workers have been indoctrinated to be a community service requiring little to no payment for the work accomplished. Social
workers often feel guilty about accepting payment for treatment. Society, including social workers, believes social work
is a job requiring little compensation. This is detrimental to
our profession. We are highly trained and highly skilled. By
charging an appropriate fee per session, we are able to accommodate the patient's needs in a private office setting,
while validating our accomplishments. As entrepreneurs, our
business is one of helping others.

Private practitioners are unable to receive immediate grati-
fication in discussing a case with colleagues. When a session
is difficult, there is no other clinician around. The responsibility of this person's treatment is solely in my hands, com-

bining a sense of power and fear. It is helpful for private practitioners to build support networks, connecting with colleagues for case discussion. This reduces the isolation.

A priority for the private practitioner is to establish a billing system. I have set up my computer with a small business software package to monitor patient billing and outstanding fees. I put time aside weekly to input data about sessions for the past week. I send invoices out two times per month to insurance companies, to keep a regular flow of income.

After seeing patients in the morning, I go to the university to perform my role as an adjunct professor. I enjoy academia, both learning and teaching. One of the most productive ways I have found to become proficient in an area of social work is to teach in that area. Students are challenging. I must be at least one step ahead of the students and have a solid understanding of my ideas to be able to relay the information.

I derive satisfaction from watching students integrate the information into their training. The role of adjunct professor is time-consuming. Preparation for a class takes between two and five hours per week. I read the material, take notes, and decide what information to put forth to the students. Highlighting the important aspects of a topic and giving examples are part of the preparation. Bringing in other citations and philosophies will encourage students to expand their research. This is a continual process of new learning for me.

Deciding on how to grade the course and what type of system to use, then making up tests or reading papers, takes several hours. Balancing a private practice with hours for preparation and review is difficult. During a semester, I do not consider my time to be my own. Every minute of the day is taken for some task to be done. Students also want time to talk to the professor. I receive calls in my office about papers and tests. The role of adjunct professor is not just the three hours I am in the classroom. I teach three classes a semester, which totals about seventy students per semester. I had to learn to manage my time appropriately to complete all tasks efficiently.

An additional role I have is one of instructor. I teach one-day to five-day workshops. Preparation for this includes making an outline and copies of all handouts to be sent to the facility. The time to prepare for workshops is done months in advance of the presentation. When the actual event comes close, only review is needed.

Moving on further in my week, I do administrative work for the continuing education department at the university. I develop workshops for clinicians who are Family Preservation Service (FPS) workers. FPS is a short-term, intensive in-home program that teaches families skills to prevent the un-necessary placement of children outside of the home. My role here is to conceptualize the training needs of the workers, locate instructors who are experts in that area, and arrange for a training site for each workshop. I then develop the bro-chure and prepare it for print.

This work really is seasonal. The main functions are done during the summer for the Fall semester and in January for the Spring semester. The remainder of the months consist of gathering statistics, writing up the quarterly reports, and monitoring workshops. This job balances out with being an adjunct professor. The time-consuming part is during the summer when classes are not in session, unless I take a sum-mer teaching position.

The last role that I take on is the role of student. I am currently attending school full time for my Ph.D. I would like a future in academia, and that is not possible without a doc-torate. My classes fit into one full day, and when I return home I go back to my office to see patients. Time needs to be put aside at some point within the week to do readings, re-search articles, or write papers. I find myself with a book, paper, or laptop computer at meals. I have found my laptop computer to be one of the most functional pieces of equip-ment to have with my lifestyle.

My various roles all have a function. Private practice never guarantees an income. I am more secure with a safety net. Private practice is my first desire, but I gain more security by having positions with a regular income. My goal is to obtain a full-time position as a professor and to maintain my private practice. Obtaining my doctorate and teaching at a university are steps toward that goal. I also have the personality of one who likes diversity. Keeping my professional lifestyle active contributes to my enjoying every minute of my work.

Chapter 30
An Office to Call My Own: Private Practice in the Lesbian Community

by Amy Blake, MSW, CSW, ACSW

On the day I walked away from the "real world" of my profession, I felt as if I had just launched myself into outer space with no way back. Leaving a hospital-based program for survivors of sexual trauma was not easy for me. I had an illusion of security there in a regular paycheck and benefits. My disagreements with the administration, the fact that my program was dissolved, and a growing awareness that that environment was killing me emotionally, physically, and spiritually brought me to a crossroad. I took a leap of faith to become self-employed in work I care about, which is helping people heal. In my dreams of private practice, I longed for the freedom but never counted on the depth to which I would have to draw on my inner strength and resources. I battle the incessant voice of doom and despair that tells me I cannot do what I am doing, that I should get a "real job" and put to rest this silly notion that I can make it on my own. Never mind that I have been able to support myself.

I was diagnosed with Chronic Fatigue Syndrome in the Fall of 1995. This has given me pause to reflect and act on my ideals of health and well-being. Private practice has helped to hold me accountable to my ideals. The more I take care of myself, the more able I am to be present for my clients. I have had to adjust to the need for midday naps, no super late hours (which, unfortunately, is when most clients need appointments), time for cooking good food, and time for my meditation practice along with yoga and Tai Chi. Some days, taking care of myself is my full-time job. I have thankfully beaten back the fear of not being able to take care of myself, and I have recovered a great deal of my energy.

I chose the world of private practice two years ago after seven years of psychiatric hospital work and a stint, which felt like a lifetime, in the geriatric division of a university medical school residency program. I also had the good fortune to experience teaching at the university level in Women's Studies. I currently work with individuals, couples, and groups for lesbian and bisexual women survivors of childhood sexual abuse. The focus of my counseling work has been healing from abuse and trauma.

As it turns out, my work is the polar opposite of my major area of study in social work school. I studied Social Policy and Planning and received a Certificate in Gerontology. One of the things I love about being a social worker is how fluid the movement can be from one aspect of social work to another. All roads can lead us to exactly where we need to be in our work and in our lives. I have found it so unfortunate and aggravating in interviews when my background was viewed as a limitation rather than a source of information and a different perspective.

My social work education prepared me to be in the trenches with people's pain. Social work school taught me about opportunities in life and about being an active participant and change agent in my own life. Being in the trenches has to be a choice. I have to want to be there and I have to be able to be present with my client's process. To do this, I have to know that I do not have to, that I have a choice to do something different.

Education aside, it was my personal healing journey that led me to clinical work and eventually private practice. Once I began experiencing the healing power of therapy, I knew I could help others. I draw deeply on the success of my own healing process when I am struggling in the face of a client's hopelessness and pain. I am not convinced that that kind of experiential knowing can be taught. The advanced training that I have found most beneficial has been that which challenges me to grow as a person and as a therapist. So far, I have been fortunate to find such an environment for personal and professional growth in a Grove Metaphor Therapy Training and consultation and currently in an IMAGO Relationship Therapy Training.

The private practice teeter-totter plays independence and isolation against one another. Having my own office and setting my own schedule is appealing—I get to work any twelve hours of the day that I choose! Hearing about people's pain and trauma can skew my view of humanity, especially if I am not careful to find a balance in my life. There is no more walking down the hall for collegial companionship. Lunches, peer supervision, and networking all need to be arranged more formally. It is very easy to become unbalanced when the last thing I want at the end of the day is to talk to people, but it is exactly what I need to challenge the day's experience of senseless violence. To battle the isolation, I talk with other therapists, and I helped to start a gay and lesbian therapists' networking group in my area.

I happen to like the slower pace and the quiet of my office. I have been able to create a space for healing, and clients and others who visit my office comment that they feel safe and they can really talk there. I am sure it is not because of my rag-tag and borrowed furnishings I've picked up along the way, although they do add a certain atmosphere.

"Hi, I got your name from the Gay and Lesbian Hotline. Do you charge for counseling?"

The financial instability of private practice is a struggle. Putting a dollar amount on my worth as a therapist and asking people to pay it is an evolving process. I generally do not work with insurance. I believe that there will always be room for high quality, confidential therapy. I have managed to keep myself out of the managed care crisis and I hope to keep it that way. Seeing clients who pay out-of-pocket creates other issues.

I work most directly with the lesbian community, and the community seems to have a love/hate relationship with therapists and therapy. At times, fees can be a major issue, and I am confronted with an expectation that my service to the community should not come with a price tag or it should be greatly reduced. My gay male colleagues do not face this same issue. To me, it is an ingrained piece of sexism where it is hard to pay a woman for emotional support, because of an expectation that it be given freely. It is a challenge to negotiate the financial rules of therapy. I have to remind myself that my sick days, vacation days, and insurance benefits come directly from the work I do and not from some company. On the other hand, I have also had the experience of having a client, who pays a low fee, decide to give me a raise because she appreciated the work she was able to do.

"Oh, you own the women's bookstore. I tried dating the other woman there and she said, 'No.' "

The "other woman" at the bookstore is my life partner and business partner. We decided our town needed a feminist, lesbian and gay bookstore and five years ago, we set about creating A Woman's Prerogative Bookstore. I saw it as a great way to focus my social work on the positive aspects of community building. It is another way for me to balance the pain and trauma side of my work. People come into the store and find themselves in ways they never expected, whether that is a growing feminist consciousness or coming to accept their gay or lesbian identity. I also get to see how there are many paths to growth and healing.

I am actively involved socially and politically in the community I serve, which poses some interesting boundary challenges. On a busy Saturday, I may see a client in group, ring up her purchase at the bookstore, and end up being seated very near her at the women's coffee house that evening. My house, my office, and my bookstore are all located within a quarter mile. I thank my lucky stars that I have a love relationship that precedes my arrival in the metro-Detroit women's community. I cannot fathom dating in such a fishbowl. Boundaries tend to be a rather frequent topic in my sessions, as well as with my peers. The tough part for me is the battle I feel around the need to assert my right to have my life and the feelings of constriction I experience when I run into a client socially. I think this setup, although not ideal, can be powerful and growth-producing when handled with extreme care and when the power dynamics are acknowledged and kept in check.

The best part about the life I've created as a social worker is that I like the foundation I have established. I get to live my life according to my values, and when I go to work and hate my boss, I have a major say so in how things change and get resolved.

PART 9:
CRIMINAL JUSTICE

Chapter 31
Prison Substance Abuse Treatment

by Timothy S. Wight, MSW

Today, the autumn morning in the Northwestern Willamette Valley is heavy with moisture and a lingering smell of yesterday's burned fields. I travel a two-lane highway toward the coast to Sheridan, Oregon, turning off just after a sign with an arrow announcing the all-male "Federal Correctional Institution." After driving past a small post with a notice proclaiming that I have entered United States government property, I scan the institution, already cognizant of the secure environment I am about to enter. Double fences with coiled razor wire surround the perimeter. Two vehicles, each carrying a correctional officer, an arsenal of weapons, and plenty of ammunition, circle the outside fence, ready to shoot any inmate attempting an escape.

I walk toward the entrance, the only place where the circumference is broken. I feel relief that everything appears normal. A few months ago, an ambulance was parked in front. As I walked inside, a stretcher was being wheeled out with a person laid out on it. Face covered in blood and breathing assisted by three EMTs, I found out minutes later it was an inmate who had been assaulted on the recreation yard by a "rock in a sock," one of several weapons inmates can utilize quickly and with minimal chances of detection. Relieved it was not a staff member, I was dismayed later when I learned it was Mr. Avila, an inmate I had interviewed a few weeks earlier for the institution's drug abuse program.

I walk inside the first door. To prevent escapes and unauthorized entry, several doors lead into the institution. Each door is electronically opened by the Control room. I stand in front of the second door, waiting for them to identify me and engage the solenoid lock. It loudly clicks and I enter. I close it, then stand in front of another door, waiting again to be identified. After another click, I walk toward the Control room. I check out keys and a radio. I loop the heavy keys on my belt, slip the radio in its pouch, then stand in front of a final door. With one more click, I am on the institution's compound.

Inmates roam the sidewalks. Many have just finished breakfast and are going to their work details.

Attention on the compound. Unicor work call. Unicor work call.

I hear Control make the loudspeaker announcement for inmates to report to Unicor, the business name of the industries in the federal prisons. This factory manufactures desks, bookshelves, and credenzas. The work is a coveted job in the institution because of its high pay; some inmates make as much as a dollar an hour. Those who don't work in the factory report to other jobs earning much less money: food services, maintenance, laundry, barber shop, education, and landscaping.

I slip a large key into the door of the Drug Abuse Programs (DAP) building. Inside, all is quiet. I unlock my office, then sit down and prepare for the morning's drug treatment group. The topic for the past two weeks has been relapse prevention. To aid in discussing their past relapses, each inmate creates a "Relapse Road Map," a pictorial representation of a past alcohol or other drug relapse.

A knock summons me to the door. I key it open, then allow a few early group members to enter.

"Good Morning, Mr. Wight," they say as they enter the building.

"Good Morning, Mr. Barrigan, Mr. Crawford, and Mr. Pollard." After over two years of this, I still consider the use of titles to be constrained, but the advantages of keeping a professional distance with prison inmates outweigh the disadvantages of becoming too informal. Staff must always be on guard for inmates who attempt to compromise the boundaries to obtain drugs or other favors.

More inmates enter, greet me, and go into the group room. I lock the front door. After a quick head count to make sure all seventeen inmates are accounted for, I begin the session.

"Before Mr. Barrigan begins with his map, are there any group issues?"

"Yeah, I got one," Mr. Harmon, an angry, defiant inmate in his early twenties speaks.

"Go ahead," I respond.

"You say we gotta have a balanced life to stay off drugs, but you admitted yourself that for the past two months you've been taking a college class after work. That sure as hell ain't balanced."

"What does the group think?" I ask, trying not to allow an annoyed smirk to surface. In every treatment group I've conducted, the same tactic is used. Addicts often attempt to thwart their own recovery by projecting their own problems onto others.

"Short-Dog's right." Using his nickname, a few quickly agree with Mr. Harmon. Some of those in agreement often defend Mr. Harmon, likely a slavish deference used to keep out of conflict with him. In non-institutional settings, those in treatment don't live in tight quarters with one another. In prison, one opinion expressed during a two-hour group could mean a fight in the housing unit hours or days later. It could also mean one being labeled as a "snitch," an inmate who cooperates with those in authority.

"Does all of the group feel that way?" I allow a long pause to force an answer.

"Well, for *me*," an ex-methamphetamine cook begins slowly, "I relapsed after I last got out of jail because my lifestyle was imbalanced. I knew I'd used in the past to keep me going on all the jobs I was working, but I set myself up to use again, because I chose to work long hours every day."

"How many hours?" I ask to get clarification.

"I'd leave at four in the morning to get my truck, then around quitting time my boss would ask if I wanted an extra run. Sometimes I didn't really want to, but I was chasin' the dollar and I couldn't say 'no.' I usually wasn't home until nine at night. I started using speed again to keep me on schedule."

"So," I begin, "there are several issues surrounding his relapse. What were they?" I go to the chalkboard to write them for emphasis, as other group members now join the discussion. Their responses tell me they understand the relapse concepts: This inmate knew that in the past he'd worked long hours and used methamphetamine to maintain that schedule. He also chose to work extra shifts every day, not just once in a while or for a limited period of time. He had difficulty being assertive with his boss to refuse the extra shifts. Finally, a group member points out that he had a thinking error when he said he *couldn't* say "no" to the extra money.

"Mine is just the opposite," Mr. Barrigan says after the discussion.

"Well, let's hear about it on your Relapse Road Map." I motion for him to come up and present his assignment. During the remainder of the group session, he explains a return to heroin use after being in a treatment program ten years ago. Mr. Barrigan was arrested a year ago after committing several bank robberies. With a $200-a-day habit, it was a convenient way to maintain his addiction.

Attention on the compound, ten minute recreation move, ten minute move.

Mr. Barrigan finishes quickly, and I unlock the door to let them return to their jobs, housing unit, educational classes, or the recreation yard. I return to my office to work on treatment reviews.

My noon group is in the Criminal Lifestyles module. With the inmates involved in treatment for a full year, the Federal Bureau of Prisons' drug abuse program focuses on many areas surrounding drug use. Cognitive skills, criminality, interpersonal relationships, lifestyle wellness, and transitioning to the community are all part of this comprehensive program.

"The conditions I grew up in were bad," an inmate from an impoverished, inner-city area begins. "My mother used drugs, my father is doin' time in the state prison for robbery, and all of my friends used and sold drugs. I just got caught up in it. Besides, there wasn't anybody affected by what I done, and I needed money to raise my son."

"Caught up in it, that's an interesting way to put it...." I begin a group discussion on thought patterns of lifestyle criminals. We address cognitive indolence, the poor reasoning skills and short-cuts criminals take to obtain money. We learn about mollification, where a criminal downplays the seriousness of an offense and justifies behaviors by pointing out external circumstances. A final topic in the two-hour session is sentimentality, the "Robin Hood Syndrome," in which law-breaking behaviors are claimed to be necessary to provide for loved ones.

After group is over, I walk to the prison's Special Housing Unit (SHU). A prison within the prison, the inmates are sent here for disciplinary reasons. Privileges are limited, and movement is confined and tightly regulated.

"What's up, Mr. Sloan?" I ask through a rectangular hole in his cell door.

"You know or you wouldn't be here," he replies indignantly.

"I need to have you sign this to remove you from the drug program." He takes the paper, and nods. Mr. Sloan is an older inmate who has been in the system a long time. He knows if you give a urine sample positive for drugs, you are removed from the program. He also knows it's nothing personal between us.

"All right, Wight." He scribbles in his name and registration number with the stubby pencil he is allowed to have.

"Can I get back in DAP? I want to get a good halfway house." He references the time he will spend in community placement, the interim between being released from prison and going home. Inmates who complete the drug program generally get more community placement time.

"Sure. When you get out of here, send us another application. We're starting another DAP group in a few months." I speak with him a few more minutes about his family and his desire to see them. I also talk with him about his relapse.

I leave SHU and go down to one of the housing units. I read the files of several inmates who will soon begin the program. It's best to have knowledge of each inmate, not only for effective treatment but for security reasons.

I read of one inmate who has several past convictions for sexual offenses and assaults. I wonder how many offenses he committed that weren't reported or that he got away with. I find out later during a poignant group session that his deceased mother was a prostitute, and he will never know who his father is, because even his mother didn't know.

I read another file of an inmate incarcerated for drug sales. As I scan the offense conduct section, I marvel at how foreign his past lifestyle is to me; carrying guns, threatening people, and getting high were all part of his daily routine. I note his strong gang affiliations, then move to the next file.

The final one is an inmate convicted of Felon in Possession of a Firearm. Unlike many inmates, his father and mother are still happily married, his father was an aerospace engineer for a large military contractor, and the inmate has a college degree. As I close the file, I am reminded again not to stereotype the men I work with. Some have excellent backgrounds but still choose to commit crimes.

When I get back to the DAP building, it's almost time to leave for the day.

"Hey Wight, what's going on?" My supervisor, a clinical psychologist, questions. I go into his office and sit down.

"I went to SHU to see Sloan. He wants back in the program."

"Good. Let's hope he makes it next time. We had one come back today from the halfway house on a dirty."

We talk about our mutual hobby of canoeing, then about the Oregon autumns.

Attention Unit Officers and outcount areas: 4:00 p.m. standup count time. Standup count time. My radio crackles with the daily announcement that signals the end of my shift.

I consider the day as I turn in my keys and radio and exit the doors armed with solenoid locks. I didn't stand a fog line today. I didn't sprint in response to a staff's need for immediate assistance. There were no fights or assaults to change the daily routine. I didn't drive a mobile patrol vehicle around the perimeter fence, make sandwiches for inmates locked down in their cells, or count inmates during an emergency count. With the Bureau's motto, "You are a correctional worker first," I have done each of those things many times, but today nothing unusual occurred. It was a typical day as a drug treatment specialist in the Federal Bureau of Prisons.

Chapter 32
A Hard Day's Night: Working with Assaultive Men in Prison

by Michael Crawford, MSW, RSW

It's only a short drive from my home to work. That's long enough for me to start focusing on the tasks ahead and just long enough at the end of the day for me to clear out the stress and strain of my work and get ready to enjoy time with family.

I used to think that prison was an odd place for me to practice my craft. Having been trained in both mental health and family therapy, I was comfortable with fifty-five minute hours spent in the privacy of a quiet, clean consulting room. In sharp contrast, the damp and dark quarters of an aging portable trailer, which, when not used for therapy groups, doubled as a school house, seemed decidedly unprofessional. Over the years, I have developed considerable comfort in places like this. Prisons are places where social workers should feel quite comfortable. We have been working in prisons since well before social work was considered a profession.

I don't work in a prison full time, but rather on a contract basis, conducting group therapy. My other job is teaching in a school of social work. I need to work hard to put the jobs I have waiting on my desk at the university out of my mind, so I can focus on the tasks at hand.

Today the sun is shining and the temperature is climbing quickly, as the sun burns the fog off the mountainside. I know that the trailer will be hot today. The breeze I always hope for never materializes and probably wouldn't help anyway. The windows in the trailer are just too small to do much good.

I walk into the minimum security farm camp with its low wire fence, through gates that are wide open during the day. The trimmed grass and ornamental bushes are beautiful, and I catch a scent from a fragrant flower bed. The men enjoy the task of caring for the grounds, as it gives them an opportunity to be outside and work at a job that is more relaxing than most.

Frank is pulling weeds today and greets me with a warm smile. His smile makes me think that people can make their own happiness, even in places where one might think there is little joy. I mumble to myself, wishing that more of the guards would show a lighter side.

I sign in and Mr. Richardson, a senior correctional officer, tells me, with what I think is a cheeky grin, that I should have a full group today. I smile and give myself permission to think that the system is working, all the while remembering that last week two of the group members were inadvertently sent out on a work party and missed the group session. Mr. Richardson and I seem to be developing an understanding about the place of social work in corrections. He was the officer who told me that licorice was contraband and that I couldn't bring it to the group, even if it was Easter. "Rules are rules," he said in response to my attempt to make sense of the declaration: "These guys aren't here because they missed Sunday School." There are so many rules in prison, and breaking them takes little effort. What's harder though, is dealing with the punitive attitudes held by many of the staff.

With pass key in hand and name tag firmly pinned to my shirt, I head over to the portable. Several men shuffle about outside waiting for the door to be opened. I see black running shoes and dark green work clothes for everyone. What an ugly color to have to wear day in and out. The men understand this for what it is. They freely describe this stripping away of their personhood as part of a systematic method that robs them of their uniqueness and individuality. There is no misunderstanding possible about who is in charge and has control here. My mind wanders back to the psychiatric hospital, where I worked many years ago and the time I was stopped at the door when trying to leave a locked ward. My protestations that I was indeed staff were not enough to free me from the steel grip of an enthusiastic and newly-hired orderly. The nursing unit manager came to my rescue and soon freed me, but not before I had a small taste of what it's like "inside." Being scared and powerless are common themes in my work with abusive men.

The therapy group consists of men who have been convicted and are now serving sentences of two years or less for assaulting their partners. Each of them has been court ordered to attend a twelve-session family violence program. I usually have about ten men in the group and work with a female colleague. Working with Sandra is great; I would hate to do this work alone. She brings some balance to the group and really challenges the men, and sometimes me, on our sexist beliefs and attitudes.

The men are restless today, and we spend the better part of the first hour dealing with a conflict that has come up between two members. It's loud and pointed. I don't want the group to get out of hand, and work as skillfully as I can toward a peaceful resolution. I wonder who in the group would get involved to break up a fight if one started, all the while knowing that there has never been any assaultive behavior in the many years that I have facilitated group sessions with abusive men. One man last week couldn't handle the conflict in any other way than to excuse himself from the group. Walking out was a giant step in the right direction for that man. This was one of the few times in his life that he had had to deal with conflict so positively. His earlier response, and one that he is struggling to change, was to start throwing punches. The other men recognized his progress and shouted some praise in his direction, as he slammed the door behind him. I make a mental note to call on him later that day. I can tell from the look on Sandra's face that she is exhausted. I am, too. We have worked hard to help the men work through this problem, and we know we have made some gains.

Today, Bob tells us that his wife has decided to leave town and head back east to be closer to her parents. His eyes are filled with tears as he tells the group that he knows this is the end of his marriage and that he probably won't see his children anymore. Some men make empathic responses and others, maybe because the issue hits too close to home, just hang their heads. Lou, whose mother has just passed away, talks about his own loss and encourages Bob to ask others for the support he'll need to deal with this in prison. Prison is so isolating. The men sit back and watch life go by on the "outside," unable to influence or control it in any way. "Letting go" is harder for some men than for others. It's particularly hard for those like Phil who are serving their first sentence.

The men struggle a bit with our presentation today. Our aim is to introduce the men to a gendered analysis of woman assault, and we use an exercise that asks them to discuss male dominance and their need for power in the relationship. This is hard for most men to do, and these men are no exception. Some struggle with the exercise and others reject our ideas entirely. One man talks about how his girlfriend must have felt living with him. However, he comes to understand her and have empathy with her victimhood, he says, by living under a correctional system that to him seems to set and enforce arbitrary and senseless rules. Great insight! I hope he is able to carry through with this and translate that thought into some behavioral changes. Other men just want to talk about how messed up the "old lady" is. Our feminism offends the sensibilities of some of the men, but we seem to have come to an arrangement in the group. Sandra and I gently invite them to consider our ideas about violence and accepting responsibility as they review their lives and plan for the future.

At lunch I am reminded again of the divisiveness that is everywhere in prisons. We eat at separate tables. The men sit on benches, while the staff are afforded more comfortable chairs near the windows. The food's good. In fact, most days the food is great! I suppose that it's used as something of a pacifier, keeping the men content. Regardless, the men like to complain about the food, but privately most agree they don't eat that well when not in prison.

I finish my day after a few interviews in which men and I plan for their continued therapy once released, some telephone calls, and of course, the requisite hour for recording. I feel good about my work today. When I first started working as a social worker, I had a boss who told me that if I really wanted to feel good about my work, I should work with clients about whom others feel most hopeless. He gave me my first opportunity to work with violent men, and I have thanked him for this many times. This is great work. Some of the men simply fight their way through therapy and gain nothing, but I don't choose to focus on those at the end of the day. The men who have had the courage to face their situations honestly and make decisions about living nonviolent lives are the ones that bring the greatest satisfaction to this job.

As I drive home, I allow myself the luxury of thinking about how torn I am between the clinical social work I practice daily and the political social work I know needs to be done. For me, it's a happy discomfort. I would hate to feel the complacency that I see in some social workers who have accepted that things don't change. Every time I walk into that prison I see the poor and the disadvantaged, the physically and the mentally ill, the alcohol and drug addicted, the uneducated, the abused and the Indian men that are disproportionately represented. I don't just see criminals, and I don't just think about how they need to change. I wonder about our social, economic and political system, and how we in Canada imprison more people than most industrial countries in the world. I wonder about a country that has so much wealth but so little interest in distributing it fairly. My work with social justice groups is important to me and provides me with the hope of systemic change, but today my clinical work brings me satisfaction.

Heading home, I wish that others could experience the happiness that I experience in my life.

Chapter 33
Residential Treatment for Adolescent Sexual Offenders

by Ronald M. Arundell, Ed.D., ACSW, LISW

I will describe an average day in the life of a social worker practicing social work in a residential treatment facility in the Midwest. This facility specializes in the treatment of adolescent males who have committed sexual crimes.

In the last decade, there has been an increased awareness of the severity and magnitude of child sexual abuse in this country. Adolescents account for approximately 30% to 50% of the cases of child sexual abuse each year and 20% of cases of rape, according to Brown and Deisher.

There is evidence that sexual offending behavior begins in adolescence. In 1989, Becker and Kaplan found that approximately 58% of adult sexual offenders first began their perpetration activity in their teens. What these data indicate is that juvenile sexual offending behavior is a serious social problem and needs attention.

Treatment for adolescent sexual offenders is provided in both community-based outpatient and residential modalities. According to the 1992 Safer Society Survey, there are 755 juvenile programs that specialize in sex offender specific treatment.

Many of these programs employ both BSW and MSW social workers. The salary range for BSWs is from $18,000 to $20,000. For MSWs, the range is $24,000 to $32,000, depending on experience and nature of the license requirements of each state.

The residential treatment center consists of 24 male adolescents ranging in age from 13 to 18. The Juvenile Court refers most of the residents who have had convictions ranging from rape to gross sexual imposition. Over 80% of the residents have convictions for other antisocial acts, such as breaking and entering, theft, possession of drugs, running away, and assault. The average length of stay is four to six months. The facility utilizes a behavioral level system common to most juvenile facilities.

The day begins at 8:30 a.m. I grab a cup of coffee and check in with the director. We briefly review issues that arose from the day before and discuss incidents that need addressing in group session this afternoon. The unit leaders are also present to report on the behavior of the residents last evening. A couple of residents had their levels dropped because of abusive language and failure to follow the rules. The team agrees that these issues need more attention in group.

At 9:00 a.m., I conduct an intake interview. In the waiting room, I introduce myself to the new resident, his probation officer, and his mother. I usher them into my office and try to join quickly with the young client, John, by asking him if he is nervous. John responds by looking at his shoes and saying, "A little." I then begin the interview by disclosing information about my experience and the overall philosophy of the treatment program. I briefly review the intake forms, rules of confidentiality, level system, and the treatment program rules and regulations. I then ask John to go with a staff person so that he can unpack his clothes and see the facility. I inform him that his mother will be over shortly to say good-bye.

I review the court documents, probation reports, and victim impact statements supplied by the probation officer. I explain to the probation officer and Mom that the first couple of weeks will involve a thorough assessment that will include psychological tests, a psychiatric consult, and a complete social and sexual history. After obtaining this data, the treatment team will develop a specific behavioral plan. The social worker will consult with Mom and the probation officer for their input and suggestions.

After answering questions that Mom has about family therapy, phone calls, and visitation, I escort her and the probation officer on a tour of the facility. We end the tour at John's unit. I say good-bye and inform John that I will see him in group.

As I walk back to my office, I have strong feelings of sadness, anger, and powerlessness. I feel for both John and his mother, who are struggling with behavior that neither understands. John sexually molested his 6-year-old sister and his 8-year-old cousin. John has his own history of sexual abuse and experienced severe physical beatings until the age of eight. His mother struggles with her own feelings of shame, guilt, and powerlessness as she attempts to do "the right thing" to help John and her daughter.

I check my messages before getting into my car to go to Juvenile Court. There is to be a hearing to review a resident's progress in treatment. As I am driving, I begin to reflect on how I became involved in the treatment of juvenile sexual offenders.

A few years back, when I was a social worker at a psychiatric hospital for children, I became aware of the extensive sexual and physical abuse that 80% to 90% of our residents experienced in their lives. This was in the early 1980s, and there was a significant level of denial about this phenomenon. Today there is more awareness, but still not enough. My own clinical social work experiences led me to a recognition that young people were acting out sexually, but mental health professionals did not seem to be addressing this behavior.

I joined the Association for the Treatment of Sexual Abusers (ATSA). I involved myself with researchers, social workers, and other mental health providers who shared a similar concern about these issues. Through conferences and personal contacts, I learned about the dynamics and treatment approaches from pioneers in the field such as Gene Abel, Judith Becker, Meg Kaplan, Bill Marshall, and Fay Honey Knopp.

My generalist social work training, coupled with the specific knowledge of the dynamics of child sexual abuse and sexual offending behavior, provides me with a solid foundation for professional practice in this special area. Although the work is stressful and discouraging at times, there is also a sense of fulfillment that comes when I witness significant behavioral change in my clients. There is also the knowledge that as a social worker, I am contributing to the prevention of sexual offending behavior in the future.

I find a place to park, grab my notes, and walk quickly to the Juvenile Court building. Outside the courtroom, I greet the resident, Bill, and the residential staff person. We review the details of the hearing. Bill and I have discussed this hearing in individual and group sessions the week before.

The bailiff calls the case and we enter a small hearing room. The referee reviews the treatment reports, asks me to comment on Bill's progress, and then asks Bill about how he is doing in treatment. There is also a discussion of future discharge plans. The referee congratulates Bill on his progress and schedules a final hearing in six months.

As I leave court to go to my car, I have a feeling of accomplishment. Bill has done well in treatment. He learned the cognitive behavioral techniques of Relapse Prevention and how to apply these techniques to his own life. He also has a good aftercare plan. His prognosis is good. The hard work by Bill, his family, and the treatment team resulted in a positive outcome. I stop at a streetside vendor, get a hot dog and a soda, and enjoy the moment.

After court, I return to the facility and attend Clinical Staffing. Our treatment team conducts clinical staffing weekly for about an hour. The social workers, psychiatrist, psychologist, art therapist, recreation therapists, and mental health technicians from the units discuss the progress of the residents in treatment. We review, discuss, and modify treatment plans. The social workers report on the progress of the residents in individual, group, and family therapy.

Clinical staffing is lively with a free exchange of ideas. There is a climate of mutual respect and support as we debate various treatment approaches. I briefly report on Court and the outcome. The team members congratulate me on the fine work I did with Bill and his family. The positive feedback feels very rewarding, and I thank the team for their support and cooperation.

After clinical staffing, I have two individual therapy sessions scheduled. The first is with Randy, where I will be completing his sexual history. The second is with Andrew, who is preparing for discharge. We will discuss his safety plans and his thoughts and feelings about returning home in the next two weeks.

When I complete the individual sessions, I prepare for group with my co-therapist Melody. Melody is a graduate social work student in her final year. Melody will be leading the group on the sexual assault cycle. She will review the cycle using charts and handouts and will have each group member report on his own sexual assault cycle that was part of his homework assignment from the day before. Melody and I discuss various approaches and strategies that we might use as co-facilitators.

Group consists of twelve adolescent males who have committed various sexual crimes. Group takes place four times a week for an hour and a half. The group uses a cognitive-behavioral model that incorporates the sexual assault cycle, thinking errors, and Relapse Prevention Model. There is a defined structure to the group, and the social workers play an active role in the group process.

Melody reviews the components of the sexual assault cycle. We both assist each resident in describing his own cycle and how it applies to his sexual offenses. The group goes well.

After group, I briefly visit with some of the residents. We discuss their progress in treatment, visits, problems at school, and discharge issues. I remind certain residents of upcoming assignments. Bantering and joking takes place between the residents and myself. I return to my office feeling very positive.

One of the interesting outcomes for me in doing this work is to experience the wide range of positive and negative emotions. In struggling to teach these young men how to get in touch with their own feelings, I learn how to do this myself in a deeper and more effective manner.

I check my messages, do some paperwork, confirm family therapy appointments, and prepare to call it a day. I feel tired but fulfilled.

This work is challenging and requires the social worker to apply social work knowledge in multiple modalities. This is a relatively new field. It offers many opportunities for social workers to be innovative and creative. This field also provides a social worker the chance to make important contributions to clients and to society.

In the years I have worked with adolescent sexual offenders, I have found this work to be exciting and growth enhancing. In the process of serving others, I have learned much about the world in which I live and myself.

Chapter 34
Forensic Social Work: Mitigating Death Penalty Cases in a Capital Defense Unit

by Lisa Orloff, ACSW

As of September 1, 1995, New York state reinstated the death penalty for certain crimes defined as first degree murder. The return of the death penalty after a 21-year absence brings with it challenges not only for the legal community, but for social workers as well.

The death penalty is the ultimate statement about the worthlessness of a human life. When a jury imposes the death penalty, it has concluded that this person's life no longer has value, sense, or purpose—a concept completely antithetical to social work. We know that a person is more than the worst thing he or she has ever done, and thus, capital cases demand a social work perspective.

I am the social worker for the Legal Aid Society's Capital Defense Unit. I work in Brooklyn, NY. The unit also includes five attorneys, two investigators, two paralegals, an administrator, several law students, and several social work volunteers. The inclusion of an in-house social worker as part of the defense team is an acknowledgment that social workers bring a special body of knowledge, skills, and abilities necessary in the representation of people charged with capital crimes. In my work, I perform traditional social work functions, and some that are not so traditional.

The most obvious role I play is that of advocate. In no uncertain terms, the state is trying to kill my client, and I advocate for my client's life: I tell the client's "story." This is called mitigation. In order for the judges, juries, and district attorneys to understand my client's actions, the actions must be placed in an extensive social history of the client's life. A social history is constructed through client interviews, collateral interviews with multigenerational family members and others, and the collection and evaluation of life history records (school, hospital, child welfare agencies). The presentation of mitigating factors can be used at different stages of a case, but it is predominantly used in the beginning. For example, the District Attorney has 120 days from a client's arraignment to decide whether or not to seek the death penalty. Along with a multitude of legal issues that can be raised during this time, the defense team can produce evidence of mitigation to persuade the District Attorney that *this* is not a death penalty case.

The range of mitigation evidence is as diverse as our clients, and the presentation of mitigating factors is written into the criminal procedure law. I explore and explain the forces acting on the client—I discuss the people, places, and things that shape a client's life. The person-in-environment perspective is crucial to this work.

At the foundation is my relationship with the clients. What I need from them is information. I need to understand them, and this is most definitely a process. Much of what will be our mitigating evidence is our client's own victimization. Getting a client to reveal horrific stories of abuse and neglect is a skill requiring good interviewing techniques, empathy, patience, and frequent contact over a long period of time. I've heard this referred to by the lawyers as "hand-holding," and I wish it were that easy. The more time I spend with my clients, the more they will trust me and the more they will tell me, and this is one of my goals. Another reason I spend so much time with them is because of what they are telling me. For example, when a client relayed the details of his father's suicide, I did not scribble in my legal pad, thank him, and wrap things up. It took some time to "debrief" with him. I'm not my clients' therapist, but I do counsel them. To do less would be exploitive. Sometimes, however, I go visit a client without an agenda. Sometimes, I go just to talk, break up their monotony, show I care.

Unique clinical issues are raised with a client who may be facing the death penalty. For example, depression is common for a client who feels as if he is waiting to die, and a challenge arises in trying to keep him engaged in the complex processes of a capital case. Often, our clients express suicidal thoughts or even attempt suicide. Consequently, sometimes my own anger is peaked. I feel, "Here I am trying to save your life, and there you are trying to end it!" I absolutely understand where it's coming from: their vision of their future is bleak, and in reality it is. In most cases, if the client does not receive the death penalty, he will spend the rest of his life in prison without the possibility of parole. The challenge is to get the client to take baby steps with you: let's get through the first 120 days, then the trial, and so on.

Collateral interviews are vital in this work. It is a huge mistake not to question what my clients tell me. Some clients will make things up because of the desperation of their situations or because of their mental illness. Some clients will not remember their own childhoods—a function of trying to repress traumatic memories.

Gathering a social history from a family most often involves convincing them to reveal painful secrets: mental illness, addiction, physical abuse within a family. Sometimes the collusion is incredibly strong. Protecting the family secret appears more important than saving the client's life. This can be ameliorated by social workers, as we are trained and educated to do not only thorough diagnostic interviews, but sensitive collateral interviews.

It is also vital to go into the homes and communities where my clients come from—to experience firsthand (albeit for a short time) the chaos and poverty. If I expect to tell my clients' stories, then I need to immerse myself in their worlds.

Reviewing client records is one of my favorite parts of the job. I learn most about my clients by reading their records, and I get independent verification of our mitigation. Records are paper trails. For example, a school record may refer to a psychiatric hospitalization a year earlier, which the client has not told me about. Or, a certain caseworker is mentioned over and over and will be contacted and interviewed. The records must be closely read and read with a creative mind and with an eye toward the future. I ask myself, *Where does this record lead? What agency record will we request next? What person from the record should we contact?* Reading records also allows me to take the information back to the client, whose memory might have faded about a significant life event.

I educate the rest of the staff with regard to the mental health or disabling conditions our clients face. For example, we discuss how to effectively communicate with a client who is mentally ill or mentally retarded, or we discuss what schizophrenia looks like. I don't think I've cringed harder than when one of our lawyers referred to a client as "weird." It was a perfectly accurate description of a very disturbed client, but after a discussion, the lawyer understood the importance of not referring to a client in this way.

I network with mental health experts. Clients frequently need psychological testing, psychiatric examinations, and neuropsychological testing. I serve as the unit's liaison with these mental health professionals. Together, we discuss what testing is appropriate.

The biggest frustration I feel revolves around our time limitation. Most often, we have 120 days to build our case; that is, to uncover and substantiate from all angles, for example, sexual abuse. This is a tall order. Most social workers know that it can take months or years for clients to even begin to discuss sexual abuse.

There are several lessons I learned very quickly in this field. The first thing I had to learn was to redefine success. I used to think success was measured in terms of how well a treatment plan worked, or how much a person's functioning improved. Success in a capital defense unit is when the state decides not to kill your client.

I also learned that the social worker in this field needs to be able to seek out support and ask for help. This was the first job I had in which I started to dream about my clients. My most personal moments were being invaded by work, and I realized some need was not being met during my waking hours. I went into therapy for the first time and bought clinical social work supervision.

I came to this work through a logical evolution. Most of my volunteer experience as an undergraduate was working with victims. I worked as a rape crisis counselor and in battered women's shelters. While living in London, I had my first experience working with "perpetrators"—male prostitutes. What I came to realize in my first week was that most of these kids (all under 21) were victims of some type of familial or stranger sexual and/or physical abuse. My first paying job out of graduate school was in the Legal Aid Society's Criminal Defense Division. Again, I was working with people accused of committing crimes instead of working with the victims of crimes. And again, I found that a huge percentage of my clients (mostly felony offenders) had been victims of trauma or were survivors, and many were re-enacting their trauma.

Legal Aid's Capital Defense Unit was assigned to the first murder one indictment in New York City. Manhattan District Attorney Robert Morgenthau appointed a committee of senior Assistant District Attorneys to help him weigh the factors in the case. Several members of the Capital Defense Unit, including me, met with this committee after I submitted an extensive psychosocial report outlining mitigating factors. In his first decision in a capital case, District Attorney Morgenthau announced that he would not seek the death penalty.

It has been shown that the death penalty is not a deterrent to violent crime. It has also been shown that it is applied capriciously and disproportionately to racial minorities. And obviously, it is irrevocable. This is the most challenging position I have held as a social worker, and by far it is the most rewarding. The pay-off is huge. It's indescribable. The feeling I had when I went to tell my client the District Attorney was not going to seek the death penalty against him cannot be duplicated.

I am proud to be involved in this difficult fight by bringing a social work perspective to death penalty work.

Chapter 35
Victim Services

by Staci A. Beers, MSW, LSW

It is 7:15 a.m. and I start the day with an hour and fifteen minute commute to work. On my morning commute, I ponder the question I get asked the most when I tell people what I do—"How did you get involved in this line of work?" I didn't exactly grow up and say, "I want to work in victim services." I just kind of fell into it.

It all began when I attended West Chester University. I majored in criminal justice and minored in women's studies. One day, a counselor from the local victim resource center came to speak to my women's studies class. She spoke about the services of the center and volunteer opportunities. It sounded interesting. I was planning on attending law school the following year. I wanted to focus on women's issues in law. I contacted the center and signed up for the next training class. The classes were quite educational. I learned a lot about myself as well as the victim experience. I began volunteering three nights per month. My role as a volunteer was to provide support for victims on the hotline or at hospitals when a victim would come into the Emergency Room for the rape exam. Every night I was on call, I waited patiently, eager to put my newly-acquired skills to work. I graduated from West Chester University five months after I became a volunteer.

I decided to attend graduate school. I was accepted at Marywood College School of Social Work in Scranton, PA. During my interview, it was clear that I would be able to gain experience with victims of crime during my internship. I interned at a comprehensive victims' center in a nearby county. The first year, I worked with sexual assault survivors in group and individual counseling, as well as on the hotline and in the emergency room. I will never forget my first "run" to the ER with an adolescent woman. She was sexually assaulted in a group home and was not sure she wanted to press criminal charges. Her caseworker brought her to the ER for the exam with the intent that criminal charges would be pursued. I explained the exam and told the young woman that the choice to prosecute the perpetrator was hers. The caseworker disagreed. I quickly learned that we, as social workers, may have the same basic training, but the agencies that we work for have many different philosophies that will mold our work ethic. I was able to diffuse the situation by separating the young woman and her caseworker and explaining the importance of choice and regaining the control that was lost from the assault. They both agreed that the choice lies within the victim.

The more I worked with sexual assault victims in the emergency room, the more I came into contact with law enforcement. I decided that my second-year internship would be within the criminal justice system. I worked in the victim witness department at the same comprehensive victims' center. I provided accompaniment to all court proceedings, assisted victims in filling out victim compensation claims, and provided training to the local law enforcement community. It was at this point in my career that I was exposed to different types of crime victims.

It was also at this point in my career that I worked with survivors of homicide. I was fortunate to co-facilitate the Adult Homicide Survivors Group. The members of this group allowed me to walk with them through their grief process. I am forever grateful that they allowed me to be with them through some of their most difficult and personal times. They taught me more than any textbook or class could teach. In the final semester of graduate school, I put together a handbook for these survivors. We received a grant, the book was professionally printed, and we used it when we met with families for the first time. The handbook covers different types of grief, the criminal justice system, and a simple glossary of terms. This handbook is available at no charge for all homicide survivors.

As a victim witness coordinator, I learned to deal with different professionals who did not necessarily share my philosophy and ethics. I worked with many police officers and detectives who were good at their jobs but lacked empathy needed to work with victims. I was able to provide the bridge that was needed to communicate between the victim and law enforcement. I also worked with many prosecuting attorneys. Again, they were good at their jobs, but some lacked the compassion it takes to work with victims of crime. Sometimes plea agreements were taken without the consent of the victim. Other times, the victim was not believed. I was fortunate that the core group of district attorneys I worked with were extremely compassionate and understanding. They worked with the victim month after month, and week after week before going to trial or taking a plea.

After working at the county level for four years, I was given the opportunity to work on behalf of victims of crime at the state level. It was a difficult decision to leave clients that I had worked with over an extended period of time, as well as the many professional relationships that I had made. However, I made the move and am now working in a newly-created office designated for victims of crime in the post-sentencing phase. Most of my work with victims is through telephone contacts. It consists of notifying victims when the inmate is eligible for parole.

It is 8:30 a.m. and I venture into the office. I begin the morning by scanning my in-box, which is overflowing from work that I never got to the day before. I try to prioritize the many things that are awaiting me. By 9:00 a.m. my two fellow co-workers and I are scanning the piles of files that are flowing into the office. We try to prioritize the piles; however, all are equally important. The piles consist of (1) files that we need to notify victims of the parole decision, (2) files that need to be checked to make sure all of the victim information is complete, so the parole decision can be made (if the information is not there, we must notify the victim), and (3) files that have come to our office because a parolee has violated his parole, come back into the system, and either brought more victims with him or we need to notify the others.

As we scan the piles, the phone rings. Soon all of us have an issue that needs immediate attention. The in-box can wait. I receive a phone call from a woman who is a domestic violence survivor and is receiving death threats from the inmate, who will soon be paroled. I try to track down the file in our file room. I find an "out card" that is unclear and must go on the first of many "file hunts" today to find out who has the file. I locate the file and immediately type up a memo to the decision makers to notify them of the new threats. I tell the domestic violence survivor that we may be able to keep him in prison a bit longer; however, he will complete his sentence in nine months, and he will walk out of prison a free man with no supervision. I refer her to her local domestic violence center, so she can start to work on a safety plan in the event that he attempts to carry out his threat on her and their children. As I hang up the phone, I feel like a Band-Aid. I am only able to stop the bleeding for a short amount of time. One day the inmate will get out, and the vicious cycle will start over again. I pray that if he enters the system again, it is not for murder.

It is lunch time and very quiet in the office. I try to dig through my in-box, separating memos from victim input. I sign letters that will notify victims of their offenders' status. Some victims will be happy that the inmate has been refused; some will be terrified that the system can no longer house their offender, who is paroled.

In the afternoon, I weed through the victim statements received in today's mail. Some speak of the abuse suffered at the hands of the inmate. Some speak of the loss of their loved ones who will never come home, because the offender decided to drive drunk. Others speak of the betrayal they feel because the offender is someone they loved and trusted. The statements are placed in a confidential file for the decision makers.

As the afternoon steamrolls ahead, I take several phone calls from anxious victims who are awaiting the parole decision. I tell them there has not yet been a decision, but we will notify them when it comes back. I encourage them to call again if they want to check on it from time to time.

I receive a phone call from a past client of mine whose brother was murdered several years ago. The murder is still unsolved. A few weeks ago, she called me and asked me to advocate for her on the state level. She gave me permission to speak to whoever I could that would help her. I contacted the District Attorney's office handling the case. The DA would not talk to me, instead relaying an answer through his staff. I was referred to the investigators. They were surprised that I was calling and inquiring about the status of the investigation. They assured me that the puzzle was beginning to fit together. Now, several weeks later, my past client is calling to tell me that my phone calls have helped a great deal. The case has not been solved, but it looks as if it will be soon. I am happy for her. I hope she soon gets the answer she deserves.

The end of the day is nearing. I have acquired some new things in my in-box that will have to wait for tomorrow. The piles have dwindled. However, I know that more files will come flowing in. It is never-ending. I never would have imagined that working at this level would be so stressful. We cope with the stress through humor. Sometimes, all I can do is laugh!

As I commute home, I am again reminded of what it takes to work in this field. First, it takes dedication and determination. I did not enter victim services for financial gain. Most victim services professionals working at a community agency start out in the high teens to low twenties salary range. Second, it takes the desire to learn. Every day is a learning experience for me. I work with so many different individuals. They are from various ethnic, socioeconomic, and educational backgrounds. They teach me what they have learned. Third, it is imperative that anyone working in this field deal with their own personal biases and issues. It is difficult to be effective as an advocate when you have not done this. Finally, it takes the perseverance to want to make a difference in the lives of others. Victim services is about helping people in need at their time of trauma and thereafter. It is about walking with them on their journey of healing—if they allow you. It is about getting their voice heard by the decision makers, including elected officials.

As I pull into my driveway, my family and my Black Labrador, Chelsea, greet me. I leash Chelsea up and we go for a very long walk, unwinding from another "typical" day.

PART 10:
OLDER ADULTS AND
THE END OF LIFE

Chapter 36
Nursing Home Social Work

by Patricia Gleason-Wynn, Ph.D., LMSW-ACP

All nursing homes or facilities are required to provide for the medically-related social service needs of each resident. Medically-related social services assist the residents in maintaining or improving their ability to manage their everyday physical, mental, and social needs. Nursing facilities with more than 120 beds are required, effective October 1, 1990, to employ a qualified social worker on a full-time basis. Facilities with 120 beds or less must provide services based upon the needs of the residents. In these homes, the social worker may be employed on a part-time or contractual basis. A qualified social worker has (1) at least a bachelor's degree in social work or a bachelor's degree in a human services field, including but not limited to sociology, special education, rehabilitation counseling, gerontology, and psychology; and (2) one year of supervised social work experience in a health care setting working directly with individuals. In many states, the individual must also be certified or licensed as a social worker to practice social work in that state.

I have worked in nursing homes for more than sixteen years. I started out as a volunteer while in college studying to be a social worker. Initially, I was offended by the unpleasant odors and frightened by the advanced age and cognitive decline of many of the residents. However, I came to realize that my caring and attention meant a great deal to the residents, and I learned much about life and also about United States history from them. I was hooked! After graduating with my

BSW, I was offered a job as the only social worker in a 180-bed nursing facility. Though I had little practical experience and training as a nursing home social worker, I took it. The job turned out to be a great learning experience, as well as very challenging. Even after obtaining my MSSW and Ph.D., I have continued to work with older adults in and out of nursing homes.

There are many things I like about my job. First, I like working with older adults. Most of the residents have a wealth of insight and wisdom about everyday living, and are willing to share if asked. The residents seem to appreciate the caring attitude and attention. As an advocate for the residents, I look for ways to help them achieve their own personal goals and wishes. I seek to empower the residents by helping the staff understand the residents' needs for autonomy and control over what remains of their lives. I believe social workers play an important role in enhancing the residents' quality of life.

The second thing I like about the job is the autonomy. Even though my administrator is not too clear about what my job as a nursing home social worker involves, she knows that I know what has to be done to meet the psychosocial needs of the residents, and provides me the freedom and flexibility to do it. A nursing home social worker needs to be self-directed and able to work independently. I have been the only social worker in all the facilities where I have worked. There are no other social workers telling me what to do next or how to get it done.

Third, I like the diversity of the job. Though the tasks may be similar day to day, I work with different residents, family members, and volunteers daily. Diversity requires one to be flexible, as well as a wise time manager. Throughout one day, I may practice a variety of social work roles—a coordinator of services, liaison between the resident or family and staff, counselor, advocate, and educator. The days are usually quite busy, and may include meeting and assessing the needs of newly-admitted residents; documenting social histories, assessments, periodic reassessments, and progress notes; consoling a resident over a recent loss, perhaps a roommate's death; attending meetings such as weekly resident care planning meetings, monthly quality assurance and periodic department head meetings; visiting with individual residents; providing weekly reminiscent group therapy; and working with the resident, family members, and community services to arrange a successful discharge to home.

Finally, I enjoy the opportunity to work as a member of an interdisciplinary team. I have to communicate and work with other nursing home personnel: nursing, dietary, activities, and ancillary services, including rehabilitative therapies. Communication is necessary in order to avoid conflict and fragmentation or duplication of services. With the other team members, I assist in directing care toward meeting a resident's physical, mental, spiritual, and social needs. It is challenging at times working with different disciplines, assuring the resident's right to choice, and meeting various expectations set forth by the administrator and corporate office.

A typical day in my life as a nursing home social worker is as follows. The facility is licensed for 90 beds, and I work part-time. I like to arrive at work by 8:00 in the morning. There tend to be fewer interruptions in the early hours. Thus, I have some time to get my paperwork done. In my mailbox, there is a note from the night shift nurse informing me that Mrs. Smith needs a new pair of house shoes, and Mr. Brown's wife died at the hospital late last night. I add Mr. Brown to my mental checklist of residents to see this morning, and make a mental note to call Mrs. Smith's niece about the shoes. A look at the resident care plan conference list indicates there are twelve residents who will be reviewed this week. I need to see these twelve residents prior to the care conference to reassess their condition, evaluate their current psychosocial needs, and document their progress made toward achieving the goals set at the last quarterly meeting.

As I leave my office, I pick up my notebook. In it, I document the various social service requests I receive from residents, staff, and family members, in addition to my own observations and interactions as I am walking through the facility. I can refer to my notes later when I am in my office, make the necessary phone contacts, and then check off the request after it has been met and documented in the resident's medical record. It keeps me organized.

I visit the three nurses' stations, review the 24-hour note-book and talk with the charge nurse about any changes in the residents' conditions, as well as any need for social work intervention. There are no referrals this morning. I breathe a sigh of relief, because I need to see the twelve residents for care planning and get their paperwork finished.

I stop to talk to Mr. Brown about his wife's death. His son and daughter are with him, and he's picking at his breakfast. I offer my condolences to Mr. Brown and his family. The son and daughter take the opportunity to go get a cup of coffee while I visit with their dad. I sit and listen while he talks about his marriage, how much he loved his wife, and how much he will miss her. He is also worried about who his next room-mate will be, now that his wife won't be returning to the room. I assure Mr. Brown that I will inform him as soon as I know about a potential roommate. This seems to give him some relief. I give him a hug and tell him I'll see him tomorrow morn-ing before the chapel service for Mrs. Brown.

As I walk toward Mary Jones' room to begin her reassess-ment for care planning, Bertha McDougal hollers out, "Honey, honey...come here, honey!" Mrs. McDougal has advanced de-mentia, probably of the Alzheimer's type. Though she does not seem to recognize who walks by her room, she calls out, because she is alone and likes to have her hand held. Signifi-cant conversation is difficult with Bertha, because she can-not follow the train of thought. She enjoys having her hand held and patting the hand of the visitor. After a couple of min-utes of pleasantries, I offer to take her to the Activity Room where other people are gathering. She goes willingly.

Before lunch, I am able to see nine of the twelve residents who are going to be reviewed at the care conference. As I com-plete the required paperwork, I am interrupted by three fam-ily members asking questions about their relatives, by a call from Mrs. Smith's niece saying she will bring the house shoes tomorrow, by a resident who is going home soon wanting to know if I have contacted the home health people yet, and by a few residents who are disoriented and want to know where to go. I plan to finish the other three residents' reassessments tomorrow morning.

There is a Quality Assurance meeting during the lunch hour. I am the secretary for the QA meeting, so I have to go. The meeting ends about 1:15 p.m. After checking my mailbox for messages, I head out to the floors to complete individual visits with residents who are room bound because of physical or medical conditions, residents who are having difficulty adjusting to placement, and residents who have been assessed as requiring social work intervention such as remotivation, supportive counseling, and social interaction. The visits are completed amid interruptions for phone calls, questions from the Admission Coordinator and Director of Nursing about potential admissions, stopping to offer reassurance to residents who are confused, and saying good-bye to Bert Black, who is going home with his wife.

I stop to see Matilda Church, who was admitted yesterday. Miss Church has no immediate family. A neighbor provided minimal care for Miss Church until Miss Church fell last week and fractured her hip. Matilda is in the nursing facility receiving physical therapy, and hopes to return home within the month. I review the Resident Bill of Rights with Matilda, provide her with a copy, and document the interaction in the social service progress notes. I make a copy of her Living Will and Durable Power of Attorney for Health Care and place them in her medical record. I obtain the information I need to complete Miss Church's social history and initial psychosocial assessment. She wants to return home as soon as her hip is healed. We discuss various options for discharge planning. I assure her that I will work with her, the staff, and her neighbor to make the discharge a successful one. It's after five o'clock; it's time for me to go home.

There are a number of challenges facing social workers who choose to work in nursing homes. One of the challenges is the lack of training or preparation for the job. In their formal education, social workers rarely receive any training in the field of aging, much less in how to provide services to the nursing home population. When confronted with the reality of the work place and what one can realistically achieve, the social worker may experience tremendous dissatisfaction. The social worker is typically confronted with time constraints and high caseload ratios.

Lack of understanding by other staff, including administrators, about the social worker's role and functions is another challenge. Social work services are not always tangible, e.g., emotional support services vs. obtaining house slippers; thus, others outside the profession do not always see or understand the importance of the social worker's job. The staff needs to be educated about the functions of the social worker and come to view the social worker as a valuable team member and trusted advocate.

As nursing home social workers, we experience death and dying daily. We are constantly saying good-bye to residents and family members or friends who have touched us significantly. We have to handle our own grief while consoling others who are grieving.

The days are busy and at times long. I believe it takes a person with strong willpower, desire, and determination to make it as a nursing home social worker. The job holds personal rewards and benefits for the social worker. These rewards include the hugs and smiles from residents and thank yous from the family and staff.

Chapter 37
Senior Adult Coordinator

by Madeline B. Cohen, MSW, CISW

My days as the Senior Adult Coordinator at the Tucson Jewish Community Center are never "typical." Each day presents new faces, new challenges, and new ideas. Join me on my daily journey into the wonderful world of seniors.

Coordinating activities for senior adults at a Jewish Community Center incorporates the basic tenets of social work practice, as well as the creativity of program planning and implementation. My scheduled activities range from "Lunch Bunch," a daily kosher lunch/socialization program for frail seniors, to "Young at Heart," a weekly lecture program for active seniors. "Lunch Bunch" includes chair exercises for seniors with limited mobility, as well as conversational Yiddish, current events, movies, and Bingo; a special luncheon complete with Hebrew ceremonial blessings is held every Friday to welcome the Sabbath. It is indeed incredible that fifteen regular members of "Lunch Bunch" are over 85 years of age. In fact, I was inspired to create the Nifty Nineties Birthday Club for any senior who reaches this special milestone.

The "Young at Heart" lecture series provides an opportunity for cultural and educational stimulation. The enthusiasm of this well-informed, politically astute group never ceases to amaze me. The members have a program committee that votes on their speakers, makes the calls to the prospective lecturers, and even writes the thank you notes. Topics range from famous artists to medical technology. Other senior activities are Bridge Club, Stamp Club, Chess Club, and Friendship Club, a senior support group. A comprehensive sports and fitness facility is also available at the Jewish Community Center to meet the seniors' recreational needs.

My daily responsibilities include developing and implementing activities, making social service referrals to appropriate community agencies, and providing emotional support. Because the elderly have very special needs revolving around their physical, emotional, financial, and social problems, a seasoned social worker is needed to assure appropriate referrals to community resources. I interface with the State Department of Family and Children's Services, mental health partial hospitalization programs, community physicians, and nursing homes on a regular basis. Family members often call me for guidance in dealing with their aging parents.

Providing growth-oriented supervision to paraprofessional staff, student interns, and volunteers is the key to a smooth operation. In addition, excellent organizational skills are a necessity in managing this fast-paced job, where each day brings new demands. I have learned that being tactful in difficult situations is imperative in establishing good rapport with older adults. I encourage monthly council meetings to allow the seniors an opportunity to verbalize and ventilate about their likes and dislikes. Since many of our participants were professionals before retirement, they need to feel a sense of empowerment in this new phase of their lives.

My interviewing skills are always put to the test when prospective members call to learn about activities. Many have just lost a spouse or recently moved to Tucson to retire. I must quickly assess each individual's needs and issue a personal invitation to at least one specific group activity. Patience is a virtue in this role. Since many seniors have no other contacts in their lives, they often want to share their thoughts, opinions, and grief with me. Empathic listening is required at all times, even if I have heard the same story one hundred times.

One of the positive aspects of this job is the opportunity for one-to-one relationships with a population that imparts wisdom, wit, and often a little "chutzpah" (nerve). Moreover, program development allows one's creativity to soar to new heights. It is always crucial to develop new activities for this population. I have found that anything is possible, from a drama club to bagel brunches. Day trips to local attractions and special holiday programs are quite popular. My position also requires planning one overnight trip each year. A scenic bus trip to a Nevada hotel/casino proved to be memorable for all of us.

Working with nearly one thousand seniors means that I will invariably run into one of "my" seniors in the community. It is indeed a treat to see a familiar face in the supermarket, mall, or library and to be greeted enthusiastically.

Unfortunately, the senior social worker must also cope with the physical deterioration of the aging and the inevitability of their deaths. My experience in bereavement counseling comes into play, as I must support the grieving family as well as the seniors who have lost a friend.

How do I cope with the emotional and physical demands of the job? The staff organizational design provides the answer. The Senior Department at the Jewish Community Center falls under the auspices of the Adult Services Department. This team concept allows for shared ideas, as well as peer support. The Center incorporates a yearly staff retreat for team building and enhanced customer service skills. I have had the privilege of serving on the planning committee, which has led to heightened camaraderie with my colleagues.

In addition to my agency, there are several organizations that provide ongoing support to the senior worker. The Pima (County) Council on Aging, a joint funding source for our kosher lunch/socialization program, sponsors periodic training on the nutritional aspects of aging, as well as governmental regulations. The National Association of Social Workers and the Institute of Continuing Education, a branch of Jewish Family and Children's Services, offer various conferences and group discussions with networking opportunities, as well as continuing education units to keep my social work certificate current.

I chose this specialty because of my commitment to community service and my desire to utilize my creative talents. My experience for this position includes years of group work in a mental health setting and enjoyable summers as a unit leader at a coeducational camp for Jewish children. Working with a vital senior population has allowed me the opportunity to grow both personally and professionally.

Chapter 38
Hospice Social Work

by Daniel Liechty, Ph.D., D.Min., LSW

Hospice medical care is a relatively new and growing field for Masters-level, licensed social workers. In other areas of medicine, social workers too often find that in the economic pinch, social work services are considered secondary in importance. Nursing professionals have been very ambitious to extend their field of activities, and RNs now perform many of those social work duties that are considered vital. This has not been the case within hospice medicine, for Medicare guidelines are very explicit about the need to preserve the interdisciplinary nature of care.

There are five core hospice disciplines, each making its own unique contribution to the care of the patient. Medical nursing services assume responsibility for the overall medical treatment. Typically this includes aggressive pain and comfort control, bowel and bladder regimen, wound care, and monitoring nutrition and fluid intake. Home health care services focus on the personal care of the patient. Volunteer services focus on social visitation for patients and also clerical or public relations functions within the hospice program. Because Medicare regulations stipulate that at least 5% of the work hours for the hospice must be done by volunteers, hospices take very seriously the task of training and coordinating volunteer services. The Volunteer Coordinator position is often filled by a Masters-level social worker. Pastoral Counseling Services are another of the core disciplines, a recognition by those formulating Medicare guidelines of the importance of spiritual issues in the face of mortality. It is with these professionals that the hospice social worker forms a patient care team, a team which closely consults, plans, and carries out the care for each individual patient.

Social work services focus on the psychosocial needs of the patient and family. This may begin with connecting the patient or family to available public and private services. The more a social worker knows about available services and the qualifications for each service (means, age, specific disease, geographic location), the more that worker can be of service in connecting the patient or family to relevant services. Individual and family counseling skills are extremely important in hospice social work. Assisting the family in organizing its available resources for caregiving is usually necessary. Family members may be available and ready to provide the care. Yet it is not uncommon for even very competent people to be stumbling all over each other. As a less emotionally involved outsider, the social worker can play a valuable catalytic role in such very concrete tasks as assisting the family in working out a schedule and assigning care tasks to specific family members.

Care for a dying loved one always stirs up death anxiety and related emotional stresses within a family. The hospice social worker remains available to the patient and to each family member for supportive counseling and for psychotherapy related to death anxiety and anticipatory grief. Such issues vary widely from family to family and are strongly influenced by such factors as age, ethnic and religious background, the patient's place in the family system, and past experiences of resolved or unresolved grief. The worker also needs to know his or her limitations, both in terms of personal expertise and limitations imposed by the function of the agency.

Most hospice cases are paid at a capitated rate. This means that the social worker does not increase agency income by making more visits. Therefore, hospice social workers should be generally less tied to productivity rates than in other agency-based work, and also have greater freedom to concentrate services on those clients most in need at any given time.

There are cases of complicated grief that are either beyond the expertise of the worker or would require an investment of time that is beyond the function of the agency. Recognizing when to refer to specialists is one of the hospice social worker's most important tasks. Hospice social work perpetually moves between practical experience and theory. The hospice social worker will be engaged in expanding his or her theoretical knowledge through studied reading and further education. It is clear that the psychosocial care of hospice patients and families demands the attentive concentration of a trained and highly professional social worker. In addition to membership in the National Association of Social Workers, affiliation with either the Council of Hospice Professionals (Social Work Section) or the Association for Death Education and Counseling (ADEC) is important for keeping you up to date.

Let us now look at an actual day, a Tuesday in February of 1996, typical in my practice. I arrive at the office by 8:00 a.m. The first thing I do each time I enter the office is to check the RIP notices. This tells me which patients, if any, have died. That information is very important, because it affects all other scheduling. If a patient has died, I prepare a discharge summary and the paperwork for bereavement follow-up. In larger hospices, bereavement follow-up is handled by a bereavement specialist, often a Masters-level social worker. But in my agency, I handle that task as well. I spend about an hour looking over paperwork, answering mail, and calling patients to schedule the appointments for that day. I see some patients on a regular schedule each week, but most patients are scheduled on the day of the visit. This allows more scheduling flexibility for me and allows the patient to easily decline a visit if he or she does not feel up to it on a given day.

Normally I begin visits by 10:00. Social work visits are not generally appreciated before the morning routine is over. This particular morning, however, will be a bit different. My hospice is hospital-based and I have been asked to lead an in-service on death, dying, and grief for the dialysis group in the hospital. Health care professionals are placed in emotionally paradoxical positions. They possess a body of knowledge and skills that makes them adequate transference objects for suffering patients seeking assurance. Yet this same body of knowledge and skills also forces them to acknowledge less-than-optimistic prognoses in many cases. Coping mechanisms for shouldering this paradox, as well as the personal death anxiety stirred up by working day in and day out with extremely vulnerable patients, is the theme of this in-service. Such in-service leadership adds a dimension to my job that would not be possible except in a hospital-based program. Another example of this added dimension is my participation as a standing member of the hospital's medical ethics committee.

The in-service runs until 10:30, so I schedule my first patient visit for 10:45. My first visit is with a 96-year-old man. Although a cancer patient, he is still active and mobile. It is the first warm day in months and, as I expected, he wants to get out for a walk. We walk out to his barn and he explains each piece of equipment to me. He has done this many times before, but each time, I encourage him to remember different stories that go with the use of each piece. This allows him to keep his mental faculties stretched and active, and also allows him to make narrative closure on his life as a whole. I finish this visit at 12 noon. My next client is scheduled for 1:00 p.m. Driving time will be about 20 minutes. I could go back to the office to write up my notes, but in this case, it makes more sense to go to the public library.

There are a few tricks of the trade a hospice social worker needs to know. One of these relates to equipment. You need a good, comfortable and reliable car, but not one so nice that it bothers you when it gets to be a total mess inside. You need a detailed map of the catchment area, one that shows every single street. The best map is the book-type with a comprehensive index. You will then proceed to mark your own landmarks on that map. These will include diners and fast food places, where you can grab coffee and a bite in a hurry; libraries, where you can do paperwork in peace and always find a public rest room; and any other public rest rooms you find. Your toolbox will also include an accordion file with at least five copies each of every form of your paperwork and documentation; a good set of black pens; a pocket dictionary of medical terms; a professional book or journal you are studying, which can be read in 5-minute slots; and back at the office, a copy of the "bible," Therese A. Rando's book, *Treatment of Complicated Mourning*.

I leave the library at 12:45 p.m. and eat my lunch in the car on the way to my next appointment. My one o'clock appointment is not actually a hospice patient, but rather a home care patient. Like my agency, many hospices find it most cost-effective to be teamed up with a home care service agency. In smaller agencies, this allows for better utilization of nursing personnel and more advantageous quantity pricing for pharmaceuticals and medical equipment. My agency employs a home care social worker—I only see home care patients if the longer term plan is to discharge them to hospice.

In this case, however, I have been asked to visit the woman to find out why she has been absolutely resistant to the presence of home health aides in her home, a form of assistance she desperately needs by all objective standards. She is 89 years old and lives with her 94-year-old husband. She suffers from advanced vaginal cancer, which has spread to the liver, and was discharged from a recent emergency hospital visit into home care. She could easily qualify for hospice services, but she is unwilling to accept hospice. I met with her a few months ago after another hospitalization to speak with her about this. She equates accepting hospice services with "just giving up." We in hospice don't see it that way at all. We see ourselves as continuing an aggressive fight against the illness. But it is a fight on another level. That is, after diagnostic medicine has done all it can to fight the illness directly, palliative medicine continues that fight on the level of combating the ability of that illness to rob the person of the maximum quality of life, however that person defines it, for the time that person has left.

The equation of accepting hospice with giving up is a common social prejudice. The price people pay for that prejudice is continuation of torturous, agonizing, and invasive treatments months after such procedures can do any good for the person and may actually be doing harm. It is sad, but as respect for patient autonomy is a cardinal hospice and social work value, it is a situation we must live with until a shift occurs in the values of the larger society.

The woman rants and raves about the inept housekeeping skills of the home health aides she had during the first two days. She angrily told them not to come back! I am lost for a way to turn. She is ethnic Italian, so I ask about her own special recipe for pasta gravy, just to make friends. Her face lights up as she explains the delicate nature of stewing red sauce and adding the right spices (at least one of which, of course, will go with her a secret to her grave). At last she sighs and says she no longer has the strength to cook like that. I sense an opening and ask her to talk about her earlier days, before she and her husband moved to this small apartment. She goes on and on about what a great housekeeper she had been. Her house, her garden were the envy of the neighborhood!

"I was strong! Not like now, worthless, useless..." I form a hunch.

"Did you help any of the older ladies in the neighborhood to cook and clean?"

"Of course, all the time! They needed me!"

"Did you view those ladies as worthless and useless because they needed your help? I can assure you, nobody views you as worthless and useless now that you really need help with your cooking and cleaning."

Once that connection was made, her attitude changed rapidly. By the end of the visit, she and I together called the home health services supervisor to request an aide for the following morning. She only asked that the aides ask her what needs to be done before just jumping in and doing it, and that they tell her where they put things when they do the cleaning. Easily respected requests.

It is a short drive to my next visit, and I arrive at 2:15 p.m. The patient is a 67-year-old man with end stage lung cancer. In many ways, this is the diagnosis I dread the most. The patient is hooked up to oxygen, has no energy, and gasps for breath with even the slightest exertion. At this late stage, there is also often a tradeoff between pain control and mental alertness. This patient has chosen pain control and is sound asleep when I arrive. I spend the session with his wife, who spends the time reminiscing about their happiest times and tearily seeking my reassurance that they are doing the right thing.

These kinds of visits wrench my guts. It is easy to see that professional burnout could be a problem in this line of work. My style is to meditate purposefully and regularly on my own mortality—not on a sweet by and by, a reincarnation or some other emotional escape, but on my own death, finality, ultimate personal limitation. I find this allows me to truly stay with people emotionally who are hurting because of their mortality, yet also relieves me of any messianic complex, of assuming responsibility to carry their pain with me constantly and to fix everything.

I'm back at the office by 3:30 p.m. If this were Monday, I would be leading a bereavement group at 7:00 p.m. As it is, however, I have just enough time to write up the paperwork on these last two visits before leaving for home at 4:30. Maybe I'll have time tonight to watch that tape of last Thursday's episode of *ER*....

Chapter 39
Home Health Social Work

by Judith J. Lacerte, MSW, LISW, G.S. (Geriatric Specialist)

Home health social work requires flexibility, patience, and a genuine concern for the elderly, the chronically ill, and their caregivers. Professionally, I came to home health social work from within a public health setting, as a result of my prior position. It introduced me to direct practice with the frail elderly and the successful collaboration between a department of social services and department of health in serving the needs of the community. Personally, I discovered during this time that I relate well to senior citizens. I especially enjoy working with the very old. On hindsight, I believe this is because of the relationship I had with my maternal grandmother.

The majority of my time is spent visiting patients in their homes, as opposed to seeing people in an office. My car acts as my office, with my beeper and car phone facilitating communication among the office, patients, and other agencies. I work as part of a multidisciplinary medical team that includes nurses, physical therapists, speech therapists, occupational therapists, nutritionists, and personal care assistants.

I have a lot of autonomy and freedom, two of the things I like best about my job. For the most part, I am the one who chooses how to use my time, and the days go according to the schedule I set. However, flexibility is still a key to enjoying this work. The best planned visit schedule may change one or more times during the day, depending on patients' availability (doctor appointments or unplanned hospital trips) and patients' needs. Although there are few social work emergencies, the work is fast-paced. Counseling for depression, anxiety, or pain management requires a more intense visit regimen than resource coordination.

I am on a beeper between 8:30 a.m. and 5:00 p.m. I choose to start my day early, at my home desk away from the commotion of a busy office, charting visits made the day before. I go to the office to hand in paperwork and to make myself available to other staff. Nurses ask questions about resources and the psychosocial impact of a particular illness or social condition on patient care. As team leader, I assist other social work staff with questions about community resources and documentation around unusual visits.

Home health work is done in a prompt and timely manner. New assessments are ideally made within three working days of the referral and not more than seven days. Charting is turned in weekly, and statistics are collected monthly. In some ways, I am always "under the gun," so I can never get very far behind. My weekly schedule of visits is in place on Monday morning, indicating slots available for new referrals. I see patients 1-2 times per week for 4-15 weeks. Visits, in combination with the follow-up paperwork, meetings, supervision times, and just being available for phone calls and questions, create a full schedule. I visit many agencies to coordinate resources. It is often easier to drop by an agency than to go back to the office and call. I have the best relationships with other agency staff that I have ever had in my 30 years of professional social work practice, because so many of the supervisors and front line staff know me personally. I work full time and have benefits, but the trend is toward pay per visit, averaging $30-50 per visit. Salaries range from $25,000-35,000, depending on where you live.

I rarely take lunch, as I am usually on a "roll" by noon. I use the car phone to confirm that patients are available for visits. I stop to pick up coffee and eat my apple, carrots, and nuts while I drive. If there is time, I return to the office to check the mail, check the referral book, and follow up on phone calls. I use my "lunch time" to run a personal errand as needed.

I evaluate all patients for community resources and long-range health care planning. I counsel patients and their family members on issues relating to behaviors that may impede optimal health or adherence to a medical regimen, or that may require changes in activities of daily living. All follow-up visits involve aspects of one or more of these areas. I pride myself that I can move easily during one day from completing a psychosocial assessment to doing a relaxation therapy session with a patient in pain to arranging for another to be connected to community resources. I continue by counseling a patient for depression, assisting a family with nursing home placement, and educating a family on techniques for managing a family member with Alzheimer's Disease.

Medicare is the primary payment source and determines how charting is done. I format goals that are behavior specific, time specific, and outcome measurable. I devise treatment plans for each goal and address them in each charting. I do progress notes every 30 days and after a hospital discharge. The entries are brief, but specific. No process reporting here! The prompt charting regime keeps me focused on patients' needs and treatment outcomes. I don't visit to visit. I know why I am there and so does the patient. My role is clear as a professional helper. I am there to do a job, and the patient and/or family member sees the result, or knows what the barriers to care have been.

A typical day could easily include the following cases and interventions:

Mrs. Smith, 88, has a diagnosis of emphysema and middle stage Alzheimer's Disease. She lives with her husband of 55 years in a well-appointed trailer. Her husband is exhausted after seven years of caregiving and refusing all offers of help. Recently, his wife has become verbally and physically abusive. Afraid he was on the verge of hurting her and himself, he accepted his physician's recommendation for home health services. *Presenting problem:* counsel spouse to cope with current situation. *Intervention:* This was considered an urgent referral and I cleared my calendar preparing for a 2-hour visit. After completing a psychosocial history and allowing time for the spouse to tell "their story," and share his feelings of guilt and grief, I identified with him the problems, needs, and possible solutions. The patient needed a way to control her outbursts, the spouse needed respite and coping skills and requested nursing home placement for his wife. From the patient's home, I called the doctor to ask for a prescription to calm the patient without sedating her. I called several nursing homes, and forms were faxed to the physician's office for prompt attention. I gave the spouse a mini-course on Alzheimer's Disease and the phone number of a 24-hour Alzheimer's hotline and support group. Our agency assured him a daily personal care assistant for his wife for two weeks. Before I left, the spouse stated he felt for the first time that there was hope, and he believed he could cope without taking drastic action.

Mr. Thomas, 81, has a history of cancer and rheumatoid arthritis with prior histories of drinking, depression, and chronic pain. He lives with his caregiver wife. He makes frequent doctor visits, but obtains little satisfaction. *Presenting problem:* chronic pain and inability to sit still. *Intervention:* I had made several prior visits to this home. During this visit, I again led the patient in a 30-minute relaxation and visualization exercise. He remained perfectly still. He stated he expected to be pain-free for several hours. During the visit, the patient agreed to purchase a cassette player and relaxation tapes for pain control.

Mrs. Williams, 90, has a diagnosis of chronic heart failure and middle stage Alzheimer's Disease. She lives with her developmentally disabled but very solicitous son, age 62, in a small town. There is a long history of community involvement from churches to government services. *Presenting problem:* Mrs. Williams is increasingly hostile, as well as having periods of refusal to speak, eat, or participate in self care activities with the personal care assistant or her son. *Intervention:* I had made two visits to this home before. During this visit, I used Naomi Feils techniques of Validation Therapy, to assist the patient in interacting with her environment. The patient was becoming responsive to me. Today, the patient started actively cooperating with caregiving activities.

Mr. Jones, 65, has recently recovered from a stroke that left him paralyzed on one side. He lives with his elderly and frail brother in a relatively new, but "broken down" mobile home. Because of his successful recovery, the nurse and personal care assistant were preparing for a required discharge. *Presenting problem:* The patient's lack of safety without a personal care assistant and need for equipment in the home for patient self care. *Intervention:* My first visit was a psychosocial assessment. I learned the toilet needed repair and that a shower bench, a shower rail, and hand shower would permit the patient to safely enter the shower stall and bathe safely without a personal assistant. The patient also needed glasses in order to read the labels on his medicine bottles. On this second visit, I brought with me a donated shower bench. I also brought a shower rail and a hand-held shower, which the patient agreed to purchase. In between visits, I called a local church, and one of its members, a retired plumber, agreed to repair the toilet and install the shower equipment. They further arranged for another member, an ophthalmologist, to obtain the glasses. The patient was discharged and able to perform his personal care needs without risk of injury.

On a day such as this, there is no time to return to the office. I go home, feeling productive and tired.

I love my job, because it is challenging and daily calls for innovative practice skills. It is undergirded with outcome-oriented charting that provides stability to fast-paced practice.

PART 11:
MANAGEMENT

Chapter 40
Life as an Agency CEO

by Judith C. Czarnecki, MSW, LISW

I awake with a start at 4:45 a.m., the remnants of my Board Chairman's words in my head and the answer to the question he had posed forming in my mind. I reach for the notepad I keep by my bed for just such occasions and jot down a few things "to do" in order to get the information needed. Most of my CEO friends report having the same type of experience. I'm one of the lucky ones, though. My inspirations usually come close to dawn instead of the middle of the night. It's 5:00—only a half hour before my usual rising time. I read the parts of the newspaper I didn't get to last night and, by then, it's time to arise. Every morning, five days each week by 6 a.m., I'm at the gym. I believe it's important to be in good physical shape in order to be a CEO. My days as CEO of a social service agency are long, and hundreds of decisions can be made within them, so I need endurance, energy, and stamina. The morning is really the only consistent time I have, because of various meetings and other events that need attention. Some days, like today, I have to cut my exercise routine short to go to early morning meetings. This week, I have only two early meetings—some weeks I have five.

My first meeting begins at 7:30 a.m. It's with two Board members at an area restaurant to discuss plans for new programs. It goes well, and I leave with minutes to record and four different program ideas to research within the next three months. I arrive at the office in time for my 9:30 meeting—a brief session with the Vice President of Finance and Administration. She has an update on the audit, which will be completed soon, and needs some financial reports signed for some of the mental health boards. We also briefly discuss the requirements for the new MIS manager we will be hiring soon. It's critically important for the CEO to keep very close tabs on the finances. This is an area most social workers learn little about in school, so it requires additional training and constant work to be sure everything is in order. A large part of it is assuring the agency has a knowledgeable, well-qualified accountant in charge of the fiscal area. The agency now has about a $3 million budget, and this is my fifth controller in six years. I think I finally have someone who really understands accounting. She has never worked in the not-for-profit sector, so both she and I spend some extra time to be sure she learns the intricacies of the requirements of our various funding sources.

At 10:30, my next appointment is waiting. The new Chairman of the United Way is making a courtesy call with the President of the United Way. They are making the rounds of the funded agencies to learn about them and get input from the executives regarding the United Way's new three-year investment plan. I proudly review the agency's services (we are the United Way's second largest investment, as we receive more UW money than any other program except the Red Cross) and share with them my concerns about the new plan. The UW has decided to withdraw its support of programs for domestic violence perpetrators, as it believes this is a criminal justice issue. Although it is too late to change the UW's plan, I present my case to help my visitors understand the impact this decision will have on our agency and services to families where domestic violence is present. I haven't decided yet how we will handle this internally and, so far, have informed only the administrative team. We're still investigating the possibility of reclassifying the program in order to get it funded. After all, we have the equivalent of two people doing that work and serving about 200 batterers per year. It would be difficult to terminate this service.

It's 11:40 when they leave—just enough time to check my messages before leaving for my noon Rotary meeting. I note that I missed a call from the VP of one of the local hospitals, whom I've been trying to contact for the last month. I also need to call the Council on Accreditation. We're up for our re-accreditation this year, and I'm a Peer Reviewer and a member of the Central Accreditation Commission—it's hard to tell which of these items needs attention today. I pull out the notes I made when I awoke this morning and put them on top of the "to do" pile.

The Rotary meeting is important for making business contacts necessary to the agency. It is a little difficult, as I am one of about 20 female members in a group that numbers more than 500. Most of the other women are also from social service agencies, so we have somewhat of a bond. All of us, however, are in Rotary for the same essential reason, so competition is common. Especially as resources (financial and personnel) become scarcer, competition increases. So far, all I have gotten for the agency from my membership is one computer set-up (about $2,400). I've tried getting funding to help with a couple of other programs, but haven't yet been successful. I really need to spend more time getting to know the right decision makers.

It's 1:20 when I return from the luncheon. It was good—I was able to connect with the President of a local bank. He will put me in touch with one of their trust officers to determine if there is a fit between some of our programs and some of their trusts. I just have time to review my notes before my 1:30 appointment with two representatives from a local foundation, who want to discuss our application. We've requested $30,000 to fund a program working with fathers of children born to teenage, unwed mothers. The representatives are here with questions from their review committee, and they want to take a look around our facility. It's really good news, because this meeting means we made the second cut in the review process and, if all goes well today, we'll probably get the grant. We won't know for another two months, but it's looking good for now.

It's 2:25. I have 35 minutes before the meeting with the United Way to review the part of the investment plan into which our Home Care program falls. I check phone messages again and return the call to the hospital VP from this morning, but he isn't available, so it's another round of phone tag. The call to the Council is more successful—they ask me to review an agency in Florida. I accept, although I'll be the "Team

Leader," which means more work. The reviews are a lot of work (about 40 hours before we get on site and another 24 or so once we're on site), but they are excellent learning experiences. Every time I do one I learn something—either a new program idea or, just as important, I learn how NOT to do something. The on-site visit won't be for three months, although the work will start when the materials arrive, in about a month. I return three more calls, leaving voice mail notes on all. It's now 2:50 and time to head downstairs for the United Way meeting.

4:45—I'm back from the UW meeting. I check my messages and find one from my Board Chairman. I forgot to make the calls I thought of this morning, so I hurriedly call another CEO friend of mine to get some background information before calling the Board Chairman. I reach him at 5:10—a good time to get him. We discuss the information I have that he needs for a meeting day after tomorrow, check a few other items, and set another time to talk.

5:45—Time to review the mail, check the rest of the messages, attend to things that need to be done, and be sure I have everything in order, as I'll be out of the office the rest of the week. I leave the office at 7:00 and head home to eat, then pack for a three-day conference in Milwaukee. Before retiring, I mentally review the day, realize there was something I forgot to tell my secretary, make a note to call her from Milwaukee, pack, read the mail and most of the paper, and retire around 10:30.

Most days are similar to the above. As the President/CEO of an agency, the only way to get time for planning and research is to block out time from the schedule. If it's not blocked out, the secretary will book it! Being a CEO is demanding, exciting, stressful, fun, frustrating, sometimes lonely, and fulfilling. It is hard to get used to the impact your words and actions carry and harder still to understand that no matter what decision you make, someone will be upset. Especially in today's ever-changing environment, there is never a dull moment. Salaries range from about $40,000 for a small organization to over $120,000 for very large (over $15 million) agencies (a few not-for-profit CEOs who head national organizations can make even higher salaries).

I am one of the "old time" CEOs who received a master's degree in clinical social work, and started out as the director of a branch office of a larger organization where I did a lot of clinical work, as well as provided administrative oversight of the office. That's back when agencies hired "executive directors" and wanted them to be "practice experts," not necessarily "expert managers and leaders." With the changes in the corporate world, Board members now have much less time to devote to agency activities, and they delegate more responsibility to the CEO. This has occurred at a time when the social services world is in the throes of major restructuring and long-range planning has been reduced to about three months. This requires more business acumen on the part of the CEO— things often not acquired in graduate schools of social work.

A recent trend in social service agencies is to indicate a preference for hiring someone with an MSW and an MBA. The second preference is to hire someone with an MBA, and the third is to hire a person with an MSW or other related degree (MPH, MPA, Ph.D). Although this preference pertains mostly to larger (over $2 million) agencies, there is a similar trend among smaller agencies in larger communities. Agencies in smaller rural areas still look for MSWs and, preferably, one who can provide a combination of administration and direct clinical work.

Being a CEO is a demanding job. However, it can be quite fulfilling. There is nothing quite as rewarding as developing a program, getting it funded, and knowing that you have been responsible for helping people change their lives in ways that may not have been possible without your agency's help. It's the spirit of social work, and it's what makes all the long hours and frustrating moments worth it.

Chapter 41
Association Management

*by Dr. Marjorie Baney, LCSW,
and Janice Fristad, ACSW, LSW, CAE*

Association management is a growth area for social workers interested in a macro practice setting. Your hosts for this tour work in the association management specialty area called chapter services. What follows is our professional journey, what we do, and options available to you in association management.

Marjorie: The up side of being a social worker in association management is the variety of opportunities available. During my 18 years with the National Association of Social Workers (NASW), I have been an executive director, a lobbyist, a management consultant, a leadership development trainer, event planner, awards judge, a field instructor, and president of Local 2382 of the Communications Workers of America, the national NASW office staff union.

The down side of association management is the lack of opportunity. Association management, in general, has a relatively high turnover rate. The current trend is to hire someone with the best package of skills to meet the association's needs for the next 3-5 years, then find someone else with a different package of skills. Your career is built not on promotion, but on progression. Opportunities to progress diminish after 5 years or so, because other associations no longer view you as a generalist, and career opportunities become limited to your own professional association. A career built on a single association is a career diminished.

Within NASW, for example, the career path for executive directors is to move from smaller to large chapters and to the national office, each progression requiring a move to another state, a barrier for many accomplished individuals and their families. Once you have progressed to the national office (less than a dozen chapter staff have done so to date), the barriers on the career ladder include a limited number of positions, with very few positions requiring a social work degree, which increases competition from others in association management (Washington, D.C. is home to the largest number of associations in the U.S.). It is important to distinguish between career opportunities and work/practice opportunities.

The up side is the incredible variety of interesting options available in your job. The down side is a constricted career—creativity and variety vs. recognition and compensation.

Janice: Associations represent the collective interests of members who have adopted a common mission and common program goals. After my employment at NASW, I quickly discovered the power of the group in decision-making and its impact for advocacy for the association. Association staff members generally understand this, realize its potential for the association, and enjoy this aspect of the job. During my tenure at NASW, therefore, I have tremendously enjoyed the experience of working with association volunteer leaders at the national, state, and local levels. One day at the state chapter level, for example, might bring meetings on recruitment and retention of social workers in state child welfare agencies, work with home health social workers on a third-party insurance issue, and advocacy with legislators on welfare reform legislation.

The ability to influence social, professional, and organizational policies was another drawing card for me to remain challenged, interested, and involved with association management as a career. Even though the policy-making role is generally reserved for association boards of directors, in reality, staff and volunteer leaders work collaboratively and are mutually supportive in policy development.

Marjorie: Association management is not for wimps. You must be able to cope with constant change. Associations are governed by boards of directors composed of association members. Each election results in a new board with as many as half of its members newly-elected. The direct impact of this annual transition is greatest on the executive director, but ripples throughout the staff and members. Surviving in this corporate environment requires flexibility.

The pace of change is set by the board and influenced by board policies, strategic plans, leadership development and orientation programs, and the personal agenda of individual members. In my seven years on the national NASW staff, I have experienced seven boards of directors, two deputy executive directors, and four executive directors. As a member of the Communications Workers of America, Local 2382, I have been through labor contract negotiations with management four times.

The ability to work as an independent professional and as a team player is another essential. Most social workers in association management do not work with other social workers. Like many clinicians in private practice, social workers in association management need to assemble a support network of colleagues outside the workplace. A good sense of humor is an asset in any workplace. The values and ethics of our profession and the clinical/people skills taught us in school guide the conduct of our work and enhance our effectiveness.

Janice: If you plan to pursue a job in association management, you need to do an assessment of your skills, find out which association positions are available, and pursue employment opportunities accordingly. The social work curriculum emphasizes and enhances communication, program development, and advocacy skills, all assets in association employment. In addition to social work classes, take advantage of administration course work offered either through your school of social work or through other sources, such as the school of business or public administration.

Why Association Management?

Janice: I was unaware that association management existed as a career. I joined NASW while enrolled as a student at West Virginia University School of Social Work, after hearing a faculty member's presentation on NASW's leadership in representing social work interests at Capitol Hill.

Upon graduating, I noticed that a position was open at the Pennsylvania State Chapter Office of NASW. It was a matter of timing, rather than one of design, that I came to work at the Pennsylvania Chapter Office as Coordinator of Membership and Legislative Activities. My job initially was defined by the director of the association. Slowly, I learned the intricacies of association management and later applied and was hired for the executive director position.

Marjorie: I never chose association management; I chose NASW. I joined on my first day in graduate school, because the application was on the table with the usual bunch of first day of school forms. We were told that representatives from NASW would come to meet with us one evening and were urged to attend. They came, I went, and a dynamic relationship began.

Both of my field placements were with NASW before we had state chapters. I was part of the first legislative involvement the association had in North Carolina, under the auspices of the NC Council of NASW Chapters. My title was Legislative Representative. I followed legislation of interest to social workers and reported to the Council's Social Action Caucus. I quickly changed my career path from clinical to metasystems, dismissing the warning of my advisor that it was hard for women to get jobs in administration. Reorganization into state chapters eventually created the opportunity to become chapter executive director. It was as a chapter executive that I began to learn about the field of association management. It was the move to the national staff that enabled me to learn about career management in associations and to convey what the ups and downs have taught me to colleagues entering association management.

A Typical Day

We work in the Office of Chapter Services (OCS) Department. The OCS facilitates chapter staff and leadership contact with, and service from, national staff. Its mission is to deliver high quality consultations, technical assistance, and training services to NASW chapter leadership and staff; to act as the chapters' advocate at the national level; and to provide an effective communications link between chapters and the National Office.

On a typical day we provide a variety of direct services to chapters, including consultation on chapter governance, management, and personnel issues; coordination of chapter requests for legal and program consultation; monitoring of compliance with chapter standards, personnel standards, and affirmative action plans; and coordinating the Chapter Development Fund, which provides grants and services to twenty-seven chapters.

So, for example, Janice might spend twenty minutes talking on the phone to a new chapter executive director who has questions about the chapter's personnel policy regarding employee performance problems, while Marjorie is on another line helping a chapter president understand why a proposed change in the chapter's bylaws is problematic, because it violates chapter standards developed at the national level. Marjorie might spend a day (or several) in California helping the chapter's search committee hire a new executive director, while Janice is in Mississippi leading a workshop for newly-elected board members.

Our department also coordinates and implements the Delegate Assembly, NASW's tri-annual meeting of chapter delegates who adopt program priority goals for the coming three years and set the association's policies on social and professional issues. This major event for the association involves a great deal of planning, along with pre-Delegate Assembly meetings on the regional level.

We also plan and implement an Annual Leadership Meeting each April, which is attended by chapter staff and presidents from all over the country. It's always a challenge to plan these major events, and it's always exciting to see them finally come together.

Administratively, we develop and maintain information on chapter organization, management, and programs. We develop and disseminate policies and procedures for chapters in areas of nominations and leadership identification, personnel, fiscal management, and bylaws. The NASW National Office receives over 4,000 phone calls per day, many from chapter staff or board members seeking information, interpretation of operating policies and procedures, or just a sounding board for the day's frustrations—one of our more popular and valuable services.

Finally, one of the most rewarding and fun aspects of what we do is the ability to develop and implement special projects.

Marjorie: In the last year, one of my special projects was the career development center at NASW's Annual Meeting of the Profession in Philadelphia, where we offered free résumé critiques, jobs listings from employers and our chapter newsletters, and computers where attendees could write a résumé or participate in a simulated interview.

Now, I've moved on to focus my energy on the development of an NASW Leadership Academy. I meet frequently with marketing staff to find creative ways chapters can recruit members for leadership positions; identifying better ways to get the message out to members that we want to assist them in using the learning opportunities NASW provides, through the Leadership Academy, to enhance their own careers; keeping all the various interested parties up to date (phone, fax, e-mail) on the Academy's progress; and assembling learning modules, designing evaluation instruments, and arranging for participants to receive certificates documenting continuing education contact hours.

Janice: Through the generosity of the Chapter Development Fund, four regional fiscal management seminars were recently held for chapter treasurers and executive directors. Marjorie and I worked with other national NASW staff to plan the curriculum, coordinate site arrangements, and conduct the training.

CDF funds also supported the creation of an in-house training video for chapter boards of directors. I worked with many staff members and leaders, as well as professional and amateur actors, to coordinate the development, filming, and editing process for this training video.

Associations—located primarily in the nation's capital and, on the state level, in state capitals—offer many opportunities for social workers interested in macro-level work. Working hand-in-hand with other staff members and volunteer boards of directors to make ideas become reality can provide challenges and rewards too many to mention here.

PART 12:
HIGHER EDUCATION

Chapter 42
Life as a BSW Educator

by Carol A. Heintzelman, DSW

As is true in most social work practice specialties, a "typical" day in the life of a baccalaureate social work educator/professor does not exist. A "typical week" in a fall semester perhaps unfolds as follows:

Monday, Wednesday, Friday

9-9:50—Teach Social Work and Women's Issues

11-11:50—Teach Social Work Practice III (Macro Level Practice)

Wednesday

6-9—Teach second section of Social Work Practice III

Tuesday, Thursday

11-12:15-Teach Interdisciplinary Introduction to Gerontology

A "typical" spring semester is very similar, differing only in the courses taught. For example, I typically teach Social Work Research I, Senior Seminar, and Field Instruction I-II in the spring semester.

In addition to teaching twelve hours a week per semester at Millersville University in Millersville, PA, I am expected to be available in my office a minimum of five hours a week spread over three days. Office hours provide excellent opportunities for students to discuss their progress in their courses and their personal or professional concerns. My academic advisees also seek advice regarding their progress toward completion of requirements for the social work major, as well as the university requirements for graduation.

I also serve on various departmental and university committees, in order to contribute my professional expertise to the ongoing daily operation of the University. In addition, in a social work department, faculty members are expected to provide service to community agencies and organizations. The board of directors of LUTHERCARE, the Lancaster County Coalition for the Prevention of Teenage Pregnancy, National Association of Social Workers (NASW), American Association of University Women, and Delta Kappa Gamma Society are some of the community activities with which I am involved.

Generally, not until late afternoon or early evening can I sit down and begin to prepare for classes, student conferences, and other activities for the next day. Periodically, exams are given and term papers are assigned. All of these need to be read, graded, and returned to the students in a timely fashion. In between all these activities, I must prepare papers for presentation at conferences, conduct research, prepare articles for publication, and so on.

In a baccalaureate social work program, I am guided in my work by two key principles: academic freedom and academic responsibility. Academic freedom means that a social work educator is entitled to full freedom in research and in the publication of results, subject to the adequate performance of his/her other academic or administrative duties. The second principle, academic responsibility, means that the concern of colleges/universities and their members for academic safeguards must extend also to requiring responsible service, consistent with the objectives of the college/university.

As an outgrowth of the above two principles, the various activities that the job entails fall into three major categories. The first area is effective teaching and fulfillment of professional responsibilities. My specific responsibilities include: effective teaching; preparation of course syllabi; student advisement; participation in the work of the department; and timely execution of expected work, both in the classroom as well as outside the classroom.

The second major area is continuing scholarly growth. My activities here include: delivering papers at national and regional meetings of professional organizations, such as NASW, CSWE (Council on Social Work Education), or BPD (Baccalaureate Program Directors); judging regional and national awards; holding offices in professional organizations; delivering invitational lectures; participating in panels at regional and national meetings of professional organizations; acquiring grants; editing professional journals; serving as a consultant; researching projects and publications; completing additional graduate work, including the Ph.D./DSW in social work or a related field; and contributing to the scholarly growth of one's peers.

Service, the third area, is defined as professional contributions to the college/university and/or the community. Some of my activities in this area include: participating in program, department, school and college-wide committees; developing new courses or programs; participating in college/university-wide colloquia; serving as a member in professionally-oriented, community-based organizations reasonably related to my discipline; lecturing; and consulting with local and area agencies and organizations. As you can see, being a full-time baccalaureate social work educator can be very busy, very demanding, and yet very fulfilling.

The major reward of being a baccalaureate social work educator is seeing your students progress from freshman nonprofessional status to seniors who graduate as "beginning professionals" ready to "take on the world." Related to this is the thrill of talking with students after they secure their first paid social work positions.

Another major "up" as an educator is receiving tenure and promotions. The "top of the academic ladder" is the promotion to professor. Faculty who receive the accolades of tenure and promotion to professor can feel good about themselves.

On the opposite side of the coin are the "downs." A major one is "crunch time." Term papers, reports, presentations, and final exams all happen within the last two to three weeks of the semester. Average class size in the social work department is 18-19 students. Also, during the course of the semester, exams and papers are assigned. So semesters may become busy and hectic for everyone, faculty as well as students.

Another frustration is the demand on teaching time by service activities to the university, community, and profession. Millersville University stresses that "the universal responsibility of the teaching faculty member is effective teaching." Unfortunately, other demands on faculty time seem to conspire against adequately fulfilling this responsibility, often to the detriment of the students.

Several personal characteristics are helpful for a person who wants to be a baccalaureate social work educator. First is being genuinely interested in the students as they struggle to master the transition from student to beginning professional. In many cases, students are also making the transitions from late adolescence to young adulthood. A willingness to reach out and give support and encouragement is necessary. In other words, enthusiasm and concern are certainly necessary characteristics.

Another needed characteristic is initiative, a willingness to take the lead in spite of obstacles. Related to initiative is persistence, especially when climbing the academic ladder and pursuing doctoral work. In addition, one needs to learn to balance the demands of a professional life against the demands of a personal life. In other words, one needs to learn to make time for oneself.

As a social work educator, I am a member and active participant in the National Association of Social Workers (NASW), the Council on Social Work Education (CSWE) (especially the Annual Program Meeting), the Association of Baccalaureate Social Work Program Directors (BPD), as well as the Pennsylvania Association of Undergraduate Social Work Educators (PAUSWE), to stay informed about social work practice, education, and accreditation.

How did I become a BSW educator? In 1970, I graduated with my MSW from Howard University in Washington, D.C. At the time, I decided to work in child welfare services for about five years to gain some work experience and then explore the possibility of teaching in a graduate school to share with students my experiences and enthusiasm about social work.

To paraphrase the poet Robert Burns, "the best laid plans of mice and men often go astray." Instead of following my "best laid plan," I worked for one year as a supervisor in a Department of Public Welfare (DPW) in Winchester, VA, located at the edge of Appalachia. Then in the spring of 1971, I decided to leave the DPW. About this time, Shepherd College, in Shepherdstown, WV, received a grant from the former U.S. Department of Health, Education and Welfare (now the Department of Health and Human Services) to start a baccalaureate social work program.

As an historical aside, in 1969, the Council on Social Work Education, as an outgrowth of the "War on Poverty," voted to begin providing social work education at the baccalaureate level—the entry level or the first professional degree. The state of West Virginia recognized the significance of this change and took advantage of the federal money made available for the development of four baccalaureate programs, including the one at Shepherd College.

I applied for the vacancy and was hired as an instructor of social welfare and sociology. As a result, I got in on the "ground floor" for the emerging field of baccalaureate social work education. I was on the faculty at Shepherd College from 1971 to 1975, teaching a variety of courses in social work and sociology, working with the program director to get the program accredited, advising students, providing service to the college and community, and beginning work on my doctor of social work degree at the Catholic University of America in Washington, D.C.

Recently, in conjunction with my sabbatical leave research project, I returned to visit the baccalaureate program at Shepherd College. It was good to see how the program has grown and developed during the last twenty-one years. The social work department had just received word that it had been re-accredited for the next eight years, till 2004, and they were very excited. Needless to say, it was a good visit.

Average annual salaries in 1994-1995 for an individual teaching in a baccalaureate social work program in a *public* college/university ranged from an average of $36,430 for an entry level instructor to an average of $59,173 for a senior level professor, with the overall average salary being $45,174, according to the *Chronicle of Higher Education*. Average annual salaries for an individual teaching in a baccalaureate social work program in a *private* college/university ranged from an average of $32,083 for an entry level instructor to an average of $54,181 for a senior level professor with the overall average salary being $41,149. The typical college/university tenure-track academic ranks are instructor, assistant professor, associate professor, and professor. Minimum faculty qualifications are a master's degree in the discipline and "good moral turpitude."

Several other items need thoughtful consideration by the social worker who decides to become a baccalaureate social work educator. First, one's primary task is educator, not therapist. I have found through experience that if a student comes for help for long-standing, deep-seated family and/or personal problems, it is usually best to refer the student to the appropriate on-campus or off-campus counseling or clinical services. Providing clinical/therapist services blurs the lines between student and teacher, which can cause difficulties for both parties inside as well as outside the classroom. This is a major struggle for most social work educators and one that you will need to resolve in order to become an effective educator.

Second, a baccalaureate social work educator in a college/university setting will need to make a commitment to pursue a Ph.D. in social work or a related field. The Ph.D. is increasingly the "union card" for continued employment and advancement at the college/university level.

Third, a minimum of two years' post-MSW practice experience is required to teach in the practice sequence in a CSWE-accredited baccalaureate program. Practice experience, however, is not required for teaching in the social welfare policy and services sequence, human behavior in the social environment sequence, research sequence, or for serving as a field instruction liaison.

A fourth consideration for many academics is working in a union environment. The union environment has both positive and negative aspects. Among the positive aspects are an excellent fringe benefit package and clearly defined expectations. On the negative side, however, are the perpetual contract negotiations approximately every three years and the resultant possibility of a strike.

Chapter 43
University Counseling Center

by Laura Crawford Hofer, MSSW, LCSW, ACSW, BCD

I anticipated an easy day today in my role as a counselor at the university's Counseling Center. I had checked the black notebook on the secretary's desk for my appointments and found that, because it was early in the semester, just three students had appointments scheduled with me today. I also had time blocked off to meet with the director of the Counseling Center about the Crisis Response Team, to prepare for a group interpretation of the Myers-Briggs Type Indicator, and to attend an Academic Leave committee meeting.

Suddenly, a hurricane appeared in the doorway. My first student was here. I invited Donna into my office. The tall, gangly, raven-haired woman in front of me described again what it had been like growing up with Attention Deficit Hyperactivity Disorder (ADHD) and not having been understood. Still hyperactive at thirty and unwilling to take medication regularly, she could barely sit still in my office on the red plaid couch. Her thoughts darted around as actively as her long, brown limbs did. Sometimes she didn't even complete sentences. It was, nevertheless, easy to hear the pain as she talked about playing basketball, her skill and love for the sport, and how often she would be prevented from going to practice by detention. Blurting something out in class or not being able to find her homework earned her detentions, even though they were due to her impulsivity and disorganization, both also hallmarks of ADHD. Today she was grieving again, as I listened, for the many years that she had been misunderstood.

Her thoughts switched to the waiver that she was hoping to secure for the math requirement at the university. An English major, she felt hopeless at math. Each math problem looked new to her. She could not remember the processes she had used before to solve a similar problem. If she didn't receive the waiver, she threatened, she would drop out of college. I knew that Donna was not willing right now to be tested for a learning disability. She was already grieving her ADHD and felt that she could not handle being diagnosed with another problem. But I also knew that without testing, Donna would be unlikely to be granted the waiver. She and I had already discussed this and she knew, too.

Suddenly she brought up her "twin" brother, Richard. Exactly one year older than she was, the two had been very close as they had grown up. Richard had died eight years ago in a car accident. The anniversary of his death would be Thursday. Donna wept as she remembered him. She longed for him to be here now so that he might understand her anew, as she was coming to understand herself and her experiences. As the session ended, Donna commented again on how tired she was after every session. Not used to experiencing feelings for anything but the briefest time, the sessions with me focused her on what was going on inside.

After Donna left and I had written a few notes on the session, I knew that I had to meet with the Director of the Counseling Center, Dr. Joanne Wells. Joanne and I had been instrumental in the development of the Crisis Response Team (CRT) at the university. It included representatives of many of the organizational units in the university: campus police, housing, faculty, students, campus ministry, health services, athletics, counseling center, the Dean of Students, the Vice President for Public Relations, and the Vice President for Student Affairs. Joanne and I had already led this group in a process that had established the purpose and basic functioning of the team and had produced a written protocol. Now she and I were responsible for the once-a-semester training.

Before we started, I told Joanne how deeply Donna's pain had moved me, how I wondered if it were really possible to resolve the profound losses that she had to bear, and how concerned I was that she might act impulsively again and drop out of the university. Joanne heard my pain, my doubts, and my questions. Then I was ready to move on.

For the CRT training, we wanted to provide a hypothetical situation that the team could respond to. We brain-stormed.

What crises had we heard on the news lately that had occurred on a college campus? We considered a sexual assault, a suicide, and an apparent love triangle where a jealous husband had assaulted a professor and left him in critical condition. This time, because we knew that there were gang members attending our university, we settled on a gang-related incident. We fleshed out the hypothetical incident. A gang member and a fraternity brother would have words in White Hall. Someone would bump into the rattled gang member. The gang member would draw a gun and shoot wildly. A nursing professor and a nursing student would get hit. We gave the student a fictitious name and laughed as we thought about the professors that we'd like to shoot and the ones that we knew that the students would like to shoot. Our good judgment won out, though, as we settled on someone who was genuinely liked and respected in all parts of the university community. We would let the team decide what happened after the shooting and how each organizational unit could best respond to this scenario. The secretary, Sally, knocked on the door. Both Joanne and I had students who were waiting to see us.

A tall man in his mid-twenties, Bruce almost always wore a black leather jacket, black jeans, small round sunglasses, and multiple silver earrings in his left ear. On warmer days he wore a ripped shirt exposing a pierced nipple. The bottom third of his head was shaved and his long hair gathered into a ponytail at the nape of his neck. Flamboyant and unconventional in his appearance, I knew Bruce also to be a gentle and thoughtful person disturbed by his relationship with his girlfriend, Danielle. A recovered alcoholic, Bruce had just begun to experience the relationship as destructive. Danielle toyed with him, he felt, and yet he couldn't give her up. Today he continued. He compared Danielle to alcohol. Bad for him but feeling so good. He knew the relationship hurt him. She hurt him when she told him that she had seen her old boyfriend and when she had hinted that they had had sex. And, she hurt him because he was not focused on studying. But he knew he would call her again. He knew that when she called him, he would respond. *What was it that made him want to call her and want to respond?* I asked in numerous ways. Bruce could see Danielle only negatively and couldn't identify right now what was magnetic about her to him.

When the session ended, Sally asked if I could see a resident assistant, or RA, who had walked in without an appointment. RAs are upperclass students who receive room free at the university in exchange for their support to a section of ten to twelve students in the residence hall. RAs generally only come to the Counseling Center if they have students about whom they have serious concerns. So I agreed to see Shelley.

An RA in our one residence hall with apartments, Shelly explained that all three of the apartment mates of another student, Rose, believed her to be bulimic. They had come together to see Shelley the previous evening and had reported that Rose often excused herself from a meal and that they could hear her vomiting in their shared bathroom. When they had confronted her, Rose had passed it off as a virus, but she had gone into the bathroom to vomit so many times now that they no longer believed her. Two of the apartment mates were nursing students and were aware of how damaging repetitive vomiting was to one's body. The woman who shared a room with Rose also had seen laxatives in Rose's purse.

That Rose was possibly using both laxatives and vomiting to control her weight made this an emergency situation. Losing so much fluid from the body could cause not only dehydration but an electrolyte imbalance, a heart arrhythmia, and death. I asked if Shelley had told her boss, the resident director (RD), what was going on. She had. I asked Shelly to set up a meeting in the Counseling Center later today or tomorrow with Rose, her roommates, and herself present. The meeting would be an opportunity for Rose's roommates to describe exactly what they had seen and heard, to express just how worried they were, to learn whether or not action was warranted, and what action would be taken.

Shelley and I then talked about how she would approach Rose about the meeting. Shelley thought she could tell Rose that her roommates were very worried about her and needed to talk with her at the Counseling Center. But she feared that Rose would deny all of what her roommates had observed and would refuse to come to the meeting or would come to the meeting and would refuse to follow through on any plan. If Rose refused at either level, I pointed out, we could use the university's judicial process to force Rose to act, since she appeared to be exhibiting behavior that endangered herself. But hopefully, I continued, Rose will be moved by her roommates' worries to worry herself and to want to act.

I knew that, depending upon what came out in this meeting, it was likely that I would be recommending to the student that she have a full evaluation for an eating disorder. She would need a physical as well as a psychosocial evaluation that included specific questions about weight and dieting history, body image concerns, and family history of eating disorders, sexual abuse, drug or alcohol use, and mood disorders in order to fully address what appeared to be a very serious problem. Shelley was relieved when she left my office. It felt good, she said, to have a plan.

Many things were crowding my mind right now. I was quite concerned about Rose and about her physical condition. I knew that I had to tell Joanne about this situation. I was concerned about Donna, since she seemed in the midst of a crisis, and about Bruce who was stuck. Then there were my kids. I had applied for this job, in part, because it offered a 10-month contract. Like school social work, I could have two months during the summer to be with my family. Except for occasional evening events, such as a workshop, class, or speaker that I was responsible for, most of my hours at work were hours that my children were in school. The starting salary, comparable to that of an assistant professor at $35,000, was also good. The university also offered an exciting, intellectual environment. But today I had to work late. I had an Academic Leave committee meeting. Tuesday meant that my 13-year-old had swim team practice after school and that my 10-year-old would be home alone for awhile. Even though she knew that I would be late and would call Sally to check in, I knew that she was likely to be apprehensive.

I had a few minutes now to begin preparing for the group interpretation of the Myers-Briggs Type Indicator for the class on interpersonal communication. I thought back to my training in the indicator and how often I had used it since then. Professors in certain classes, RAs, and sorority presidents had all requested that I do an interpretation for their groups. A useful tool to help people sort out some innate differences in behavior, the indicator also teaches respect for those differences. I enjoyed watching groups learn, for example, that some people think and talk almost simultaneously while others process their thoughts internally for a while before they are ready to speak.

Sally broke into my thoughts, asking if I would take a call from a professor who was concerned about a student. A professor in the business school, Dr. Foster, had a student who had become increasingly withdrawn. Friends of the student's had told Dr. Foster that his father had died two years ago and his mother had died just last month. The friends were worried that he was drinking excessively and might be suicidal. Dr. Foster had observed that he was participating less in class and had stopped handing in homework. Dr. Foster himself had had a friend commit suicide and was worried that this student might be at risk. He wondered what he should do. We talked first about setting up a meeting with the student. Dr. Foster needed to talk with the student about the change in his behavior in class and about what might have precipitated it. With the permission of the other students, or if the student said anything to indicate that he might be suicidal, Dr. Foster could address that question directly. Dr. Foster wondered if he could make the student think about something that might not yet have crossed the student's mind. I explained that if the student were not thinking about suicide, he would simply dismiss the idea. If he were thinking about it, he would probably be relieved that someone had asked. If he were thinking about it, I continued, the professor should escort him to the Counseling Center. Someone would see him immediately. *And today was supposed to be easy!* I mused to myself, as I hung up.

My next student was waiting. Denise entered my office almost soundlessly. She sat without moving on the couch, but I knew that beneath her surface calm she struggled with profound and disturbing feelings. Today she talked again about her decision to file sexual harassment charges against a staff member at the university. He had touched her and tried to kiss her. She had been frightened and tried to avoid him at first. A year ago, she said, she would not have been able even to consider confronting him. Now she was angry. She described her anger as being like a volcano within her. She never knew quite when it was going to erupt. Sometimes, she said, she was afraid of her anger, but it was better, she said, than the feelings of helplessness that she had endured for so long. I was reminded of Denise's history of being raped twice, of not being able to tell anyone because of her shame and fear, and of not having had words for many years for these parts of her experience. She had certainly come a long way.

As I wrote up notes on my session with Denise, a very relieved Dr. Foster called me again. He reported that the student was sad but had said that he was not thinking about suicide. He had also been referred by his boss to a therapist and had started therapy during the past week.

Sally reminded me that I was now due at the Academic Leave committee meeting. I sighed. I felt like I hadn't had a moment's breathing space all day. As I walked to Berkshire Hall, I thought back over the applications that I had reviewed: the English professor who had requested time for the final chapters of a book on the medieval Norman author, Marie de France; the librarian who had requested two summers' leaves to investigate and write about the life of Deems Taylor, an American composer, critic, and author from the '30s; the art professor who wanted time to explore the Basque region in Spain, his ancestral home, and hoped to produce a visual record of what his trip meant to him. While these were written in a layperson's English, one application about rainfall patterns and el Niño from the meteorological department was so technical, I knew that I would be relying on the expertise of other committee members to help determine how significant a study it was and whether or not it was worthy of a sabbatical.

I thought back to starting on the committee. I had felt uncertain of my place at first, but I had learned quickly that my comments were heard and respected. The group had a norm that encouraged everyone's active participation and disagreement. I looked forward to lively discussion.

After the meeting, I walked quickly through the light rain and stopped by the office briefly to check my schedule for tomorrow: five students on the calendar. It looked like Shelley had been able to put together a meeting for Rose and her roommates, and Donna wanted to see me again.

I looked forward to tomorrow.

PART 13:
INTERNATIONAL
SOCIAL WORK

Chapter 44
Consulting in Armenia

By Jerry L. Johnson, Ph.D.

Suddenly, it seemed, I was standing in front of the city council building on a sunny March morning trying to shake off the fogginess of jet lag. I needed to pay close attention in my first meeting. After a 36-hour trip, I had arrived in Yerevan Armenia at 4:00 a.m., just five hours earlier. As a consultant for the United Nations Development Programme (UNDP), I thought that my job was to develop and implement a region-wide media campaign against substance abuse. Yet, I have discovered that nothing is certain in international practice.

In five minutes, I had a meeting with my hosts from the city council and UNDP—assuming, of course, I had found the correct building. I was supposed to have a driver, but he failed to appear at the hotel that morning. So I walked the three miles to what I hoped was the city council. Simply walking around a busy city, hearing the noise, nearly choking on the overwhelming smell of car exhaust, and listening to the melody of an unrecognizable language is a learning experience. I'm glad the driver didn't show up.

I walked past the guard at the door and up three flights of marble stairs to the office of International Affairs. I knocked on the closed door. A woman answered, and in halting English said she was in another meeting, but I was welcome to sit in while she finished. The room was a busy place. People were talking, others were knocking and entering, and one woman was grinding coffee beans by hand. How can these people hear each other?

Ninety minutes later, after sitting in a smoke-filled room unable to understand even one spoken word, my meeting still had not begun. In Armenia, as well as many countries around the world, time means very little. The telephones and public transportation did not work well, so people simply showed up hoping to squeeze in at least one minute at some time during the day. If I wanted to telephone someone, I had several people try to call all day, hoping that at least one person would be lucky enough to get a message through. I was lucky to get one meeting completed during any given workday. It was normal for 9:00 a.m. meetings to begin after lunch. Waiting is a fact of life. Everybody waits up to several hours for meetings, food, and transportation. This is a difficult lesson for time-obsessed Americans to learn. For me, it is easier on my mental health to leave my wristwatch and planner at home.

When I accepted the assignment in Armenia, I had been a social worker for 15 years. I worked as a therapist, community organizer, administrator, and consultant during that time. Yet, I did not really learn to be a social worker until I began international practice. It is stimulating, challenging, and exciting, while at the same time quite humbling. You see, many years of practice experience in the United States are not always helpful outside the United States. I believe that theory and practice are, for the most part, contextual. In other words, my expertise in substance abuse prevention and treatment ended as soon as my airplane crossed out of United States airspace.

To be successful, social workers in international settings must carefully study the culture, politics, and lifestyle of the locals. They must be willing to make plans and develop strategies "on the fly," relying heavily on local needs, wants, and volunteers. Pre-planning is normally a useless exercise, often leading to a dangerous single-mindedness that when implemented results in an ugly version of practice colonialism. It certainly results in little or no success.

A social worker should take nothing for granted in international practice—even the assignment. In fact, I am more surprised when things go as planned than when they don't.

Thus, on this assignment, I was not surprised by what transpired next. After two hours and two cups of very strong Turkish coffee, my meeting finally began. My hosts began by telling me what I was partially expecting: my assignment was not what it appeared. I was not in Armenia to work on substance abuse prevention after all. This was a ruse in order to get a social worker with community-based experience into the country. Substance abuse prevention was the only pocket of untapped money locals had left to pay for a consultant, so they developed the substance abuse prevention project. It worked.

I was actually in Armenia to help UNDP and local leaders with "democracy building" efforts. They wanted me to develop a project to stimulate local interest and participation in community service through volunteerism. In addition, they wanted my ideas the next day.

Finally, some of my training and experience was helpful. As an advanced generalist practitioner, I was prepared to work closely with different systems at different levels of society in order to develop a project that best fit local needs. If it were not for the jet lag and personal intercultural adjustment dilemma faced by all social workers in international settings, this would be easy. However, in international practice, social workers not only have to learn to work differently, but their efforts are confounded by the sometimes overwhelming task of learning to live in the foreign setting. That can be a daunting task, indeed.

Just as we were beginning to discuss different project ideas, we were interrupted by a harried-looking woman who, after one loud knock at the door, rushed in and grabbed me by the arm. She wanted me to go somewhere, but she was speaking in hurried Armenian and I had no idea what she wanted, or why she was grabbing me. Through a translator, I discovered that I was now very late for another meeting my hosts had scheduled that day with 20 police officers from the surrounding area. They wanted to know my ideas, and had many of their own to share. Great! I am off to meet with a group of people about a project I just learned is not the project I had planned.

For me, the most important thing for a social worker to accomplish before intervention planning is to learn about the country and its people. Armenia was no exception. My first trip to Armenia came during one of the most difficult times in its long and interesting history. In the seven years prior to this trip, Armenia had survived one of the most deadly earthquakes in world history, the breakup of the Soviet Union, war with Azerbaijan, and complete blockade as a result of the war by Azerbaijan and Turkey leading to a complete collapse of its economy and way of life.

When I arrived, the Armenian people had lived four years with less than two hours of electricity per day, and they had survived harshly cold winters with no heat source. Food and water were scarce. Basic services were nonexistent, meaning that schools were closed, garbage was left to pile and rot, and transportation was a nightmare. People were living day-to-day simply trying to feed their children and survive. They did not have the time, money, or inclination to abuse drugs, or volunteer for community service, for that matter.

After a harrowing car ride through the city, dodging huge potholes and oncoming traffic on streets without functioning traffic signals, we arrived at an older-looking stone building for the meeting. My translator, Sona, the harried woman from the city council, informed me as the meeting began that I was her first subject as a translator, but I had no reason to worry. She would do her best.

We sat around a large wooden table, all in overcoats, as there was no heat and winter's chill still made it uncomfortable, even indoors. As is typical in meetings all across the former Soviet Union, I opened the meeting by telling about my project, explaining my credentials, and describing my experience. Then, I listened as each person made his or her statement. Since I had no idea what this project was at that point, my opening remarks were brief.

Sona did a nice job translating as people stated their ideas about community service. A good job, that is, until one woman in military uniform seized the floor. She stood at her seat and proceeded to give a twenty-minute speech, punctuated by yelling and fist pounding. After about five minutes, Sona stopped translating. Now, this usually means that the translator does not want me to hear what the person is saying. Therefore, I assumed the woman was telling me to leave Armenia on the same plane I flew in on earlier that day. I kept tugging gently at Sona's arm saying, "What is she saying?" I was reading her body language and, in America, she was unmistakably angry.

Fortunately, I was wrong. She was vigorously saying that the work I was intending to do—as yet undefined—was needed in these difficult times and that they (the police) should do whatever they can to help. However, she warned me that any efforts to organize people might be mistaken as Communist policy, so I should expect difficulty getting people to trust the sincerity of the effort. This was, in fact, prophetic.

This experience demonstrates how unfamiliarity with the local language is a significant barrier in any international setting. I misread words and body. I had a translator, but as I found out in this instance, translation is unreliable and difficult. It takes time and experience together to build the relationship of trust needed to make third-person translation work well. I did develop this type of relationship with Sona later; however, the trust was not present at this meeting. When I spoke, did she translate me accurately? What if she did not like my ideas—would she change them? Would she make me sound foolish, and would she let me in on any nuances of speech and communication that might be unfamiliar? These were only a few of the questions racing through my mind as the meeting progressed.

At meeting's end, each person shook my hand and offered his or her assistance before leaving. It turned out to be a successful meeting, despite my limitations and lack of ideas. Yet, participants in this meeting agreed that I should develop projects to address the growing problem of idle youth. The blockade and power shortage had forced the closing of schools during late fall, winter, and early spring. In addition, the end of the Soviet regime also ended the existence of a large network of youth clubs and activities. As such, youths had nothing to do but idly "hang out" on the streets. The police (and most others I interviewed in the coming weeks) believed this was a dangerous precursor to crime and delinquency. This ultimately became the organizing theme of my work over the next two years in Armenia.

By this time, it was well past noon. After a short lunch break, we went to meet the director of the Department of Social Work at Yerevan State University. After waiting for nearly an hour to no avail, we learned that she had been unable to get to the office that day because of transportation and electrical problems. This was typical. When the power went down, the subway did not run. Often, public buses simply ran out of gasoline, leaving people to walk from wherever they stopped. So, we rescheduled for another time.

Without power, days end early in Armenia. By 4:00 p.m., it was time to go home before it became dark and impossible to travel. Therefore, I walked the two miles back to my hotel, hoping to write notes about the day's events. That night, like every night for six weeks, I made handwritten notes by flashlight instead of typing them on my portable computer. Nights were long and dark; so dark that I could not detect the city outside my hotel window. It is a strange experience to sense the presence of a city, but be unable to see it. For more than five years, over three million Armenians lived without light.

After six weeks, I (with much help from my hosts) recruited 25 local people to serve as volunteer organizers. We developed a grassroots youth center, run by adults, that provided youths with cultural and community service opportunities. While changes in local politics ended the youth center after one year, the initiative demonstrated by the local people did not die. Out of the core group of volunteers, two other nongovernmental organizations (NGOs) were born. One group of women completed the first qualitative study of women's lives in Armenia in 1997, while the other publishes and distributes literature to help educate and motivate the citizenry to vote in democratic elections.

Yet, in the beginning, the task was difficult and the barriers plentiful. Culture, politics, economics, and history conspired to make democracy-building in Armenia hard. It is a challenge to motivate people to care about the community when it is questionable whether they will have food or heat on any given day. However, the spirit of the local volunteers was remarkable and admirable.

I have worked in other countries (Albania, Belarus, and Russia), but few have had the difficulties of the Armenians.

Therefore, in this culture, at this time, with all the barriers present in daily life, it is difficult to accomplish much in one day. By international practice standards, this day—my first in a new land—was successful indeed.

Chapter 45
Working with Raskal Gangs in the Highlands of Papua New Guinea

by Gerhard J. Schwab, MSW

I wake up in the house of John Taka, a former "raskal" gang leader. He lives in a typical Highlands "bush-house," which is made of local timber, bamboo, and grass. The entire house is basically one big room with a fireplace in the center. The roof is the highest above the fireplace and rests on a circular wall that is low and does not have windows. As all other houses in the village, John's house does not have electrical power, water supply, or any of the other conveniences that we are used to in the industrialized world. During my village visits, I sleep in my sleeping bag, which I always carry with me. However, after years of living in Papua New Guinea, I am still getting annoyed by fleas that find their way into my sleeping bag, suck my blood, and keep waking me up during the night. So it was this night. I did not sleep well and although I know it is morning, I am still tired. Hence I try to rest as well as I can for the time left until I hear people starting to prepare fire to boil sweet potatoes and coffee for breakfast.

Through the little door, the only opening in the house, I see that it is dawning outside. I get up, go to the river, and take a bath in refreshingly cold water. After my river bath, I enjoy sitting at the river shore. As the warmth of the sun energizes my body, I reflect on my situation and think about what an interesting and challenging job I have. I am employed by the Austrian Institute for Development Cooperation and am part of an effort to build an association of criminal youth gangs, "raskals" as they are called in Papua New Guinea. The primary goal is to develop income-generating projects with gangs so they cease criminal activities. The salary I get for my work is split into two parts. About US $450 are paid every month into a savings account in my home country. The purpose of this is that I have enough savings for my reintegration when I return home. In Papua New Guinea, the actual place of my work, I get free housing, food, and a pocket money allowance. In terms of social security and health care, I have the same benefits as any public servant employed by the Austrian state. Funds for this project are provided by the Austrian federal government, the Catholic Bishops Conference, and the local Catholic Church in Papua New Guinea.

When I come back to John's house, I see that he and his family are already sitting around the fire, drinking coffee and eating sweet potatoes. I join them and immediately get a plate of sweet potatoes and a big cup of coffee. Our conversation turns into a review of plans we have worked out over the last few days to develop a business to farm potatoes in John's village and sell them in a town at the northern coast of Papua New Guinea. However, my mind is eager to move the conversation to our plans for today. We are going to meet with two other gang leaders to prepare a conference with gangs of several other tribes in a particular valley. I am very excited about these kinds of conferences we conduct in more or less regular time periods. Over a couple of days, we meet with raskal gangs and analyze economic, political, and social structures and developments in the Highlands. Within this community framework, we then move on to learn about the reasons why they engage in criminal activities. This broadened understanding of Highland communities and criminal gang activities then provides a base to develop economic projects utilizing relational and social recourses of raskals to generate income for gang members and their families.

It takes us nearly two hours to get to the place of our planned meeting. The road is in bad condition and requires 4-wheel-drive cars to get through to the village at the end of the valley. The car we are using is a 4WD Suzuki; it was donated by a Catholic aid organization and belongs to the Catholic Archdiocese of the Highlands province. Along the road, women and children are walking to their gardens, carrying gardening tools in their hands; men we see are carrying axes. Naturally, many of them would like to get a ride, but they have to recognize that our car has only limited seating. We are aware that we would have to walk with them for at least a whole day to get to our meeting place, if no people in Catholic churches around the world would donate money for cars in "mission countries."

As soon as John and I arrive at the village, we are greeted by village elders and church leaders. We briefly talk about the purpose of our coming to their village and are then taken to the house of a village elder. They obviously are pleased about our coming and have already prepared a meeting place. Two village elders and three church leaders sit with us and we all wait for the arrival of the two raskal-gang leaders we are supposed to meet with. I have learned to view these times as opportunities to learn about people and their communities. However, in this situation these village leaders are more interested in hearing from us than telling us about themselves and their village. They are eager to find out what other projects we have started with raskals from other areas. We are proud to tell them about some of the projects we have started and are very open with failures and frustrations we have experienced. Our most successful projects are farming projects, primarily vegetables and coffee, and work contracts with governments, such as road maintenance. The biggest problems we have are a few members of our raskal association who secretly continue to engage in criminal activities after they have become members of the raskal association. This puts the legitimization of our association at serious risk and endangers our positive working relationship with governmental and business organizations.

When the raskal leaders arrive, the village elders tell us that they now know enough, promise us their full support, and leave. Initially, the two gang leaders are suspicious, but are willing to engage in a discussion about the goals of our work as soon as they find out that several well-known raskals have joined our association and have started viable businesses. We share with them our main reason for wanting to meet with them: to invite them to co-sponsor a conference for raskals of their valley. They very quickly realize that we do not come to "save their souls," but that we want to work with them on a specific project, a conference to analyze the reasons why young men form raskal-gangs. The more they hear about what we want to learn from them and the more they see how we define their possible roles in the proposed conference, they realize that we are willing to engage in a partnership with mutual risks and dependencies. After about two hours of talking with each other, I hope that we have enough of a common denominator to agree on organizing a conference that will take into account new ideas that we have generated during the meeting. I am somehow disappointed that we are not able to set a time and place for the proposed conference, but nevertheless I am glad that we all agree to meet again in two weeks.

In the late afternoon we drive back to John's house. I drop him there and drive on to the main township in the area to have dinner with the Archbishop and three priests. These four men constitute the community I live with when I am in town. They are a great group of men, and I enjoy being affiliated with them. They are all "movers and shakers" and are deeply dedicated to values of human dignity and social justice. There is no doubt in my mind that our association of raskal gangs only could get started because of the full backing of the Archbishop. Dinner with them is always fun and serious at the same time. We freely talk about our personal issues, laugh with each other, challenge each other, and do business at the dinner table. Tonight, among other things, we talk about arrangements I need to make in order to duplicate the budget of the provincial government with a commentary I wrote about it. Budget analysis of provincial and national government is a key element in our raskal conferences. My friends at the dinner table help me in thinking through some possible budget implications and give me valuable help in improving my commentary. Additionally, one of them edits my commentary and thus helps me to improve my writing skills in Pidgin, one of the three official languages in Papua New Guinea.

After dinner, everybody gets out for their evening engagements. I have scheduled a meeting with an Australian business man, who operates a hardware store in town. We meet in his house in a very pleasant living room. He knows I am Austrian and puts on Mozart's *Eine Kleine Nachtmusik* to make me feel comfortable. Our discussion circles around gang activities and the problems they cause for his business. He wants to explore with me ways for him to get involved with our raskal association. After I point out to him some of the difficulties gangs have in managing their businesses, he suggests that he will design an accounting course for project leaders. He personally will attend the next conference to get to know some of the raskals and then design a course, which will be implemented by his staff together with a selected group of raskals.

It is close to midnight when I leave his house and go home to a small two-bedroom house in town that the Catholic Church provides for me. I share the house with two Papua New Guineans who are students at the nearby teachers' college. When I enter the house, they are already asleep. I greatly enjoy my first warm shower after several days and am looking forward to sleeping in a bed without fleas. In bed, I read a few pages in Saul Alinsky's *Rules for Radicals* and a few pages in the Bible. I use these readings to help me reflect on the day past and to live with the conflicts, complexities, and paradoxes of doing international social work in Papua New Guinea.

PART 14:
WORKING IN COMMUNITIES

Chapter 46
Community Organizing for Social Change

by Asherah Cinnamon, MSW, LCSW

My favorite part of my work is getting to know and have close relationships with a very diverse group of people in my community, and working with them to empower the community toward change. The most satisfying part of the work is being able to do something effective and positive about the problems of racism, sexism, classism, anti-Semitism, and all the other "isms." I am able to do the work that has my heart, and get paid to do it. As a social change agent and community organizer, I get to be involved with a wide variety of people working toward systemic change.

I am Director of the East Tennessee Chapter of the National Coalition Building Institute, and serve as one of its national trainer/consultants. I've been with NCBI since it began in 1984. NCBI is a nonprofit organization that builds teams of local community leaders and future leaders and trains them to handle controversial issues and intergroup tensions in their own organizations, among their own identity groups, and in the community as a whole. This training, team building, and outreach to community leaders are all part of my job. I coordinate the activities of the chapter with a completely volunteer team of 20-30 local community leaders and students, whom I have recruited and trained over the past three years. I have no paid staff, which also makes me a Jill-of-all-trades.

Three days in January, though not routine for me, never-theless represent the culmination of three years of local orga-nizing and relationship-building. At 8 p.m. on a Monday night, I hear that a black church in our city has been burned to the ground in the early morning hours. Recovering from shock, outrage, and grief about this, I begin making phone calls to find out more about it and learn that the church is one of more than 20 that have been burned to date in the Southeast USA in the past 16 months. I spend two hours on the phone with a Methodist minister, who is a volunteer on my NCBI chapter team. That same night, we put together a statement of support to present to the congregation of the burned out church as quickly as possible. Calls go back and forth at 10 p.m. with the first draft of the statement, to check in with the NAACP president and several chapter members to make sure that the statement is appropriate and will indeed be seen by the African community as a genuine offer of support.

Early the next morning I begin faxing the statement out to key community leaders, especially white church and syna-gogue leaders, for their signatures. By sheer luck, it is time for all the Methodist ministers in the district to hand in their year-end reports, so we obtain permission to meet with the district superintendent the same morning, and we have a copy of the support statement ready for signatures. At noon, we have over 50 signatures from district ministers and the bishop. Other signatures come in by fax from the Catholic Bishop, the Director of the Jewish Federation, the Presbytery, the Epis-copal Bishop, a rabbi, and several Baptist ministers and lay leaders. I make more phone calls to encourage other local leaders to sign the statement in time for the next church meet-ing, and pass it along to others.

I talk with the Director of the local Neighborhood Devel-opment Center, an active member of my NCBI team, about possible workshop offerings to bring people together around this event and the issue of racism in our community. She and the NAACP president, who has participated in one of our trainings two years earlier, agree to co-sponsor the first work-shop. I find free space, get a team member to agree to lead the workshop with me, and we set the date.

The vast majority of people I speak with thank me for giv-ing them the opportunity to show their support. Many say they did not know what to do, and their shock kept them immobile until I called. A few are not eager to sign or join the coalition of workshop sponsors—they are cautious. One of the frustrations of this work and its most important challenge is to overcome the fear and hopelessness that masquerade as caution. Equally challenging is the internalized oppression of members of groups who have been the target of prejudice and find cooperation difficult. This can disable whole organizations from taking effective, cooperative action when it is clearly needed. Others, often with political pressures on them, are unable to take what is for them a bold step, for fear of making a mistake and being criticized for it publicly. Given our cultural propensity to trash leaders as soon as we think they have goofed, I can't entirely blame them, though I would like to indulge in that comforting pastime.

Not all caution leads to refusal or opposition. A key religious leader calls in response to my fax to ask if we should be sending a statement about the racist motives behind the arson before we have proof of them. I point out that our support statement has been worded specifically not to depend on such proof, but to give local leaders the opportunity to make a renewed commitment to fight racism in the community, regardless of the motive for the arson. I inform him that late-breaking news reports say racist graffiti was found on the scene of the arson and has been linked to the time of the arson. He thanks me for my patience and signs the statement immediately, telling me the name of another leader to contact and giving me permission to say that he encourages his colleague to sign. I am elated. Often, people who may seem to be fighting what we are doing turn out only to need more information and some listening time to join in fully.

I make many calls trying to reach the minister of the burned church or his associate pastor, whom I met earlier in the year when he interviewed me on the church-run music and talk radio station. The station had been broadcasting from the building adjacent to the church. It too has been destroyed in the fire, along with a brand new church-sponsored day care center. Finally, I reach the associate pastor, who remembers me and says he is sure the congregation would like to receive our statement of support that same evening at its service. He says he will check with the minister, who has been deluged with calls and is having difficulty returning them all, including mine. I am pleased to hear that he is receiving mostly supportive calls.

That evening, I meet with the Methodist minister who helped me draft the statement, to attend the prayer service in the parking lot of the burned out church. It is a freezing January night, and I am grateful for my New England training in how to dress for cold. Still, it is not enough, and our toes feel frozen soon after we arrive. We are introduced to the presiding minister, who welcomes us and invites us to read our statement of support after the service. I do so and then list some of the community leaders who have signed. I notice the faces of the 50 or so congregants who are gathered in this place of violent destruction. As I read, I see one woman elbow her friend with an excited air as she hears the names of the signers. Others nod their heads solemnly, moved, and also still numb from the shock of the violation of their sacred building and the destruction of their base in the community. One woman's eyes sparkle with unshed tears. She watches intently as I read the list of signatories. It is a small thing, really, to put words together and send around a statement of support. But for these people, it is a sign of hope, and a contradiction to their isolation as victims of violence and their isolation as members of a minority group in the midst of a majority culture which has too often let them down.

The statement of support is only a first step in our response. We quickly begin plans for a series of workshops to teach bridge-building skills to some of the people who signed the statement and members of the burned church. Three months later, 70 people participate in the first Leadership for Diversity Workshop, including members of local law enforcement, who have been criticized by the Black community for not doing enough to apprehend the arsonists, and an FBI administrator, who has just moved into town in the midst of it all and has not yet met anyone. He sits down unknowingly behind the minister of the burned church, and the group gasps in anticipation of tension, as they see the chance placement of the two men. As we go around introducing ourselves, the minister turns and shakes hands with the FBI agent, showing much grace, and breaking the tension for us all. The rest of that workshop day would be a jewel in the life of any social worker. Participants are honest, kind to each other, and unusually open to each other's point of view.

As I have become more experienced in this work, I have also been invited to present workshops for the profession at national conferences and for national groups. This gives me the added perk of meeting people from all over the country in my field, and making lifelong friendships that endure even when I move to a new state. Similarly, the fact that the organization I work for has grown to international scope gives me at least semi-annual contact with people who do the same work I do from all over the U.S., Canada, and Europe. The National Association of Social Workers and the National Association of Human Rights Workers are additional networking resources for me.

As is true for staff in many social change/community organizations, my job includes fund raising and grant writing, activities that are necessary to raise the money to pay myself and the organization's expenses. Most of the time, I work on contract, with no benefits, and I have a lot of independence to set the direction for my chapter in conjunction with my local team. I have earned anywhere from $9,000 to $37,000 per year doing this work part time to full time. Contract work is not for the timid. It varies widely and there are seasonal and geographic swings, as well. As the mother of a young child, this seasonality has given me time off during holidays and much of July. So it has its advantages.

On the other hand, the hours are irregular. Evening and weekend work are not uncommon, since reaching out to a whole community means going to community events and scheduling meetings when people who volunteer and have paying jobs elsewhere can attend. Sometimes, there is a push for a certain event, a workshop or training, and I am enfolded in my job for days and nights at a time. My family is not always thrilled, even though they are supportive. My husband volunteers with our chapter, and I have recruited my mother-in-law to make phone calls for us once a month. My daughter and my mother have participated in our workshops and other community events. One benefit of community organizing is being able to include my family in some aspects of my work. This feels more natural to me than the rigid division of family from work, though it does not suit everyone, and it requires clear boundaries nevertheless.

This fall, I will have an MSW student in field placement with me. I have always found it a very mutually rewarding experience for myself, my organization, and the student. As our local volunteer team develops, the growing sense that I am not alone in this work makes all the hard work especially worthwhile. Social change is often best done at the local level, changing attitudes and bringing people together across traditional barriers. Working cooperatively with neighbors, making new friends, overcoming obstacles on the way to goals we choose together from the depths of our hearts—that is the best kind of work I can imagine.

Chapter 47
It Takes a Village: Reclaiming Our Youth Through Community Partnerships

by Scott P. Sells, Ph.D., LCSW, LMFT

I will never forget the statements that changed my life and how I viewed the world: "Children and teenagers live in families and families live in communities," and "We must strive for academic excellence with the students we teach." These statements were made by different people within the space of a single month during August of 1997. These statements would eventually intertwine with one another and change my life and those of my students forever.

The first statement, *"Children and teenagers live in families and families live in communities,"* came from the dean of my university, Dr. Otis Johnson. When he made this statement, it was as if a light bulb went off inside my head. All my life, I had been a micro practitioner and believed that I would be more effective treating one family at a time. I thought that macro community practice should be left up to the administrators and child welfare policy professionals, not direct practice social workers. Besides, I thought, how can one individual make a difference? The problems at a community level were so vast that I was afraid to try. However, Dr. Johnson's statement made be rethink my position. I suddenly realized that I was only able to treat the multitude of child and adolescent problems as they came thundering out of the lip of a giant faucet. To be more effective, I needed to treat the faucet or where the source of the problems emerged on a community level. My current practice of one family at a time would have only limited impact. Only two questions remained: how and by what means would I implement these ideas? These questions would soon be answered.

The second statement, *"We must strive for academic excellence with the students we teach,"* came from the university president, Dr. Carlton Brown, during faculty orientation. During his presentation, Dr. Brown said that faculty must do more than just lecture in the classroom. Faculty have a responsibility to demonstrate "academic excellence" to their students by integrating concepts from a textbook into the real world. A "town meets gown" process would move faculty out of the comfort of their ivory towers and into the community. Students would then become involved in projects that improved the lives of residents in the community. As I listened, it was as if God were hitting me over the head with a 2x4.

The statements by Dr. Brown and Dr. Johnson came together into one idea. I could strive for academic excellence by forming a bridge from the classroom to the community. In the process, I would learn from my students and find a way to reach children and adolescents from a community perspective.

It was a leap of faith, but the next day, I went to the director of my social work department and made the following request:

> Dr. Jackson, I realize that I have been hired to teach micro clinical practice courses, and that I have no experience teaching macro community organization classes. In fact, if someone had told me that I would be making such a request even a month ago, I would have thought they were crazy. However, crazy or not, I want the opportunity to teach a course in community organization and, together with my students, find a community in trouble. I want to teach a concept from the textbook one day, and transform that same concept into real life practice the next. I am not yet sure how this transformation will occur, but I want to try.

At first, Dr. Jackson thought I was joking. However, I told her I was very serious. Dr. Jackson eventually agreed to my request. For the next week, I poured over everything I could read concerning community practice. During my readings, two main principles stood out.

First, a thorough needs assessment had to be accomplished before attempting any changes or interventions. Never assume to know what the community wants or needs based on statistics from a book or a quick drive through the community. One must interview the residents in the community and let them tell what they need and how the problems should be solved. Any proposed programs must fit their stated needs, not yours. In the process, one must move slowly and gain trust before making any sudden changes or movements.

Second, residents within the community must have shared ownership of the project and help run the programs that will solve their own problems. If programs are agency-based and agency-driven, the chances of long-term sustainability are "slim to none." In fact, the risk is great that these agency programs will help create a "learned helplessness" mentality. Residents will learn to become dependent on these services, rather than struggle to find their own solutions. In time, a mindset of helplessness may set in and result in an inability to solve one's own problems. This helplessness and dependency can then trickle down from the parents and be passed on to the children, creating a potential vicious cycle of poverty and emotional problems.

With these two cardinal principles intact, I met my first class of undergraduate social work students in a class entitled "Community Organization." Only four students showed up and all of them were equally skeptical and cynical about making a difference in any community. I was not prepared for such resistance, and I began to second guess my choice to teach this class. However, I refused to give up. For the next five weeks, the students and I attempted to find a community that would allow us to work with them. Just when it looked hopeless, the president of the Midtown Neighborhood Association responded to our call, and invited us to set up and conduct a town meeting. We could then do a needs assessment from a resident's perspective.

This invitation became the pivotal turning point in the project. Students suddenly became excited and less skeptical as we started our preparations for the town meeting. From the textbook, we learned how to construct a well-written press release to draw both newspapers and television stations to the event. The textbook also showed us how to prepare for and conduct a successful town meeting. Students got excited when they found out that our project was newsworthy and that the press wanted to interview them.

We also realized the importance of our work after we walked through the Midtown neighborhood and witnessed the high number of abandoned buildings. Our perceptions were confirmed when we obtained the following statistics:

- The Midtown Community contains 3,952 people — 97% African-American — with an average household income of only $17,096, compared with $28,000 citywide.

- Only six communities out of 89 possible communities in Savannah, GA have higher crime rates than Midtown.

- 65% of children under six lived in poverty, as did 48% of those under 18.

- Midtown had the third highest rate of substandard housing, with 38% of all residential homes abandoned or in need of one or more major repairs.

At the town meeting and beyond, miracles started happening, and the students began to change right before my eyes. I also began to change right along with them. The following is a summary of these miracles through the course of only one year:

1) On December 10, 1997, residents told students that they were tired of talk and that it was time for action. Residents stated that they were no longer a community and that most people stayed locked up in their houses, too afraid to leave. To solve this problem, they needed a highly visible symbol, a community center, that they could build with their own sweat labor. The act of building the center could bring the community back together.

2) The original four students were so affected by the town meeting, that they stayed with the project even after the course was completed. They presented their experiences to the next community organization class and outlined the next series of steps.

3) Students heard about this class through the grapevine, and the enrollment suddenly jumped to 16 students. These students decided to invite Midtown residents to their next class and conduct focus groups to brainstorm ways to locate and rehabilitate an existing abandoned building.

4) On February 8, 1998, a miracle happened. While the students and residents were making their presentations, an elderly Midtown resident, grandmother of 23 and great grandmother of five, stood up and donated a building she had purchased with her life savings to be used as the Midtown Community Center.

5) On June 10, 1998, the students worked collaboratively with the community to solicit the help of key business leaders. They raised $55,000 in private money from several corporate sponsors. Architects agreed to donate their services to design the center, and contractors agreed to build the center.

6) On July 17, 1998, the residents and students met to design two essential programs for the community center. The first program would feature a community family counseling clinic where residents and their children would receive counseling and support services at no charge. It would be called "community" counseling, because an entire family's network (friends, neighbors, ministers) would be assembled in one room to support the parents in efforts to solve their child or teenager's behavior problem. Social work students would conduct an internship rotation on-site under the supervision of a faculty member. The second program would feature a senior center, owned and operated by Midtown resident seniors. The program would feature a greenhouse to teach children horticulture and a mentorship and after-school program.

7) On September 1, 1998, residents, students, and I wrote a grant to receive funding from the Department of Housing and Urban Development. We received the second highest score out of all the applicants and were awarded $361,000.

8) On September 28, 1998, residents and students were so empowered by these efforts, that they joined forces with the local police force to organize a peaceful march at 1:00 a.m. The goal was to close a sports bar that served as a magnet for crime and drugs before the new Community Center was built. Over 200 residents showed up to march.

9) On December 17, 1998, the city revoked the owner's liquor license, and the bar was closed down.

10) On March 1, 1999, the ground-breaking ceremony took place.

Reflections

The spiritual component within this community and their faith over the years has really been incredible to witness. It has changed my life in the process. I now see the world through a different pair of glasses. I see how the empowerment of one community has had a ripple effect on so many more lives than one person can possibly make. It truly does take a village to change a community and in the process change the life of an individual child.

These changes can best be summed up in a recent paper written by one of my students last semester:

> Before I began the project, I thought the Midtown community was hopeless. I am a Savannahian and every time I drove through that community, I looked and thanked God that I did not live there. However, after taking part in many of the activities, I have a new outlook on things. I no longer see the Midtown community as hopeless. I saw people who were needing a hand up and who were willing to give a hand. They may not be out of their houses yet, but that day is coming and I helped make that happen.

Academic excellence and community practice are now alive and well at Savannah State University. We successfully followed the two cardinal community principles of a thorough needs assessment and community ownership from a grassroots level. As a result, things have begun to change in a small community known as Midtown.

If you come to Savannah, we invite you to drive by the corner of 35th and Reynolds. But I must warn you. You will not recognize the place as a community in need. Children will be outside playing, and the homes will look like new.

Chapter 48
A Day in the Life of a Policy Practitioner

by Joan M. Abbey, MSW

Stepping out of the shower, and reaching for a towel, my brain runs down today's schedule while the towel rubs down the body. It is going to be a long day, and I have to be in several places at once. I am not sure how I will do it, but I will try. Working as a child advocate is never easy.

The Governor's Executive Budget recommends eliminating the entire Division of Day Care Licensing. I once worked as a child care provider, so I understand the importance of licensing to assure quality child care for working families in our state. While driving to the State Capitol, I wonder what will be the outcome of today's public hearing on this Executive Budget recommendation. Arriving at the hearing room at 7:45 a.m., I can barely get in the door. In addition to child care providers, advocates, bureaucrats, and concerned parents, there are a number of journalists jammed into the hearing room. It seems the discrete phone calls to the press telling them about the hearing got results. There is no place to sit. Inching up to the front of the room, I lean against the wall.

At 8:00 a.m., the public hearing begins. From his body language, it is clear the director of the department that houses Day Care Licensing is uncomfortable with the presence of so many media and people holding signs protesting the Executive Budget's recommendation. The director explains the rationale for the recommendation in the Executive Budget. In turn, the committee members ask a number of pointed questions. Point and counterpoint, time wears on. My feet begin to hurt, and I wish I had worn flats. The director and committee chair are speaking loudly, neither swaying the other's position on this issue. Catching the attention of one of the committee staff members, I slip her a question. *Who will be responsible for investigating abuse and neglect allegations in child care centers if the Division is eliminated, since this function is the responsibility of Day Care Licensing?* A few years back, responsibility for investigations in day care settings moved from Children's Protective Services to Day Care Licensing. If the state should abolish Day Care Licensing, an entire class of children in our state will not receive equal protection under the law. In essence, the state will violate the Fourteenth Amendment of the U. S. Constitution. The department director is new to the state and may not know about this policy. The staff person slips the question to the committee chair. He glances at it and shoves it under a stack of papers. After a few more heated exchanges between the director and committee members, the committee chair asks the U.S. Constitution question. The director looks stunned, his voice falls several decibels, and he answers, "That function will not be covered." The audience gasps with the realization of the import of this statement. The chair strikes his gavel and announces the hearing is adjourned. The media swarms the director. I head to the door. It is noon and I am already an hour late for a board meeting.

Arriving at the board meeting, I apologize for my tardiness, drop into a chair, and slip off my shoes. I hate being late for anything. As the lone social worker on this board and as a general membership representative, I always want to make a good impression with this group of health care providers and administrators. Worrying that my tardiness works against that, I quickly scan the agenda, while listening to the conversation to figure out which item is being discussed. The issue under discussion is lead screening and abatement. A municipality in the state is about to lose federal funds to enable the safe removal of lead from older homes. There are problems with public outreach to identify unsafe homes, and the local health department is experiencing personnel problems. We vote to write letters to the federal government, the Mayor, and the local health department director encouraging cooperation among all parties and expeditious action. Also, we agree to use our networks to distribute fliers to parents educating them about the danger to children from lead poisoning in older homes. The fliers will also tell parents where they can call for lead screening and abatement assistance.

The board moves through the remaining agenda items, and I hope no one notices my stomach growling. It has been a long time since that breakfast bagel and coffee. When the meeting ends, I grab a sandwich from the lunchroom and head back to the office.

I place a call to several children's legal rights organizations and ask their opinion about whether abolishing day care licensing is grounds for a class action suit on behalf of children in child care. They confirm this to be the case and offer their assistance to the local early childhood organization in drafting and filing the suit. I call the director of the local early childhood organization and put him in touch with the legal rights groups.

It is after 4:00 p.m. The security guards will lock the building and set the alarms at 6:00 p.m. I have just enough time to dash off a couple of letters and return some of the calls in my voice mail box. The other calls will have to wait until tomorrow, and I will respond to my e-mail from home tonight.

Driving home, I turn on the radio to catch some late local news and traffic. The reporter is saying that the Governor's office is swamped with phone calls from parents and others concerned that children in child care will not be protected from abuse and neglect. It has been a long day, and it is not over yet. No one told me in graduate school that to be a policy practitioner, I would have to be a press agent, politician, legal expert, and budget analyst rolled into one. It would be nice if the job paid the salaries of all four jobs rolled into one, but the work has other rewards.

Pulling into the driveway, I stop and collect the evening paper and the mail. Glancing at the newspaper headlines, I see that the day care public hearing made the front page. Inside the house, I kick off my shoes and think out loud. "Sometimes you lose, sometimes you win, and we may win this one after all."

P.S. After receiving 10,000 letters and phone calls, the state did not eliminate the Division of Day Care Licensing.

Chapter 49
Homeless Community Outreach

by Seth Rosenberg, MSW

I am a master's level social worker employed at the Veterans Administration Medical Center in Tucson, Arizona in a program called Health Care for Homeless Veterans (HCHV). The program was previously known as Homeless Chronically Mentally Ill, and this is probably a more accurate description, as most of our resources are reserved for the mentally ill or substance abusers, and not for the medically needy, as the current unit title might suggest.

The pay for professionals working with the homeless is often the lowest in the social work field. The Veterans Administration, however, pays very well. A master's in social work is required. Entry into the VAMC for non-veterans is much easier if you have done a placement through your graduate school at a VAMC.

There are five social workers in my unit. Two of the social workers are part of a specialized long-term housing program involving intensive case management, known as VASH (Veterans Administration Supported Housing). There is also a housing resource specialist, a generalist, and an outreach worker. I fill the last position.

Outreach involves making contact with those eligible clients who would not normally avail themselves of the services we offer. This is a three-fold process. First, it means reaching them at the places they frequent. The world of the homeless often revolves around shelters, jails, parks, soup lines, camps, and temporary labor halls. Second, outreach must include an appreciation of the factors that are preventing the population from accessing services. Many veterans do not know that they are eligible for benefits or what those benefits are. As well, within the homeless population there exists a great deal of cynicism and alienation from many institutions, if not society as a whole. While there are many reasons for this, it is common to hear the homeless complain of prior ill-treatment by bureaucracies. They are, accordingly, wary of initiating contact unless it is absolutely necessary. Travel to an agency is often arduous because of the lack of transportation. Once they arrive, they also claim to be under-served or rudely served (implicitly because of their appearance or homeless status).

Finally, a worker must be cognizant of the issues that serve to keep the homeless in poverty. The homeless are a diverse population. While a recent study by the Arizona State Homeless Coordination Office found 61% of the homeless in Tucson to be white, middle-aged males, the reasons for their homelessness were varied. A February 1995 survey by the Tucson Planning Council for the Homeless found that alcohol and drug abuse were the single most important factors involved in homelessness, with 31% of Tucson's homeless reporting problems with such abuse. I believe that the incidence of alcohol and drug abuse was under-reported, as this survey relied on client self-report, and was administered in shelters with well-publicized policies to discourage drug and alcohol use. My own experience in Tucson has convinced me that substance abuse is overwhelmingly the most important factor in keeping people homeless in Tucson. A knowledge of substance abuse issues is thus essential.

While substance and alcohol abuse are dominant factors, they are by no means the only ones. Unemployment, lack of health insurance, lack of affordable housing, inadequate mental health care, and few programs to prevent homelessness are also viewed as significant contributors to homelessness. I have heard numerous hard luck stories, with cases of people becoming disabled and ending up on the street. Unable to work, they run through all of their resources (financial and social) well before Social Security is eventually granted. They wind up living in camps or shifting from shelter to shelter for extended periods of time, while the Social Security Administration determines their fate. Others previously had employment without health insurance, fell ill, lost their jobs, and then their homes. Some of these people will end up living in their vehicles, eating at soup lines, and trying to get back on their feet working day labor through a temporary service—an almost impossible task. Domestic violence drives a surprising number onto the streets. Some homeless individuals are too severely and/or chronically mentally ill to effectively manage their lives and wind up living outside.

I begin a typical outreach day by loading up the VA truck with supplies to take out to local camps. I take water, food, clothing, bedding, and any other items I can procure through community donations or our limited cash funds. The delivery of food is not often required. Tucson has an excellent food distribution network, and the homeless are well-served in this area.

A point-in-time study conducted by the Tucson Planning Council at soup lines in 1995 showed that of the 1800 homeless people counted that day, 756 would have to sleep outside. The numbers are actually significantly greater. Any homeless person with a day job would not be present at the feeding sites, as they are conducted during regular working hours. Many others shun the sites because they do not like the food or the atmosphere or have another regular supply of food. Whatever the calculation, hundreds must camp out, and numerous multi-party camps exist. Camps vary in size from just several people to several hundred. One camp in Tucson that I regularly worked had as many as 150 people there at times.

Camps offer a homeless individual protection and a social life amidst those similarly situated. Until recently, many of the sites were tolerated by the police. Many camp residents came to believe that they would be able to squat on city property indefinitely. Accordingly, they came to consider it their home over which they had some rights.

An example of this social development was A-Mountain camp, the largest and oldest. While this camp was eventually demolished in a midnight raid by the police, when it existed, its core was composed of about 15 veterans, several with spouses. Some had lived there for as long as nine years. When I originally went to this camp, I approached them as homeless people. Some were offended and taught me that they were not homeless, just so poor that they could not afford to rent or own housing and had to squat on city land. They had shacks, stoves, and beds. They considered this camp site their home, although it was city property. Many worked through day labor offices or sold newspapers. Quite a few were disabled and waiting for approval of their Social Security—those tended to be the panhandlers and heaviest drinkers. A belief in the camps' permanence had also led to a sense of community among the long-term residents, who had forced the post office to give them a street address and then proceeded to register to vote in local elections!

I generally find camp dwellers to be extremely alienated from mainstream society. They have long since given up on the idea that they will ever hold regular full-time jobs or reside in apartments. As a rule, they have been homeless longer than any other subgroup and have settled into the lifestyle that they believe is their lot. They scrounge for money to buy the things they cannot get with their food stamps (mainly beer and dog food), and live a simple and free existence. It is a hard life with severe limitations on the lifespan and it offers little dignity.

"Selling" the idea that things can be different, and better, is a hard task. In delivering the supplies, I employ the tactic of "gift giving" to gain their trust. I want them to believe that I can help with practical things in their lives. I try not to be too pushy about the substance abuse, but it is always there under the surface. I concentrate on helping them with Veteran's pensions and subsidized housing. Many only need a little help to make major changes. Helping them in any way to reintegrate with society may rekindle the hope that it is possible. And with this hope, I can sometimes get the camp dwellers to let me help them address core issues that keep them homeless.

After I leave the camp, I then drive to the half-dozen city parks that lie along a corridor of town where a majority of the homeless live and services to them are rendered. At the parks, I approach homeless people, establish who are veterans, and talk to them about the various services offered through the Veterans Administration, such as employment, medical, housing, mental health, substance abuse, and other programs. I have to be familiar with the whole range of services, as the needs of the homeless are as varied as they are.

The homeless who are found at parks contain a proportion of people who are recently homeless. I have found that the newer a person is to the streets, the easier it is to get him to try a program that might get him back inside with a job. This group has not grown cynical of yet another "program" and are much more anxious to resume a more mainstream life. I try to concentrate on the newer individuals, and have had very good success in engaging clients in the parks and having them follow through.

Inevitably, any outreach trip ends with a visit to either the morning or afternoon soup line. As the homeless congregate at the soup lines in large numbers, these sites represent a tremendous outreach opportunity. In order to engage potential clients, I will sometimes bring a doctor from the VAMC who offers limited medical intervention. Primarily, however, I attempt to "sell" the VA's program through persistence, pamphlets, and persuasion in the same way that I do at the parks.

I have tried without success to get the police to refer homeless clients to my program. I have established excellent relations with all other agencies serving the homeless, from crisis shelters to food banks to temporary labor agencies, and receive many referrals from them. I make regular appearances at an agency that serves as a mail drop for the homeless, and I make night visits to crisis shelters. I was formerly employed both at the county jail and at the Superior Court and have received a number of referrals from Pretrial Service workers anxious to reduce the overcrowding at the teeming county jail.

When I return to the office, it takes me 20-30 minutes to process a half-day of outreach. I write progress notes on the veterans that I've seen and perform other administrative tasks. On an average day, I spend half the day in the field and the other half in the office conducting walk-in interviews and case managing regular clients. My caseload has gone into the two and three hundreds. On a given day, I will have had sufficient contact with about 25-30 veterans to justify writing a treatment note on them. Of these, probably fifteen are seen by me in my office during a three-and-a-half-hour period.

If I had to generalize the "walk-in" population, I would do so into three broad categories. First are those I am currently case managing. They reside either in contract half-way houses, one or another HUD program, or are receiving an extended stay at a shelter. When they come into the office, usually by appointment, we discuss their case plans. Case plans have to encompass a wide variety of circumstances. Involvement with substance abuse or mental health services is common. Disability claims, employment, and affordable housing are also prominent themes. They all will have a plan that seeks to address their primary needs, and they will be expected to take steps toward achieving their goals on a regular, weekly basis. I am quite strict about compliance with treatment plans. It is estimated that there are 1000 homeless veterans on any given night in Tucson. While not all of them seek housing through the VA, we only have 60 apartments and beds, a fraction of the need. Thus, we usually pass over anyone who we do not feel is committed to change.

In the second group are those who are seeking services on a crisis basis. I use the term "crisis" in the sense of a problem that can be satisfied by one intervention. Often, this is just the provision of a food box, local bus pass, or psychotropic medication refill. These crisis cases can be varied and interesting. I have had veterans ask me to pick up their mail because someone is waiting at the post office to kill them, while others want someone to buy them candy from the canteen.

The third category consists of new clients. The processing of this group involves the majority of the paperwork, but even here it is not overly burdensome. The first step of intake is to ensure that the client has been enrolled into the "system," a process by which you can get "credit" for the visit. "Credit" for visits, or "stop codes" as they are known at the VA, are believed by the staff to be very important in justifying their utility. Registering large numbers of stop codes is equated with productivity, something the administration is reputed to be very concerned about.

Once veterans have been put in the system, I interview them using a standardized questionnaire which covers substance and alcohol use, mental health, income, employment patterns, and homeless history. A psychiatric diagnosis is asked for, based on a standardized mental status exam and client self-report. As a new client will not necessarily be assigned to the walk-in worker, the practice at the VA is to address only the immediate, crisis situation, such as obtaining a detox or shelter bed, and to pass the vet on to his case manager as soon as is possible for the development of a long-term plan.

And so might end my day. As can be seen, the work is varied. I must be prepared for a mixture of very challenging problems in each case. The key is to be flexible, but that is not all. I would say that the personal and professional qualities necessary to be a good outreach worker with the homeless are reliability, consistency, a nonjudgmental approach, a thorough knowledge of local resources, a practical nature, and a sense of humor. These are probably the same for many other areas of social work. Of particular importance is reliability. Cynicism runs deep with the homeless. They have been promised many things many times by many people and agencies. It is thus essential that I be straightforward and follow through on what I say I am going to do. Only by doing what I say I am going to do can trust and respect develop. After all, I ask the homeless to take a chance on me and the HCHV program. If they feel that I am being dishonest or do not follow through, then I will be lumped into that large group of useless professionals they feel live off of their misery.

Chapter 50
Mucho Gusto en Conocerle
(I'm Pleased to Meet You):
Working with Migrant Farm Families

by Pamela J. Wilshere, LSW

I was a newly-hired social worker in an agency where I had completed a short internship. I felt wonderful because my last semester, a full internship, would be paid. I felt as if I had the world by the tail. I was going to do something challenging, something meaningful, and something that I thought would combine my eclectic interests. I was a social worker.

My family repeatedly struggled with what it was I was going to be doing, exactly. It was the most difficult thing I had ever tried to explain to anyone. I would be working with families. I had counseled a white family regarding the mom's concern over her husband's sexual interest in their young daughter. But my caseload was going to be primarily Hispanic migratory farmworkers and their families. They are people who come here in late May to pick fruit, they stay through October, sometimes November, and then they travel on up and down the eastern seaboard picking fruit. Most of my caseload would not speak English, and I ended up doing much translation. I thought at the time it was funny that no one seemed to want to learn the language of the workers. I was excited to be able to use extensively the Spanish I had taken in school. The salary was good, although there were no benefits, and I liked working outside. I had no desire to be confined in an office.

In the texts, the vision I had was driving up to someone's home, knocking on the door, being greeted by a family member, and getting started. So, I took the directions for the first assignment. They read, "Take this road to the fork, bear left, look for the crooked apple tree (okay, *all* apple trees are crooked), follow dirt road to white house." After driving around the apple orchard for what seemed like hours, I finally found the correct crooked apple tree, and met the family. The most beautiful woman I had ever seen appeared. She carried a young child on her hip. She talked to me and was very friendly. So why did all the texts spend so much time on the resistive client? I returned to the office feeling very excited. I went out next with the social worker whose place I was taking, and she took me to a camp, where she introduced me to a very impoverished family. They talked so fast, I had no idea what was being said. I tried to smile politely, and prayed my counterpart would fill me in later. On the way out, the father said to me that he was pleased to meet me, and I needed the other social worker to tell me how to respond. I felt horribly clumsy. I never wanted to be impolite to others, and here I was making a huge blunder. The self doubts set in.

I think every job I have ever had has started with some memorable story and eventually, I settle in to do the more routine tasks. At the migrant program, often families arrived and they brought with them health issues, educational issues, and family problems. My task, globally, was to satisfy those needs as much as possible. I assisted the nurse at the program in addressing issues such as lice, ringworm, and other diseases. People have these afflictions not because they are dirty or poor or of a particular culture, but oftentimes the last camp they lived in had no water or bathroom, or they have been fleeing a country for political reasons and haven't had the facilities for proper hygiene. Our summer children's camp would begin with washing the children's heads to rid them of lice and then sending supplies home for the camps where they lived to be fogged. It was a whole new world that the textbook never told me about.

One day, I was working with a family that had many children. They were not black or Hispanic as the stereotypes lead one to believe. This family came from up north. They were legal citizens by birth. They had a child who may have had a disability. They owed the electric company tons of money, and could not pay. In the course of this family's work, I tried to get them connected to a new program that the electric company was starting. They would match donations for that family. So I contacted area churches, and made a plea for help. I raised enough money, so that the utility would not be cut off. It was hard work. When I went to send in the donations, the woman I had been working with at the electric company told me that the donations could not be credited to a specific account. The funds would go to a general fund. My family would not see the benefit of this at all. I was devastated. I angrily went to the program coordinator. We set up a meeting. We met. The woman was hostile and denied that she ever told me anything. The coordinator and I settled for half of the money being credited to the family's account.

A local grower called and informed me that he had some old roosters and hens that he wanted to get rid of. Did I know of any family who could use them for free food? That evening, the aide and I went over to the farm at dusk in my pickup truck. I had my first lesson in chicken catching—one has to get them at dusk when they roost. One holds the bag and quickly reaches out and grabs the legs of the chicken and stuffs it into the bag. I would like to add that there is much squawking and flapping of the wings. The hens were delivered to the family who found use of them in stews.

I had the unique opportunity to eat lunch with Mr. Rogers of the Pittsburgh-based TV show *Mr. Rogers' Neighborhood.* He came to interview several families and complete a segment on migrant farmworkers. He was very much the person I see on television, complete with bow tie. I chose several families who represented "typical" families. The grower had to give permission to have his camp filmed. The children were excited to be on TV. Mr. Rogers ate lunch with the children at the summer school program, and saw our educational programs, which were designed to keep children out of the orchards where it was dangerous.

Food was a big part of this work. I was offered whatever the meal was, often being treated to the best. At one table, I alone was given the lettuce. It is hard to accept food from people whom I perceive as having less than enough to eat. But I sat, smiled, thanked them for their hospitality, and ate. And ate. And ate. I gained so much weight working there, sometimes eating two or three dinners a night because it was impolite not to. I have eaten pigs' ears (yuck) and avocados (yum), pigs' feet (never again), and many unidentifiable dishes. I have put a drop of hot sauce on my plate that made me weep and watched a 5-year-old pour the same stuff on hers without missing a beat.

I struggled with the cultural aspects of working with several males who were domineering, angry, controlling men who ruled the lives of the women in their households. One of these women was a white wife, who had to get the husband to meet me prior to my working with her. One was a daughter who headed the household and longed to be free. One was a wife with eight children, all under ten years old, who was being abused (my value) by her husband. It was hard to separate out what was acceptable in Mexico and other countries, such as beating a child with a belt, and what was abuse. In the USA, I believe most people would classify such beatings as abuse, but they are very common in other countries. I often wonder where these families are now.

There were several Haitian and Jamaican families around. I worked with a woman who spoke French who translated for me. I had to think about Voodoo, and our stereotypes of this practice. It really is not the black magic that it is portrayed to be. Mostly, it is ancient herbal medicine that is practiced in a land where there is little in the way of doctors, medical facilities, or traditional medicine. It is very important in social work to put aside one's own beliefs and values and open eyes toward what is different.

I do not think it is possible to be in social work without coming in contact with policy, laws, and outside influences. I struggled with these things, and continue to think about my experiences and the faces I have long left behind. Immigration is a big issue. It is complex. Many of our services went to persons who were here illegally. Some were legal. Some came in search of work, money, happiness, and the good life. Some came to flee a country whose leaders sought to annihilate them because they were of Indian blood. I spoke to a family whose 8-year-old son watched as his father was decapitated. Today, the subject of immigration continues to perplex our country. We turn away "boat people," and have harder times enforcing the Mexico-USA border. I have no answers, nor do

I have a strong opinion on whether our services, tax supplied, should be offered to illegals. It is hard to formulate an opinion when our country supplies arms to countries that do these things to people. It is hard to know these people to whom others want to deny health care. It is obvious that our standard of living is envied, and if we share it among more people, it means a decline in our own holdings.

So when my family asks me what it is that I did for people while working there, I simply smile, and reply, "I worked with families and their children." I helped to provide educational experiences through the summer that kept children out of the fields where they could easily be hurt, and we provided English as a Second Language classes and remedial education to help children catch up as they changed schools as much as eight times a year. I helped translate for them at other services. They nodded politely, as if they understood. I was challenged. I did do something meaningful. It was wonderful.

Appendix A—Organizations of Interest to Social Workers

This is a partial listing of professional associations and other organizations that may be useful in exploring social work in general or specific areas of practice. They provide a variety of services, including professional conferences, job listings and placement services, and publication of professional journals and other reading materials.

Alliance for Children and Families
11700 W. Lake Park Drive
Milwaukee, WI 53224
414-359-1040
http://www.alliance1.org

American Association for Marriage and Family Therapy
1133 15th Street, NW, Suite 300
Washington, DC 20005
202-452-0109
http://www.aamft.org

American Association of State Social Work Boards
400 S. Ridge Parkway, Suite B
Culpeper, VA 22701
540-829-6880
800-225-6880
http://www.aasswb.org

American Association of Suicidology
4201 Connecticut Avenue, NW, Suite 408
Washington, DC 20008
202-237-2280
http://www.suicidology.org

American Board of Examiners in Clinical Social Work
21 Merchants Row
Boston, MA 02109
800-694-5285
http://www.abecsw.org

American Counseling Association
5999 Stevenson Avenue
Alexandria, VA 22304
703-823-9800
http://www.counseling.org

American Family Therapy Academy
2020 Pennsylvania Avenue, NW, Suite 273
Washington, DC 20006
202-994-2776
http://www.afta.org

American Foundation for AIDS Research (AmFAR)
5900 Wilshire Blvd., Suite 3025
Los Angeles, CA 90036
323-857-5900
http://www.amfar.org

American Humane Association
63 Inverness Drive E.
Englewood, CO 80112-5117
303-792-9900
http://
www.americanhumane.org

American Network of Home Health Social Workers
1187 Wilmette Avenue, #139
Wilmette, IL 60091
847-853-9204
http://
www.homehealthsocialwork.org

American Professional Society on the Abuse of Children (APSAC)
407 S. Dearborn St., Suite 1300
Chicago, IL 60605
312-554-0166
http://www.apsac.org

American Public Health Association
1015 15th Street, NW
Washington, DC 20005
202-789-5600
http://www.apha.org

American Public Human Services Association
810 First Street, NE, Suite 500
Washington, DC 20002
202-682-0100
http://www.aphsa.org

American Society on Aging
833 Market Street, Suite 511
San Francisco, CA 94103-1824
415-974-9600
http://www.asaging.org

American Society of Association Executives (ASAE)
1575 I Street, NW
Washington, DC 20005-1168
202-626-2723
http://www.asaenet.org

American Society for Reproductive Medicine
1209 Montgomery Highway
Birmingham, AL 35216
205-978-5000
http://www.asrm.org

Association for the Advancement of Social Work with Groups (AASWG)—An International Professional Organization
John H. Ramey, General Secretary
School of Social Work
University of Akron
Akron, OH 44325-8050
800-807-0793 or
330-836-0793
http://dominic.barry.edu/
~kelly/aaswg/aaswg.html

Association for Ambulatory Behavioral Healthcare
301 N. Fairfax Street, Suite 109
Alexandria, VA 22314-2633
703-836-2274
http://www.aabh.org

Association of Baccalaureate Social Work Program Directors
c/o Mildred Joyner, President
West Chester University
Social Work Department
McCoy Center
West Chester, PA 19383
610-436-2486
http://www.rit.edu/
~694www/bpd.htm

Association for Community Organization and Social Administration (ACOSA)
c/o Alice K. Johnson
Treasurer
8567 Sugar Tree Drive
Novelty, OH 44072
http://www.acosa.org

Association for Death Education and Counseling
343 N. Main Street
West Hartford, CT 06117-2507
860-586-7503
http://www.adec.org

Association for Experiential Education
2305 Canyon Boulevard, Suite 100
Boulder, CO 80302-5651
303-440-8844
http://www.aee.org

Association of Jewish Center Professionals
15 E. 26th Street, 10th Floor
New York, NY 10010
212-532-4949
http://www.jcca.org

Association of Jewish Family and Children's Agencies
P.O. Box 248
Kendall Park, NJ 08824-0248
800-634-7346
http://www.ajfca.org

Association of Oncology Social Work
1910 E. Jefferson Street
Baltimore, MD 21205
410-614-3990
http://www.aosw.org

Association of Reproductive Health Professionals
2401 Pennsylvania Avenue, NW, Suite 350
Washington, DC 20037-1718
202-466-3825
http://www.arhp.org

Association of State and Territorial Public Health Social Work
Gail Harper, President
Department of Health and Rehabilitative Services
2020 Capitol Circle SE, BIN A13
Tallahassee, FL 32399
850-488-2834

Association of Traumatic Stress Specialists (ATSS)
7338 Broad River Rd.
Irmo, SC 29063
803-781-0017
http://www.atss-hq.com

Association for the Treatment of Sexual Abusers (ATSA)
10700 SW Beaverton-Hillsdale Hwy., Suite 26
Beaverton, OR 97005-3035
503-643-1023
http://www.atsa.com

Bertha Capen Reynolds Society
Columbus Circle Station
P.O. Box 20563
New York, NY 10023
http://www.aztlan.net/bcrs/

Canadian Association of Social Workers
383 Parkdale Avenue, Suite 402
Ottawa, ON, Canada K1Y 4R4
613-729-6668
http://www.casw-acts.ca

Child Welfare League of America
440 First Street, NW, 3rd Floor
Washington, DC 20001-2085
202-638-2952
http://www.cwla.org

Clinical Social Work Federation
P.O. Box 3740
Arlington, VA 22203
703-522-3866
http://www.cswf.org

Council of Nephrology Social Workers
National Kidney Foundation
30 E. 33rd Street
New York, NY 10016
800-622-9010
http://www.kidney.org/
professionals/CNSW/
index.cfm

Council on Social Work Education
1600 Duke Street, Suite 300
Alexandria, VA 22314-3421
703-683-8080
http://www.cswe.org

Employee Assistance Professionals Association
2101 Wilson Boulevard, Suite 500
Arlington, VA 22201
703-522-6272
http://www.eap-association.com

Ernest Becker Foundation
3621 72nd Avenue, SE
Mercer Island, WA 98040
206-232-2994
http://weber.u.washington.edu/
~nelgee

Family Therapy Networker
7705 13th Street, NW
Washington, DC 20012
202-829-2452
http://
www.familytherapynetwork.com

Farmworker Health Services, Inc.
1234 Massachusetts Avenue, NW, Suite C1017
Washington, DC 20005
202-347-7377
http://
www.farmworkerhealth.org

Federation for Children with Special Needs
1135 Tremont St., Suite 420
Boston, MA 02120
617-482-2915
http://www.fcsn.org

Gay, Lesbian, and Straight Education Network (GLSEN)
121 W. 27th St. #804
New York, NY 10001
212-727-0135
http://www.glsen.org

The Gerontological Society of America
1030 15th St. NW, Suite 250
Washington, DC 20005
202-842-1275
http://www.geron.org

Institute for the Advancement of Social Work Research
750 First Street, NE, Suite 700
Washington, DC 20002
202-336-8385
http://www.sc.edu/swan/
iaswr/index.html

International Center for Clubhouse Development (ICCD)
425 West 47th Street
New York, NY 10036
212-582-0343
http://www.fountainhouse.org

International Federation of Social Workers
P.O. Box 4649
Sofienburg
N-0506 Oslo, Norway
47-23-06-11-52
http://www.ifsw.org

International Society for Traumatic Stress Studies
60 Revere Drive, Suite 500
Northbrook, IL 60062
847-480-9028
http://www.istss.org

Joint Commission on Accreditation of Healthcare Organizations
1 Renaissance Blvd.
Oakbrook, IL 60181
630-792-5000
http://www.jcaho.org

National Alliance for the Mentally Ill
200 N. Glebe Road, Suite 1015
Arlington, VA 22203-3754
703-524-7600
http://www.nami.org

National Association of Addiction Treatment Providers
501 Randolph Drive
Lititz, PA 17543-9049
717-581-1901
http://www.naatp.org

National Association of Alcoholism and Drug Abuse Counselors
1911 N. Fort Myer Drive
Suite 900
Arlington, VA 22209
703-920-4644
http://www.naadac.org

National Association of Black Social Workers
8436 W. McNichols
Detroit, MI 48221
313-862-6813

National Association of Child Advocates
1522 K Street, NW, Suite 600
Washington, DC 20005
202-289-0777
http://www.childadvocacy.org

National Association of Family-Based Services
6824 5th Street, NW
Washington, DC 20012
202-291-7587
http://www.nafbs.org

National Association for Home Care
228 7th Street, SE
Washington, DC 20003
202-547-7424
http://www.nahc.org

National Association of Human Rights Workers
Leon Adams, President
423 North Cedar Street
Lansing, MI 48912
517-372-4075
http://www.fairhousing.com/nahrw/

**National Association of
Lesbian and Gay Alcoholism
Professionals (NALGAP)**
1147 S. Alvarado Street
Los Angeles, CA 90006
213-381-8524

**National Association of
Sentencing Advocates (NASA)**
c/o The Sentencing Project
918 F Street, NW, Suite 501
Washington, DC 20004
202-628-0871
http://
www.sentencingproject.com/
nasa/

**National Association of
Social Workers**
750 First Street, NE, Suite 700
Washington, DC 20002-4241
800-638-8799
http://www.socialworkers.org

**National Center for Prosecu-
tion of Child Abuse**
99 Canal Center Plaza
Suite 510
Alexandria, VA 22314
703-739-0321

**National Coalition Building
Institute (NCBI)**
International Office
1835 K Street, NW, Suite 715
Washington, DC 20006
202-785-9400
http://www.ncbi.org (national)
http://www.korrnet.org/ncbi
(East Tennessee Chapter)

**National Coalition for the
Homeless**
1012 14th Street, NW
Suite 600
Washington, DC 20005-3410
202-737-6444
http://nch.ari.net/home.html

**National Youth Advocacy
Coalition (NYAC)**
1711 Connecticut Ave., NW
Suite 206
Washington, DC 20009
202-319-7596

**National Hospice Organiza-
tion, Council of Hospice
Professionals**
1901 N. Moore Street, # 901
Arlington, VA 22209
703-243-5900
http://www.nho.org

**National Information Center
for Children and Youth with
Disabilities**
P.O. Box 1492
Washington, DC 20013-1492
800-695-0285
http://www.nichcy.org

**National Institute for Social
Work**
5 Tavistock Place
London, WC1H 9SN
0171-387-9681
http://www.nisw.org.uk/

**National Network for Social
Work Managers**
1316 New Hampshire Avenue,
NW, Suite 602
Washington, DC 20036
202-785-2814
http://
www.socialworkmanager.org

**National Organization of
Forensic Social Work**
P.O. Box 174
Milan, MI 48160
734-439-7960
http://www.nofsw.org

National Organization for Victim Assistance (NOVA)
1757 Park Road, NW
Washington, DC 20010
202-232-6682
http://www.try-nova.org

National Parent Network on Disabilities
1130 17th Street, NW
Washington, DC 20036
202-463-2299
http://www.npnd.org/index.htm

North American Association of Christians in Social Work
P.O. Box 121
Botsford, CT 06404-0121
888-426-4712
http://www.nacsw.org

Organization Development Institute
11234 Walnut Ridge Road
Chesterland, OH 44026
440-461-4333
http://members.aol.com/odinst

Outward Bound USA
100 Mystery Point Rd.
Garrison, NY 10524-9757
914-424-4000
800-243-8520
http://www.outwardbound.com

Parents, Families and Friends of Lesbians and Gays
1101 14th St. NW #1030
Washington, DC 20005
202-638-4200
http://www.pflag.org

Project Adventure, Inc.
International Headquarters
P.O. Box 100
Hamilton, MA 01936-0100
978-468-7981
http://www.pa.org

RESOLVE, Inc.
1310 Broadway
Somerville, MA 02144-1779
617-623-1156
http://www.resolve.org

School Social Work Association of America
P.O. Box 2072
Northlake, IL 60164
http://www.sswaa.org

Society for Social Work Leadership in Health Care
c/o American Hospital Association
One North Franklin
Chicago, IL 60606
312-422-3000
http://www.sswlhc.org

Appendix B—Additional Reading

General

Doelling, C. N. (1997). *Social work career development: A handbook for job hunting and career planning.* Washington, DC: NASW Press.

Fox-Piven, F. & Cloward, R. (1982). *The new class war.* New York: Pantheon Books.

Ginsberg, L. H. (1998). *Careers in social work.* Needham Heights, MA: Allyn & Bacon.

Grant, G. B. & Grobman, L. M. (1998). *The social worker's internet handbook.* Harrisburg, PA: White Hat Communications.

Reyes, J. (1999). *Guide to selecting and applying to master of social work programs, 1999 edition.* Harrisburg, PA: White Hat Communications.

Shulman, L. (1979). *The skills of helping individuals and groups.* Itasca, IL: F.E. Peacock.

Wells, C. C. (1982). *Social work day-to-day: The experience of generalist social work practice.* New York: Longman.

Chapter 1—Social Work in the Emergency Room

Soskis, C. W. (1985). *Social work in the emergency room.* New York: Springer.

Chapter 2—Managing a Hospital Social Work Department

Berkman, B. (1996). The emerging health care world: Implications for social work practice and education, *Social Work, 41*(5), 541-551.

Ell, K. & Northen, H. (1990). *Families and health care: A psychosocial practice.* New York: Aldine de Gruyter.

Kayser, K., Hansen, P. & Groves, A. (1995). Evaluating social work practice in a medical setting: How do we meet the challenges of a rapidly changing system? *Research on Social Work Practice*, 5(4), 485-500.

Osman, H. & Perlin, T. M. (1994). Patient self-determination and the artificial prolongation of life. *Health and Social Work*,19(4), 237-244.

Toby-Brown, J. S., & Furstenberg, A. L. (1992). Restoring control: Empowering older patients and their families during health crisis. *Social Work in Health Care*, 17(4), 81-101.

Chapter 3—Social Work in the Neonatal Intensive Care Unit

Mankita, S. & Alalu, R. (1996). Hospital social work: Challenges, rewards. *The New Social Worker*, 3(1), 4-6.

McGoldrick, M. & Gerson, R. (1985). *Genograms in family assessment*. New York: Norton.

Chapter 4—Social Work in an Infertility Clinic

Lauritzen, P. (1992). *Pursuing parenthood: Ethical issues in assisted reproduction*. Bloomington, IN: Indiana University Press.

Mazor, M. D., & Simons, H. F. (1984). *Infertility: Medical, emotional, and social considerations*. New York: Human Sciences Press.

Salzer, L. (1986). *Surviving infertility: A compassionate guide through the emotional crisis of infertility*. New York: Harper-Perennial.

Seibel, M.M., Slessling, A.A., Bernstein, J., Levin, S.R. (Eds.). (1993). *Technology and infertility: Clinical, psychosocial, legal, and ethical aspects*. New York: Springer-Verlag.

Simons, H. F. (1995). *Wanting another child: How to cope with secondary infertility*. New York: Free Press.

Valentine, D. (1988). *Infertility and adoption: A guide for social work practice*. New York: Haworth Press.

Chapter 5—Working with Pregnant Women in Public Health

Combs-Orme, T. (1990). *Social work practice in maternal and child health*. New York: Springer.

Chapter 6—Managing in Managed Care

Sharfstein, S. S. (1992). *Managed care: Ethical dilemmas in psychiatry* (videorecording). Belle Meade, NJ: Carrier Foundation.

Chapter 7—Private Practice With Urban Gay Men: With a Subspecialty in HIV/AIDS

Appleby, G. & Anastas, J. (1998). *Not just a passing phase: Social work with gay, lesbian and bisexual people.* New York: Columbia University Press.

Aronstein, D. & Thompson, B. (Eds.). (1998). *HIV and social work: A practitioner's guide,* Binghamton, NY: The Haworth Press.

Cabaj, R. & Stein, T. (Eds.). (1996). *Textbook of homosexuality and mental health.* Washington, DC: The American Psychiatric Press.

Cadwell, S., Burnham, R. & Forstein, M. (Eds.). (1994). *Therapists on the front line: Psychotherapy with gay men in the age of AIDS.* Washington, DC: The American Psychiatric Press.

Mallon, G. (Ed.). (1997). *Foundations of social work practice with lesbian and gay persons,* Binghamton, NY: The Haworth Press.

Shernoff, M. (Ed.). (1996). *Human services for gay people: Clinical and community practice.* Binghamton, NY: The Haworth Press.

Shernoff, M. (Ed.). (1999). *AIDS and mental health practice: Clinical and policy issues,* Binghamton, NY: The Haworth Press.

Chapter 8—A Very Special Nursing Home in the Bronx

Boyd-Franklin, N., Steiner, G. L. & Boland, M. G. (1995). *Children, families, and HIV/AIDS. Psychosocial and therapeutic issues.* New York: Guilford Press.

Center for Disease Control and Prevention. (1997). Update: Trends in AIDS incidence, death and prevalence—United States, 1996. *Morbidity and Mortality Weekly Report,* 46, 165-173.

Gomberg, E. S. L., & Nirenberg, T. D. (1993). *Women and substance abuse.* Norwood, NJ: Alex Publishing.

Gould, P. (1993). *The slow plague: A geography of the AIDS pandemic.* Oxford, UK: Blackwell Publishers.

Halett, M. A. (1997). *Activism and marginalization in the AIDS crisis.* Binghamton, NY: The Harrington Park Press.

Hoffman, M. A. (1996). *Counseling clients with HIV disease.* New York: The Guilford Press.

Inciardi, J. A. (1996). HIV risk reduction and service delivery strategies in criminal justice settings. *Journal of Substance Abuse Treatment, 13,* 427-428.

Jonsen, A. R., & Stryker, A. (1993). *The social impact of AIDS in the United States.* Washington, DC: National Academy Press.

Leukefeld, C. G. & Fimbres, M. (Eds.). (1989). *Responding to AIDS: Psychosocial initiatives.* Silver Spring, MD: National Association of Social Workers.

Odets, W. (1995). *In the shadow of the epidemic: Being HIV-negative in the age of AIDS.* Durham, NC: Duke University Press.

Perrow, C., & Guillen, M. F. (1990). *The AIDS disaster: The failure of organizations in New York and the nation.* New Haven, CT: Yale University Press.

Shilts, R. (1989). *And the band played on: Politics, people and the AIDS epidemic.* New York: Penguin Books.

Winchester-Vega. M. (1992). *Substance abuse: Considerations for social workers.* Boston: Copley Press, Inc.

Chapter 9—Pediatric HIV Research

Leukefeld, C. G. & Fimbres, M. (1987). *Responding to AIDS: Psychosocial initiatives.* Silver Spring, MD: National Association of Social Workers.

National Institute of Mental Health. (1993). *AIDS research: An NIMH blueprint for the second decade.* Rockville, MD: U.S. Department of Health and Human Services, Public Health Service, National Institutes of Health.

Chapter 10—Elementary School Social Work

McGowan, L. (1994). School social work: Can you make the grade? *The New Social Worker, 1*(1), 9-11.

Chapter 12—Social Work in a Rural Community

Allen-Meares, P., Washington, R. O., & Welsh, B. L. (1996). *Social work services in schools, second edition.* Needham Heights, MA: Allyn & Bacon.

Ginsberg, L. H. (Ed.). (1993). *Social work in rural communities: A book of readings.* New York: Council on Social Work Education.

Chapter 13—Urban Child Protective Services

New Jersey Governor's Task Force on Child Abuse and Neglect. (1996). *Child abuse and neglect: A professional's guide to identification, reporting, investigation, and treatment.* NJ: Author.

Schene, P., McDaniel, N. & Filip, J. (Eds.). (1992). *Helping in child protective services.* Englewood, CO: American Humane Association.

Senkowsky, S. (1994). The ups and downs of public child welfare. *The New Social Worker,* 1(2), 7-9.

Chapter 15—Working With Gay and Lesbian Youth

Futterman, D. & Ryan, C. (1998). *Lesbian and gay youth: Care and counseling.* New York: Columbia University Press.

Mallon, G. (1997). *Foundations of social work practice with lesbian and gay persons.* Binghamton, NY: The Haworth Press.

Morrow, D. (1993). Social work with lesbian and gay adolescents. *Social Work,* 38(6): 655-660.

Peters, A. J. (1997). Themes in group work with lesbian and gay adolescents. *Social Work with Groups,* 20(2): 51-69.

Chapter 16—Child Welfare Ombudsman

National Commission on Children. *Beyond rhetoric: A new American agenda for children and families.* (1991). Washington, DC: U.S. Government Printing Office.

Chapter 17—Family Advocacy in the Military

Kaslow, F. & Ridenour, R. (Ed.). (1984). *The military family: Dynamics and treatment.* New York: Guilford.

Chapter 18—Employee Assistance Programs

Briar, K. H. & Vinet, M. (1984). Ethical questions concerning EAP: Who is the client? Company or individual?" In Samuel H. Klarriech (Ed.), *The human resource management book*. New York: Praeger.

Donovan, R. (1987). Stress in the workplace: A framework for research and practice. *Social Casework*, 68, 259-266.

Garvin, C. D. & Tropman, J. E. (1992). Social work in the workplace. In *Social work in contemporary society*. Englewood Cliffs, NJ: Prentice Hall.

Googins, B. K. & Davidson, B. N. (1993). The organization as client: Broadening the concept of employee assistance programs. *Social Work*, 38(4), 477-84.

Googins, B. K. & Godfrey, J. (1987). *Occupational social work*. Englewood Clifffs, NJ: Prentice Hall.

Johnston, N., Rooney, G., & Carter, I. (1995). Occupational social work. In H. Wayne Johnson (Ed.), *The social services: An introduction*. Itasca, IL: F.E. Peacock.

McClellan, K. & Miller, R. E. (1988). EAPs in transition: Purpose and scope of services. *EAP Quarterly*, (3/4) 25-42.

Popple, P. R. & Leighninger, L. (1993). The workplace. In *Social work, social welfare and American society*. Needham, MA: Allyn-Bacon.

Ramanthan, C. S. (1992). EAP's response to personal stress and productivity. *Social Work*, 37(3), 234-239.

Rooney, G. D. (1994). *Employee assistance programs and the changing composition of the workforce*. Unpublished doctoral dissertation, University of Minnesota.

Chapter 19—Developmental Disabilities

Marsh, J. D., & Boggis, C. (Eds.). (1995). *From the heart: On being the mother of a child with special needs*. Bethesda, MD: Woodbine House.

Pueschel, S. M., Bernier, J. C., & Weidenman, L. E. (1988). *The special child: A source book for parents of children with developmental disabilities*. Baltimore, MD: P. H. Brookes.

Chapter 21—Involuntary Admission: A New Worker's Introduction to the "603"

Rodgers, A. (1995). *A shining affliction.* New York: Viking Penguin.

Sullivan, D. & Everstine, L. (1983). *People in crisis: Therapeutic interventions.* New York: Brunner/Mazel.

Chapter 22—Partial Hospitalization

Budman, S. H. & Gurman, A. S. (1988). *Theory and practice of brief therapy.* New York: Guilford.

DiBella, G. A. W. (1982). *Handbook of partial hospitalization.* New York: Brunner/Mazel.

Gendlin, E. T. (1982). *Focusing.* New York: Bantam.

Kiser, L. J., Lefhovitz, P. M., Kennedy, L. L., & Knight, M. A. (1996). *The continuum of ambulatory behavioral healthcare services.* Unpublished paper. Alexandria, VA: Association for Ambulatory Behavioral Healthcare.

Kottler, J. A. & Blau, D. S. (1989). *The imperfect therapist: Learning from failure in therapeutic practice.* San Francisco: Jossey-Bass.

Miller, J. K. (1992). *Compelled to control: Why relationships break down and what makes them well.* Dearfield Beach, FL: Health Communications.

Smith, K. G. (1994). How Christian therapists can deal with and learn from their mistakes. *Journal of Psychology and Christianity,* 13(1), 76-83.

Chapter 23—Social Work in a Clubhouse

Beard, J. H., Propst, R., and Malamud, T. J. (1992). The Fountain House model of psychiatric rehabilitation. *Psychosocial Rehabilitation Journal,* 5(1).

Vorspan, R. (1988). Activities of daily living in the clubhouse: You can't vacuum in a vacuum. *Psychosocial Rehabilitation Journal,* 12(2).

Chapter 24—Life as a Group Home Manager

Moorman, M. (1992). *My sister's keeper: Learning to cope with a sibling's mental illness.* New York: Norton.

Winerip, M. (1994). *Nine Highland Road.* New York: Pantheon Books.

Chapter 25—Disaster Mental Health Services

Myers, D. G. (1994). *Disaster response and recovery: A handbook for mental health professionals.* (SAMHSA Publication No. SMA 94-3010). Rockville, MD: CMHS.

Weaver, J. D. (1995). *Disaster mental health: Detailed information* [Document posted on the World Wide Web]. Retrieved from World Wide Web: http://ourworld.compuserve.com/homepages/ johndweaver/dmhi.htm.

Weaver, J. D. (1995). *Disasters: Mental health intervention.* Sarasota, FL: Professional Resource Press.

Chapter 26—Dual Diagnosis: Substance Abuse and Mental Health in an Inpatient Setting

Daley, D. (1994). *Dual diagnosis workbook.* Independence, MO: Herald House.

Daley, D., Moss, H., & Campbell, F. (1989). *Dual disorders: Counseling clients with chemical dependency and mental illness.* Center City, MN: Hazleden Foundation.

Daley, D., & Thase, M. (1994). *Dual disorders recovery counseling.* Independence, MO: Herald House.

Evans, K., & Sullivan, M. J. (1990). *Dual diagnosis: Counseling the mentally ill substance abuser.* New York: Guilford.

Gorski, T., & Miller, M. (1986). *Staying sober: A guide for relapse prevention.* Independence, MO: Herald House.

Gorski, T. (1989). *Passages through recovery.* New York: Harper House.

Ries, R. (1994). *Assessment and treatment of patients with coexisting mental illness and alcohol and other drug abuse* (Publication No. SMA 94-2078). Rockville, MD: Dept. of Health and Human Services.

Chapter 27—Social Work in the Alaskan Bush

Bruchac, J. (Ed.). (1991). *Raven tells stories: An anthology of Alaska native writing.* Greenfield, NY: Greenfield Review Press.

Napoleon, H. (1991). *Yuuyaraq: The way of the human being.* Fairbanks, AK: Center for Cross-Cultural Studies, University of Alaska, Fairbanks, College of Rural Alaska.

Wallis, V. (1994). *Two old women.* New York: HarperCollins.

Chapter 28—Adventure-Based Practice

Chase, N. K. (1981). *Outward bound as an adjunct to therapy.* Denver, CO: Colorado Outward Bound School.

Davis-Berman, J. & Berman, D. S. (1994). *Wilderness therapy: Foundations, theory, & research.* Dubuque, IA: Kendall/Hunt.

Gass, M. A. (Ed.). (1995). *Book of metaphors: Volume II.* Dubuque, IA: Kendall/Hunt.

Gass, M. A. & Dobkin, C. (Eds.). (1991). *Book of metaphors: A descriptive presentation of metaphors for adventure activities.* Boulder, CO: Association for Experiential Education.

Itin, C. (1993). Linking Ericksonian methods to adventure therapy: Application of the Diamond model to adventure therapy. In S. Wurdinger & M. Gass (Eds.). *Partnerships: Proceedings of the 21st international conference for experiential education.* Boulder, CO: Association for Experiential Education, 33-45.

Itin, C. (1995). Adventure therapy and the addictive process. *Journal of Leisurability,* 22(2), 29-37.

Itin, C. (1995). Utilizing hypnotic language in adventure therapy. *The Journal of Experiential Education,* 18(2), 70-75.

Kaplan, L. (1979). Outward bound: A treatment modality unexplored by the social work profession. *Child Welfare,* 58(1), 37-47.

Chapter 29—Private Practice and the Eclectic Social Worker

Linsley, J. (1996). The business of private practice. *The New Social Worker,* 3(2), 4-7.

Chapter 30—An Office to Call My Own: Private Practice in the Lesbian Community

Boston Lesbian Psychologies Collective. (1987). *Lesbian psychologies: Explorations and challenges.* Urbana, IL: University of Illinois Press.

Falco, K. L. (1991). *Psychotherapy with lesbian clients: Theory into practice.* New York: Brunner/Mazel.

Hendrix, H. (1992). *Getting the love you want: A guide for couples.* New York: HarperPerennial.

Loulan, J. (1984). *Lesbian sex.* Duluth, MN: Spinsters Ink.

Chapter 31—Prison Substance Abuse Treatment

Beck, A. T., Wright, F. D., Newman, C. F., & Liese, B. S. (1993). *Cognitive therapy of substance abuse.* New York: Guilford Press.

Ellis, A., McInerney, J. F., DiGiuseppe, R., & Yeager, R. J. (1988). *Rational emotive therapy with alcoholics and substance abusers.* Needham Heights, MA: Allyn & Bacon.

Harris, G. A. (1995). *Overcoming resistance: Success in counseling men.* Lanham, MD: American Correctional Association.

Yochelson, S., & Samenow, S. E. (1976). *The criminal personality: Vol. 1. A profile for change.* Northvale, NJ: Jason Aronson, Inc.

Chapter 33—Residential Treatment for Adolescent Sexual Offenders

Barbaree, H., Marshall, W., and Hudson, S. (1993). *The juvenile sex offender.* New York: Guilford.

Becker, J., and Kaplan, M. (1989). The assessment of adolescent sexual offenders. In R. Prinz (Ed.). *Advances in behavioral assessment of children and families.* Greenwich, CT: JAI Press.

Bolton, F., Morris, L., and Maceachron, A. (1989). *Males at risk: The other side of child sexual abuse.* Newbury Park, CA: Sage.

Deisher, R., Wenet, G., Paperny, D., Clark, T., and Fehrenbach, P. (1982). Adolescent sexual offenses behavior: The role of the physician. *Journal of Adolescent Health Care, 2,* 279-286.

Freidrich, W. (1990). *Psychotherapy of sexually abused children and their families.* New York: Norton and Company.

Knopp, F. H., and Freeman-Longo, R. (1992). *Safer society survey.* Orwell, VT: Safer Society Press.

U.S. Department of Justice. (1984). *Sourcebook of criminal justice statistics.* Washington, DC: U.S. Government Printing Office.

Chapter 34—Forensic Social Work: Mitigating Death Penalty Cases in a Capital Defense Unit

Prejean, H. (1993). *Dead man walking.* New York: Random House.

Von Drehle, D. (1995). *Among the lowest of the dead.* New York: Random House.

Chapter 36—Nursing Home Social Work

Gleason-Wynn, P., and Fonville, K. (1993). *Social work practice in the nursing home setting: A primer for social workers.* LaGrange, TX: M&H Publishing.

Mercer, S. D., Garner, D., and Leon, J. (1991). *Geriatric case practice in the nursing home.* Thousand Oaks, CA: Sage.

Chapter 38—Hospice Social Work

Becker, E. (1985). *Denial of death.* New York: Free Press.

Liechty, D. (1995). *Transference and transcendence: Ernest Becker's contribution to psychotherapy.* Northvale, NJ: Aronson.

Morgan, E. & Morgan, J. (Ed.). (1994). *Dealing creatively with death: A manual of death education and simple burial, 13th Edition.* Bayside, NY: Zinn Communications.

Rando, T. A. (1993). *Treatment of complicated mourning.* Champaign, IL: Research Press.

Ruitenbeek, H., (Ed.). (1995). *Death and mourning.* Northvale, NJ: Aronson.

Simos, B. (1979). *A time to grieve.* Milwaukee, WI: Families International.

Chapter 39—Home Health Social Work

Feil, N. (1992). *Validation: The Feil method—How to help the old, old.* Cleveland, OH: Edward Feil Productions.

Greene, R. R. (1986). *Social work with the aged and their families.* Hawthorne, NY: Aldine De Gruyter.

Chapter 40—Life as an Agency CEO

Carver, J. (1990). *Boards that make a difference: A new design for leadership in nonprofit and public organizations.* San Francisco: Jossey-Bass.

Congram, C. (Ed.). (1991). *The AMA handbook of marketing for the service industries.* New York: American Management Association.

Drucker, P. F. (1990). *Managing the nonprofit organization.* New York: HarperCollins.

Gross, M. J. (1995). *Financial and accounting guide for not-for-profit organizations.* New York: Wiley.

Chapter 41—Association Management

Encyclopedia of Associations, 31st edition. (1996). Detroit, MI: Gale Research.

Chapter 42—Life as a BSW Educator

Macy, H. J., Flax, N., Sommer, V.L. & Swaine, R. L. (1995). *Directing the baccalaureate social work program: An ecological perspective.* Jefferson City, MO: Association of Baccalaureate Social Work Program Directors (BPD).

Pohek, M. (1970). *Teaching and learning in social work education.* Alexandria, VA: Council on Social Work Education.

Chapter 43—University Counseling Center

Garland, P. H. (1985). *Serving more than students: A critical need for college student personnel services.* Washington, DC: ERIC Clearinghouse on Higher Education, Association for the Study of Higher Education.

Chapter 44—International Social Work

Johnson, J. (in press). *Visitor in a foreign land.*

Chapter 45—Working with Raskal Gangs in the Highlands of Papua New Guinea

Alinsky, S. D. (1972). *Rules for radicals: A practical primer for realistic radicals.* New York: Vintage Books.

Dinnen, S. (1994). *The criminal justice system in Papua New Guinea: A factual review.* Boroko, Papua New Guinea: National Research Institute.

Kammer, F. (1991). *Doing faith justice: An introduction to Catholic social thought.* New York: Paulist Press.

O'Collins, M. (1993). *Social development in Papua New Guinea, 1972-1990.* Canberra, Australia: Australian National University.

Shuman, M. (1994). *Toward a global village: International community development initiatives.* London: Pluto Press.

Chapter 46—It Takes a Village: Reclaiming Our Youth Through Community Partnerships

Brueggemann, W. G. (1996). *The practice of macro social work.* Chicago: Nelson-Hall.

Kahn, S. (1982). *Organizing.* New York: McGraw Hill.

Specht, H. & Courtney, M. (1994). Social work in the 21st century: Replacing psychotherapy with community education. In H. Specht & M. Courtney, *Unfaithful angels: How social work has abandoned its mission* (pp. 130-152). New York: The Free Press.

Chapter 47—Community Organizing for Social Change

Brown, C. R. (1984). *The art of coalition building: A guide for community leaders.* New York: American Jewish Committee. (Out of print, but available through NCBI International Office, 1835 K Street, NW, Suite 715, Washington, DC 20006.)

Jacobs, C. and Bowles, D. (Ed.). (1988). *Ethnicity and race: Critical concepts in social work.* Washington, DC: NASW Press.

Chapter 48—A Day in the Life of a Policy Practitioner

The Children's Defense Fund. (1998). *The state of America's children yearbook 1998*. Washington, DC: Author.

Fernandez, H. C. (1980). *The child advocacy handbook*. New York: The Pilgrim Press.

Jansson, B. S. (1999). *Becoming an effective policy advocate: From policy practice to social justice, third edition*. Belmont, CA: Wadsworth Publishing.

O'Hare, W. P., et al. (1998). *The 1998 KIDS COUNT data book*. Baltimore, MD: Annie E. Casey Foundation.

Sherman, A. (1994). *Wasting America's future. The Children's Defense Fund report on the costs of child poverty*. Boston, MA: Beacon Press.

Chapter 49—Homeless Community Outreach

Baum, A. S. (1993). *A nation in denial: The truth about homelessness*. Boulder, CO: Westview Press.

Chapter 50—Mucho Gusto a Conocerle: Working with Migrant Farm Families

Abalos, D. (1986). *Latinos in the United States*. Notre Dame, IN: University of Notre Dame Press.

Anderson, E. (1990). *Streetwise: Race, class and change in an urban community*. Chicago, IL: University of Chicago Press.

Appendix C—Internet Resources

The Internet offers information on virtually any subject, including many related to social work. Listed in this Appendix are some Web sites related to the various topics covered in this book. There are many more, and new sites are developed every day. This list is provided as a starting point. You will find many more as you explore the Web.

Information on the Internet comes from a variety of sources. Some sites are published by well known and respected organizations. Others are published by individuals who are seeking to express a particular bias or point of view. Over the years, it has become very easy to publish on the Web, and much of the information does not go through any type of peer review process. For that reason, it is necessary to evaluate for yourself the information you find online, and to decide which sites are valuable to you and which ones are not. Some criteria to look at include the scope of the site, the authority of the author and/or publisher, how the information is presented, how up-to-date the site is, accuracy, and quality of the overall structure of the site.

For more information on critically evaluating Web sites, see *Bibliography on Evaluating Internet Resources* by Nicole Auer, available at *http://refserver.lib.vt.edu/libinst/critTHINK.HTM*. Another helpful resource for evaluating health information on Web sites is *Criteria for Assessing the Quality of Health Information on the Internet. A Health Summit Group Policy Paper* (H. Rippen, et al., 1998) available at *http://hitiweb.mitretek.org/docs/criteria.html*

In addition to Web sites, the Internet offers mailing lists (electronic discussion groups) on a variety of topics. There are many related to social work. Subscribing to most Internet mailing lists is free and open to anyone. Once subscribed, one can send an e-mail message to all members of the list at one time. Additionally, the subscriber will receive as e-mail all messages sent to the entire group. As an example, many of the contributors to this book heard about the opportunity to contribute through announcements on Internet mailing lists. To find Internet mailing lists on a particular topic, search the Liszt site (*http://www.liszt.com*).

To find additional Web sites, you can search Altavista (*http://www.altavista.com*) or other search engines. Again, the Web sites listed here represent a small sample of all that is available online. Also, keep in mind that this book's publication date is Fall 1999. Internet addresses sometimes become outdated. For more up-to-date listings of social work-related Web sites, see *THE NEW SOCIAL WORKER ONLINE* (*http://www.socialworker.com*) and the other sites listed under "General Social Work Web Sites." For more information on Internet use in social work, see *THE SOCIAL WORKER'S INTERNET HANDBOOK* (1998) by Gary B. Grant and Linda May Grobman.

GENERAL SOCIAL WORK WEB SITES

The New Social Worker Online
http://www.socialworker.com

SWAN
http://www.sc.edu/swan/

World Wide Web Resources for Social Workers
http://www.nyu.edu/socialwork/wwwrsw

PART 1—HEALTH CARE

American Public Health Association
http://www.apha.org/

AMSO Managed Healthcare Forum
http://www.amso.com/

Department of Health and Human Services
http://www.os.dhhs.gov/

Healthfinder
http://www.healthfinder.gov

HealthGate
http://www.healthgate.com/index.shtml

The HMO Page
http://www.hmopage.org

Society for Social Work Leadership in Health Care
http://www.sswlhc.org

PART 2—HIV/AIDS

The Body: An HIV and AIDS Information Resource
http://www.thebody.com

Centers for Disease Control and Prevention Divisions of HIV/AIDS
Prevention
http://www.cdc.gov/nchstp/hiv_aids/dhap.htm

Children with AIDS Project
http://www.aidskids.org

HIV/AIDS Content for Social Workers
http://www.geocities.com/CollegePark/7113/

HIV InSite
http://hivinsite.ucsf.edu/

Marty Howard's HIV/AIDS Home Page
http://www.smartlink.net/~martinjh/

Michael Shernoff's Web Site
http://www.gaypsychotherapy.com

PART 3—SCHOOL SOCIAL WORK

School Social Work Association of America
http://www.sswaa.org

School Social Work Home Page
http://www.doe.state.in.us/sservices/socwork.htm

PART 4—CHILDREN, YOUTH, AND FAMILIES

Alliance for Children and Families
http://www.alliance1.org

Child Welfare League of America
http://www.cwla.org

Children Now
http://www.childrennow.org

Coming Up Taller: Arts and Humanities Programs for Children
and Youth at Risk
http://www.cominguptaller.org

Difficult.net
http://www.difficult.net

Family Preservation and Child Welfare Network
http://www.familypreservation.com

The National Assembly of National Voluntary Health and Social
Welfare Organizations (National Assembly)
http://www.nassembly.org/

U.S. Administration for Children and Families
http://www.acf.dhhs.gov/

U.S. Department of Justice
http://www.usdoj.gov

PART 5—DISABILITIES

Administration on Developmental Disabilities
http://www.acf.dhhs.gov/programs/add/index.htm

The Disability Link Barn
http://www.accessunlimited.com/links.html

March of Dimes
http://www.modimes.org/

National Easter Seal Society
http://www.seals.com

National Institute of Neurological Disorders and Stroke
http://www.ninds.nih.gov/

PART 6—MENTAL HEALTH

American Red Cross
http://www.redcross.org/

Behavior Online
http://www.behavior.net/index.html

Mental Health Net
http://www.cmhc.com/

The National Mental Health Services Knowledge Exchange Network
http://www.mentalhealth.org/

U.S. National Institute of Mental Health
http://www.nimh.nih.gov

PART 7—SUBSTANCE ABUSE

Christian Marcel Itin's Site
http://www.du.edu/~citin/home.html

Join Together Online
http://www.jointogether.org/

National Association of Alcoholism and Drug Abuse Counselors
http://www.naadac.org

National Clearinghouse for Alcohol and Drug Information
http://www.health.org/index.htm

National Institute on Alcohol Abuse and Alcoholism
http://www.niaaa.nih.gov

National Institute on Drug Abuse
http://www.nida.nih.gov

Substance Abuse and Mental Health Services Administration (SAMHSA)
http://www.samhsa.gov/

PART 8—PRIVATE PRACTICE

Clinical Social Work Federation
http://www.cswf.org

Psychotherapy Finances
http://www.psyfin.com

PART 9—CRIMINAL JUSTICE

Corrections Connection Network
http://www.corrections.com/

Family and Corrections Network
http://www.fcnetwork.org

U.S. Department of Justice Federal Bureau of Prisons
http://www.bop.gov

PART 10—OLDER ADULTS AND THE END OF LIFE

Alzheimer's Association
http://www.alz.org

Crisis, Grief, and Healing Page
http://www.webhealing.com/

Eldercare Web
http://www.elderweb.com

National Hospice Organization
http://www.nho.org

National Prison Hospice Association
http://www.npha.org

SeniorNet
http://www.seniornet.org/

PART 11—MANAGEMENT

American Society of Association Executives
http://www.asaenet.org

National Network for Social Work Managers
http://www.socialworkmanager.org

PART 12—HIGHER EDUCATION

American College Personnel Association
http://www.acpa.nche.edu

Council on Social Work Education
http://www.cswe.org

PART 13—INTERNATIONAL SOCIAL WORK

AmeriCares Foundation
http://www.americares.org/

Arminco Global Telecommunications
http://www.arminco.com

InterAction
http://www.interaction.org/

ReliefNet
http://www.reliefnet.org/

ReliefWeb
http://www.reliefWeb.int/

A Student's Guide to Planning a Career in International Social Work
http://caster.ssw.upenn.edu/~restes/isw/chapter52.html

PART 14-WORKING IN COMMUNITIES

Alliance for National Renewal
http://www.ncl.org/anr/

Center for Campus Organizing
http://www.enviroweb.org/cco/current/links.html

Center for Law and Social Policy
http://www.clasp.org

Children's Defense Fund
http://www.childrensdefense.org

National Association of Child Advocates
http://www.childadvocacy.org/index.html

Are you thinking about getting a master's degree in social work?

Find out from a former admissions director how you can improve your graduate school application. In *The Social Work Graduate School Applicant's Handbook,* you will learn about the admissions process from an insider's perspective. Discover what will help (and hurt) your chances of being accepted to the school of your choice, and find tips on deciding which school is right for you.

Read this book and find out:
* What factors to consider when determining your interest in a school of social work
* What admissions committees look for in an applicant
* Whether your GPA and test scores matter
* How to gain social work related experience that will help your application
* Who to ask for letters of reference (and who not to ask)
* What to include in your personal essay
* Which schools are accredited by the Council on Social Work Education, and why this is important
* Where to find out about social work licensing in your state.

The author, Jesús Reyes, AM, ACSW, is Director of the Social Service Department of the Circuit Court of Cook County, IL. As former assistant dean for enrollment at one of the top ranked schools of social work in the U.S., and as a private consultant to MSW applicants, he has advised thousands across the country on their school applications and personal statements and on ways to improve their chances of getting into the school of their choice.

Price: $19.95 plus $5.00/shipping (to U.S. addresses) for first book, $1.00 shipping each additional book, $12/shipping per book to addresses outside the U.S.
306 pages   5 1/2 x 8 1/2

Order the current edition of this book from:
WHITE HAT COMMUNICATIONS
P.O. Box 5390, Dept. D2
Harrisburg, PA 17110-0390

Questions? Call 717-238-3787.
Credit card orders: call 717-238-3787 or fax 717-238-2090
or order online at http://www.socialworker.com
or use order form in the back of this book.

The "Best of THE NEW SOCIAL WORKER" Series

BECOMING A SOCIAL WORKER:
Reflections on a Clinician's Transformative Journey
by Manfred J. Melcher

 Manfred J. Melcher shares the unique, as well as the universal, experiences he encountered as a master's level social work student. He reflects on his process of "becoming"—of transforming into not only a new social worker, but a new person. Includes "Suggested Reflections" and "Reflections" pages you can use to chart your own thoughts about becoming a social worker.

126 pages • 5 1/2 x 8 1/2 • ISBN 1-929109-07-5 • 2002
$17.95 plus shipping

THE FIELD PLACEMENT SURVIVAL GUIDE:
What You Need to Know to Get the Most
From Your Social Work Practicum
edited by Linda May Grobman

Field placement is one of the most exciting and ex-hilarating parts of a formal social work education. It is also one of the most challenging. This book brings together in one volume over 30 field placement-related writings from THE NEW SOCIAL WORKER magazine. A goldmine of practical information that will help social work students take advantage of all the field placement experience has to offer.

253 pages • 5 1/2 x 8 1/2 • ISBN 1-929109-10-5 • 2002
$21.95 plus shipping

Order from White Hat Communications, P.O. Box 5390, Dept. D2, Harrisburg, PA 17110-0390 with order form in the back of this book.

ORDER FORM

I would like to order the following:

Qty.	Item	Price
_____	Becoming a Social Worker @ $17.95	_____
_____	Days in the Lives of Social Workers @ $17.95	_____
_____	Field Placement Survival Guide @ $21.95	_____
_____	Social Work Grad. School App. Hdbk. @ $19.95	_____
_____	New Social Worker Subscription (1yr/2yr/3yr)	_____

Please send my order to:

Name _____

Organization _____

Address _____

City_____ State____ Zip _____

Telephone _____

Please send me more information about ❑social work and ❑non-profit management publications available from White Hat Communications.

Sales tax: Please add 6% sales tax for books shipped to Pennsylvania addresses.

Shipping/handling:
❑Books sent to U.S. addresses: $5.00 first book/$1 each add'l book.
❑Books sent to Canada: $7.00 per book.
❑Books sent to addresses outside the U.S. and Canada: $12.00 per book.

Payment:
Check or money order enclosed for $_____
U.S. funds only.

Please charge my: ❑MC ❑Visa ❑AMEX ❑Discover

Card #: _____

Expiration Date _____

Name on card: _____

Billing address (if different from above): _____
_____

Signature: _____

Mail this form with payment to:
WHITE HAT COMMUNICATIONS, P.O. Box 5390, Dept. D2
Harrisburg, PA 17110-0390
Questions? Call 717-238-3787.
Credit card orders: call 717-238-3787 or fax 717-238-2090
or order online at http://www.socialworker.com